COOPERATION UNDER ANARCHY

Written under the auspices of the Center of International Studies, Princeton University. A list of other Center publications appears at the back of this book.

COOPERATION UNDER ANARCHY

Edited by
KENNETH A. OYE

PRINCETON UNIVERSITY PRESS

CONTENTS

THE CONTRIBUTORS

KENNETH A. OYE is Assistant Professor of Politics at Princeton University and an Editor of *World Politics*. He is co-editor, with Robert J. Lieber and Donald Rothchild, of *Eagle Defiant: U.S. Foreign Policy in the 1980s* (1983).

DUNCAN SNIDAL is Assistant Professor of Political Science and Co-Director of the Program on Interdependent Political Economy at the University of Chicago. He is currently completing a book entitled *International Cooperation: A Game Theory Analysis of Regimes and Interdependence*.

ROBERT JERVIS is Professor of Political Science at Columbia University. His most recent books are *The Illogic of American Nuclear Strategy* (1984) and, with Richard Ned Lebow and Janice Stein, *Psychology and Deterrence* (1985).

STEPHEN VAN EVERA is the Managing Editor of *International Security*, and a research fellow at the Center for Science and International Affairs, Harvard University. He is currently working on a book on the prevention of war.

GEORGE W. DOWNS is Professor in the Political Science Department and the Graduate School of Administration, University of California, Davis. He specializes in models of nonmarket decision making, and his most recent book is *The Search for Government Efficiency: From Hubris to Helplessness* (forthcoming, 1985).

DAVID M. ROCKE is Associate Professor in the Graduate School of Administration, University of California, Davis. Much of his research has focused on robust statistical methods.

RANDOLPH M. SIVERSON is Professor of Political Science and Chair of the Department at the University of California, Davis. His main research interests are in the area of international conflict.

JOHN CONYBEARE is Associate Professor of Political Science at Columbia University. He is currently completing a book entitled *Trade Wars*.

CHARLES LIPSON is Associate Professor of Political Science at the University of Chicago and Co-Director of the University's Program on Interdependent Political Economy. He is the author of *Standing Guard: Protecting Foreign Capital in the Nineteenth and Twentieth Centuries* (1985).

ROBERT AXELROD is Professor of Political Science and Public Policy at the University of Michigan. His most recent book is *The Evolution of Cooperation* (1984).

ROBERT O. KEOHANE is Professor of Government and an Associate of the Center for International Affairs at Harvard University. His most recent book is *After Hegemony: Cooperation and Discord in the World Political Economy* (1984).

PREFACE

The problem of explaining and promoting international cooperation encompasses many of the principal questions in the disciplines of political economy and security studies. Yet, cooperation among political economists and security analysts has been limited. The contributors joined in this symposium to integrate major arguments that informed the study of international relations in the early 1980s, to apply a common analytic framework to important cases in both fields, and to use discrepancies between theory and evidence as a prod to theoretical innovation.

To maximize intellectual coherence, this has been a collaborative effort from the beginning. The contributors presented and discussed the analytic framework, the chapter outlines, and the draft chapters at working conferences sponsored by Princeton University's Center of International Studies in March and August of 1984, and provided extensive comments on chapters at every stage of development. To minimize the risk of premature intellectual closure, we sought external criticism at several points. Michael Mandelbaum and Robert Gilpin evaluated our plans at the March conference; Glenn Snyder, as well as many commentators from the floor, evaluated draft chapters at the 1984 American Political Science Convention; and Joanne Gowa provided a critique of the entire manuscript in January 1985. Finally, to minimize stylistic infelicity, Elsbeth Lewin edited the manuscript in the spring of 1985. Chapters were thoroughly revised in response to these substantive and stylistic suggestions.

The editor and authors acknowledge with gratitude the contribution of the Center of International Studies and the John D. and Catherine T. MacArthur Foundation to this undertaking. Without the institutional and financial support of the Center and the MacArthur Foundation, this project would not have been possible.

Kenneth A. Oye
Princeton, New Jersey
September 1985

EXPLAINING COOPERATION UNDER ANARCHY:
Hypotheses and Strategies

By KENNETH A. OYE*

I. INTRODUCTION

NATIONS dwell in perpetual anarchy, for no central authority imposes limits on the pursuit of sovereign interests. This common condition gives rise to diverse outcomes. Relations among states are marked by war and concert, arms races and arms control, trade wars and tariff truces, financial panics and rescues, competitive devaluation and monetary stabilization. At times, the absence of centralized international authority precludes attainment of common goals. Because as states, they cannot cede ultimate control over their conduct to an supranational sovereign, they cannot guarantee that they will adhere to their promises. The possibility of a breach of promise can impede cooperation even when cooperation would leave all better off. Yet, at other times, states do realize common goals through cooperation under anarchy. Despite the absence of any ultimate international authority, governments often bind themselves to mutually advantageous courses of action. And, though no international sovereign stands ready to enforce the terms of agreement, states can realize common interests through tacit cooperation, formal bilateral and multilateral negotiation, and the creation of international regimes. The question is: If international relations can approximate both a Hobbesian state of nature and a Lockean civil society, why does cooperation emerge in some cases and not in others?[1]

The contributors to this symposium address both explanatory and prescriptive aspects of this perennial question. *First, what circumstances favor the emergence of cooperation under anarchy?* Given the lack of a

* I am grateful for comments by Jeff Frieden, Ralph Ginsberg, Joanne Gowa, Stephen Krasner, David Lake, Timothy McKeown, Paul Quirk, Arthur Stein, and the other contributors to this volume.

[1] The essays presented here focus on nation-states as primary actors in world politics, treat national preferences as sovereign, and assume that any ultimate escape from international anarchy is unlikely. Our focus is on non-altruistic cooperation among states dwelling in international anarchy.

central authority to guarantee adherence to agreements, what features of situations encourage or permit states to bind themselves to mutually beneficial courses of action? What features of situations preclude co-operation? *Second, what strategies can states adopt to foster the emergence of cooperation by altering the circumstances they confront?* Governments need not necessarily accept circumstances as given. To what extent are situational impediments to cooperation subject to willful modification? Through what higher order strategies can states create the preconditions for cooperation?

The problem of explaining and promoting international cooperation encompasses many of the principal questions in the disciplines of political economy and security studies. However, divergent terminological conventions and substantive applications have impeded the comparison of answers. In the essays presented here, a unified analytic framework, derived from elementary game theory and microeconomics, has been superimposed on cases in international security and economic affairs. This use of the austere abstractions of game theory and microeconomics offers several advantages.[2] First, superficial differences often obscure the parallelism of questions, explanations, and prescriptions in the two fields. By reducing concepts to fundamentals, the use of elements of game theory and microeconomics permits ready identification of parallels. Second, intrinsic differences between the politics of war and the politics of wealth and welfare may give rise to divergent explanations and prescriptions. A unified analytic framework facilitates explicit recognition of differences in the extent and causes of, and prospects for, cooperation in security and economic affairs. Finally, uneven intellectual development may give rise to divergent explanations and prescriptions. A unified analytic framework fosters transference of useful concepts between the fields.[3]

In this introductory essay, I submit that three circumstantial dimensions serve both as proximate explanations of cooperation and as targets

[2] In this essay, I use elementary game theory in a purely instrumental fashion. First, although some references to the formal literature are provided, the text does not furnish formal proofs on the existence or location of equilibrium points in different categories of games. As Thomas Schelling notes, the equilibrium solutions identified by formal game theorists may stabilize convergent expectations among mathematicians, but unless equilibria can also be reached through "alternative less sophisticated routes," such solutions may have little influence on international outcomes. See Schelling, *The Strategy of Conflict* (London: Oxford University Press, 1963), 113-14. Accordingly, the contributors search for "alternative less sophisticated routes" to reach mutually beneficial equilibrium points and for simple strategies to restructure situations to create mutually beneficial equilibrium points.

[3] For an extended discussion of the uses and abuses of game theory in the empirical study of international politics, see Duncan Snidal, "The Game *Theory* of International Politics," in this collection.

of longer-term strategies to promote cooperation. Each of the three major sections of this piece defines a dimension, explains how that dimension accounts for the incidence of cooperation and conflict in the absence of centralized authority, and examines associated strategies for enhancing the prospects for cooperation.

In the section entitled "Payoff Structure: Mutual and Conflicting Preferences," I discuss how payoffs affect the prospects for cooperation and present strategies to improve the prospects for cooperation by altering payoffs. Orthodox game theorists identify optimal strategies *given* ordinally defined classes of games, and their familiar insights provide the starting point for the discussion.[4] Recent works in security studies, institutional microeconomics, and international political economy suggest strategies to *alter* payoff structures and thereby improve the prospects for cooperation.[5]

In the next section, entitled "Shadow of the Future: Single-play and Iterated Games," I discuss how the prospect of continuing interaction affects the likelihood of cooperation;[6] examine how strategies of reciprocity can provide direct paths to cooperative outcomes under iterated conditions;[7] and suggest strategies to lengthen the shadow of the future.[8] In addition, this section shows that recognition and control capabilities— the ability to distinguish between cooperation and defection by others

[4] For the definitive classification of ordinally defined games, see Anatol Rapoport and Melvin Guyer, "A Taxonomy of 2 x 2 Games," *General Systems* 11 (1966), 203-14. For an extended reinterpretation of crisis bargaining in light of payoff structures, see Glenn H. Snyder and Paul Diesing, *Conflict Among Nations: Bargaining, Decisionmaking, and System Structure in International Crises* (Princeton: Princeton University Press, 1977).

[5] For examples, see Robert Jervis, "Cooperation under the Security Dilemma," *World Politics* 30 (January 1978), 167-214; Oliver E. Williamson, "Credible Commitments: Using Hostages to Support Exchange," *American Economic Review* (September 1983), 519-40; John Gerard Ruggie, "International Regimes, Transactions, and Change: Embedded Liberalism in the Postwar Economic Order," in Stephen D. Krasner, ed., *International Regimes* (Ithaca, N.Y.: Cornell University Press, 1983).

[6] For orthodox game-theoretic analyses of the importance of iteration, see R. Duncan Luce and Howard Raiffa, *Games and Decisions* (New York: Wiley, 1957), Appendix 8, and David M. Kreps, Paul Milgram, John Roberts, and Robert Wilson, "Rational Cooperation in Finitely-Repeated Prisoner's Dilemma," *Journal of Economic Theory* 27 (August 1982, 245-52. For the results of laboratory experiments, see Robert Radlow, "An Experimental Study of Cooperation in the Prisoner's Dilemma Game," *Journal of Conflict Resolution* 9 (June 1965), 221-27. On the importance of indefinite iteration to the emergence of cooperation in business transactions, see Robert Telsor, "A Theory of Self-Enforcing Agreements," *Journal of Business* 53 (January 1980), 27-44.

[7] On how iterated Prisoners' Dilemmas environments literally select for Tit-for-Tat strategies, see Robert Axelrod, *The Evolution of Cooperation* (New York: Basic Books, 1984). For a formal statement on the effects of reciprocity on equilibrium outcomes in iterated games, see Drew Fudenberg and Eric Maskin, "The Folk Theorem in Repeated Games with Discounting and with Incomplete Information," *Econometrica*, forthcoming.

[8] On enhancing iterativeness through decomposition of payoffs over time, see Schelling (fn. 2), 43-46, and Axelrod (fn. 7), 126-32.

and to respond in kind—can affect the power of reciprocity, and suggests strategies to improve recognition capabilities.[9]

In the third section, "Number of Players: Two-Person and N-Person Games," I explain why cooperation becomes more difficult as the number of actors increases; present strategies for promoting cooperation in N-actor situations; and offer strategies for promoting cooperation by reducing the number of actors necessary to the realization of common interests. Game theorists and oligopoly theorists have long noted that cooperation becomes more difficult as numbers increase, and their insights provide a starting point for discussion.[10] Recent work in political economy focuses on two strategies for promoting cooperation in thorny N-person situations: functionalist analysts of regimes suggest strategies for increasing the likelihood and robustness of cooperation *given* large numbers of actors;[11] analysts of *ad hoc* bargaining in international political economy suggest strategies of bilateral and regional decomposition to *reduce* the number of actors necessary to the realization of some mutual interests, at the expense of the magnitude of gains from cooperation.[12]

Each of the three circumstantial dimensions serves both as an explanation of cooperation and as a target of strategies to promote cooperation. The concluding section of this essay provides a roadmap to our efforts to test these preliminary explanations and strategies. By applying this common analytic framework to cases in economic and security affairs and by searching for explicit parallels and differences in the incidence, causes, and prospects for cooperation, the authors hope to contribute to a deeper understanding of international cooperation.

II. Payoff Structure:
Mutual and Conflicting Preferences

The structure of payoffs in a given round of play—the benefits of mutual cooperation (CC) relative to mutual defection (DD) and the benefits of unilateral defection (DC) relative to unrequited cooperation (CD)—is fundamental to the analysis of cooperation. The argument

[9] *Ibid.*, 139-41.

[10] See Martin Shubik, *Games for Society, Business and War: Towards A Theory of Gaming* (New York: Elsevier, 1975). For a formal statement on the importance of the number of players to cooperation in iterated games, see Fudenberg and Maskin (fn. 7).

[11] See Robert O. Keohane, *After Hegemony: Cooperation and Discord in the World Political Economy* (Princeton: Princeton University Press, 1984), and Krasner (fn. 5).

[12] See John A. C. Conybeare, "International Organization and the Theory of Property Rights," *International Organization* 34 (Summer 1980), 307-34, and Kenneth A. Oye, "Belief Systems, Bargaining, and Breakdown: International Political Economy 1929-1936," Ph.D. diss. (Harvard University, 1983), chap. 3.

proceeds in three stages. First, how does payoff structure affect the significance of cooperation? More narrowly, when is cooperation, defined in terms of conscious policy coordination, necessary to the realization of mutual interests? Second, how does payoff structure affect the likelihood and robustness of cooperation? Third, through what strategies can states increase the long-term prospects for cooperation by altering payoff structures?

Before turning to these questions, consider briefly some tangible and intangible determinants of payoff structures. The security and political economy literatures examine the effects of military force structure and doctrine, economic ideology, the size of currency reserves, macroeconomic circumstance, and a host of other factors on national assessments of national interests. In "Cooperation under the Security Dilemma," Robert Jervis has explained how the diffusion of offensive military technology and strategies can increase rewards from defection and thereby reduce the prospects for cooperation. In "International Regimes, Transactions, and Chance: Embedded Liberalism in the Postwar Economic Order," John Ruggie has demonstrated how the diffusion of liberal economic ideas increased the perceived benefits of mutual economic openness over mutual closure (CC-DD), and diminished the perceived rewards from asymmetric defection relative to asymmetric cooperation (DC-CD). In "Firms and Tariff Regime Change," Timothy McKeown has shown how downturns in the business cycle alter national tastes for protection and thereby decrease the perceived benefits of mutual openness relative to mutual closure and increase the perceived rewards of asymmetric defection.[13]

In the present symposium, ideological and cognitive determinants of national preferences are emphasized in Stephen Van Evera's essay on the origins of the First World War and Kenneth Oye's chapter on monetary conflict during the 1930s. Robert Jervis's essay on the emergence of concert following systemic wars elucidates international structural determinants of payoffs. John Conybeare's comparative study of trade wars, Kenneth Oye's study of monetary conflict in the 1930s, and Charles Lipson's study of bankers' dilemmas examine macroeconomic determinants of payoff structure. George Downs, David Rocke, and Randolph Siverson investigate domestic structural determinants of payoff structure in their essay on cooperation in arms races. Payoff structure

[13] See Jervis (fn. 5); Ruggie (fn. 5); Timothy J. McKeown, "Firms and Tariff Regime Change: Explaining the Demand for Protection," *World Politics* 36 (January 1984), 215-33. On the effects of *ambiguity* of preferences on the prospects of cooperation, see the concluding sections of Jervis (fn. 5).

serves as an intervening variable between cognitive, domestic, and international structural factors and international cooperation.

A. PAYOFF STRUCTURE AND COOPERATION

How does payoff structure determine the significance of cooperation? More narrowly, when is *cooperation*, defined in terms of conscious policy coordination, *necessary* to the realization of *mutual benefits?* For a *mutual benefit* to exist, actors must prefer mutual cooperation (CC) to mutual defection (DD). For coordination to be *necessary* to the realization of the mutual benefit, actors must prefer unilateral defection (DC) to unrequited cooperation (CD). These preference orderings are consistent with the familiar games of Prisoners' Dilemma, Stag Hunt, and Chicken. Indeed, these games have attracted a disproportionate share of scholarly attention precisely because cooperation is desirable but not automatic. In these cases, the capacity of states to cooperate under anarchy, to bind themselves to mutually beneficial courses of action without resort to any ultimate central authority, is vital to the realization of a common good.

Many international situations do not fall within this class of games. First, consider cases in which cooperation will not be necessary to the realization of mutual interests. If actors prefer unrequited cooperation (CD) to unilateral defection (DC), no incentive to cheat exists. The pursuit of self-interest, without regard to the action of others, will automatically lead to mutual gains. For example, pure economic liberals—more common on economics faculties than in trade ministries—believe that unrequited openness is preferable to unilateral protection. Irrespective of the actions of others, a liberal believes that openness is best. In a world of pure liberals, policy coordination will not be necessary to the realization of openness. In such situations, where interests are in full harmony, the capacity of states to cooperate under anarchy is irrelevant to the realization of mutual benefits.[14]

Second, consider cases where no mutual benefit can be realized through cooperation. If at least one actor prefers nominal mutual defection (DD) to nominal mutual cooperation (CC), "policy coordination" cannot lead to mutual gain; the term "cooperation" becomes inapplicable. Symmetric and asymmetric games of Deadlock fall into this category. For example, if both the Soviet Union and the United States prefer arms racing to arms control, conflict is inevitable. Or consider a trade example: a believer in autarky will prefer mutual protection to mutual openness. To speak of cooperation between a pure liberal and a believer in autarky

[14] For an extended discussion of the distinction between cooperation and harmony, see Keohane (fn. 11), 51-55.

is nonsense. Where harmony prevails, cooperation is unnecessary to the realization of mutual interests. Where deadlocks exist, the term "cooperation" is devoid of meaning, and conflict is inevitable. Neither harmony nor deadlock has attracted substantial attention from game theorists—precisely because cooperative and conflictual outcomes follow so directly and simply from the payoff structure.

What function do games of Harmony and Deadlock serve in this collection? In courses on diagnosis, medical students are taught, "When you hear hoofbeats, think horse before you think zebra." Harrison Wagner has offered similar advice to analysts of international relations.[15] He warned that Stag Hunt, Chicken, and Prisoners' Dilemma are often inappropriate models of international situations. When you observe conflict, think Deadlock—the absence of mutual interest—before puzzling over why a mutual interest was not realized. When you observe cooperation, think Harmony—the absence of gains from defection—before puzzling over how states were able to transcend the temptations of defection. By devoting substantial attention to the specification of payoff structures, the contributors seek to heed these warnings.

In the class of games—including Prisoners' Dilemma, Stag Hunt, and Chicken—where cooperation is necessary to the realization of mutual benefits, how does payoff structure affect the likelihood and robustness of cooperation in these situations? Cooperation will be less likely in Prisoners' Dilemma than in Stag Hunt or Chicken. To understand why, consider each of these games in conjunction with the illustrative stories from which they derive their names.

Prisoners' Dilemma: Two prisoners are suspected of a major crime. The authorities possess evidence to secure conviction on only a minor charge. If neither prisoner squeals, both will draw a light sentence on the minor charge (CC). If one prisoner squeals and the other stonewalls, the rat will go free (DC) and the sucker will draw a very heavy sentence (CD). If both squeal, both will draw a moderate sentence (DD). Each prisoner's preference ordering is: DC > CC > DD > CD. If the prisoners expect to "play" only one time, each prisoner will be better off squealing than stonewalling, no matter what his partner chooses to do (DC > CC and DD > CD). The temptation of the rat payoff and fear of the sucker payoff will drive single-play Prisoners' Dilemmas toward mutual defection. Unfortunately, if both prisoners act on this reasoning, they will draw a moderate sentence on the major charge, while cooperation could have led to a light sentence on the minor charge (CC > DD). In single-

[15] Wagner, "The Theory of Games and the Problem of International Cooperation," *American Political Science Review* 70 (June 1983), 330-46.

play Prisoners' Dilemmas, individually rational actions produce a collectively suboptimal outcome.

Stag Hunt: A group of hunters surround a stag. If all cooperate to trap the stag, all will eat well (CC). If one person defects to chase a passing rabbit, the stag will escape. The defector will eat lightly (DC) and none of the others will eat at all (CD). If all chase rabbits, all will have some chance of catching a rabbit and eating lightly (DD). Each hunter's preference ordering is: CC > DC > DD > CD. The mutual interest in plentiful venison (CC) relative to all other outcomes militates strongly against defection. However, because a rabbit in the hand (DC) is better than a stag in the bush (CD), cooperation will be assured only if each hunter believes that all hunters will cooperate. In single-play Stag Hunt, the temptation to defect to protect against the defection of others is balanced by the strong universal preference for stag over rabbit.[16]

Chicken: Two drivers race down the center of a road from opposite directions. If one swerves and the other does not, then the first will suffer the stigma of being known as a chicken (CD) while the second will enjoy being known as a hero (DC). If neither swerves, both will suffer grievously in the ensuing collision (DD). If both swerve, damage to the reputation of each will be limited (CC). Each driver's preference ordering is: DC > CC > CD > DD. If each believes that the other will swerve, then each will be tempted to defect by continuing down the center of the road. Better to be a live hero than a live chicken. If both succumb to this temptation, however, defection will result in collision. The fear that the other driver may not swerve decreases the appeal of continuing down the center of the road. In single-play Chicken, the temptations of unilateral defection are balanced by fear of mutual defection.[17]

In games that are not repeated, only ordinally defined preferences matter. Under single-play conditions, interval-level payoffs in ordinally defined categories of games cannot (in theory) affect the likelihood of cooperation. In the illustrations above, discussions of dominant strategies

[16] Kenneth Waltz borrowed Rousseau's parable of the staghunt to illustrate the infeasibility of realizing mutual interests under international anarchy. Rousseau used the staghunt to illustrate the possibility of cooperation during his first period of primative social interdependence. He argued that individuals could cooperate on "mutual undertakings" to realize "present and perceptible interest" through "some kind of free association that obligated no one and lasted only so long as the passing need that formed it." This essay returns to Rousseau's use of the staghunt. See Waltz, *Man, the State, and War* (New York: Columbia University Press, 1959), and *Jean Jacques Rousseau: The First and Second Discourses*, trans. Roger D. and Judith R. Masters (New York: St. Martins, 1964), 165-67.

[17] The illustrative preference orderings strike most mature observers as perverse: the drivers need not place themselves in the game.

do not hinge on the magnitude of differences among the payoffs. Yet the magnitude of differences between CC and DD and between DC and CD can be large or small, if not precisely measurable, and can increase or decrease. Changes in the magnitude of differences in the value placed on outcomes can influence the prospects for cooperation through two paths.

First, changes in the value attached to outcomes can transform situations from one ordinally defined class of game into another. For example, in "Cooperation under the Security Dilemma" Robert Jervis described how difficult Prisoners' Dilemmas may evolve into less challenging Stag Hunts if the gains from mutual cooperation (CC) increase relative to the gains from exploitation (DC). He related the structure of payoffs to traditional concepts of offensive and defensive dominance, and offensive and defensive dominance to technological and doctrinal shifts. Ernst Haas, Mary Pat Williams, and Don Babai have emphasized the importance of cognitive congruence as a determinant of technological cooperation. The diffusion of common conceptions of the nature and effects of technology enhanced perceived gains from cooperation and diminished perceived gains from defection, and may have transformed some Prisoners' Dilemmas into Harmony.[18]

Second, under iterated conditions, the magnitude of differences among payoffs *within* a given class of games can be an important determinant of cooperation. The more substantial the gains from mutual cooperation (CC-DD) and the less substantial the gains from unilateral defection (DC-CD), the greater the likelihood of cooperation. In iterated situations, the magnitude of the difference between CC and DD and between DC and CD in present and future rounds of play affects the likelihood of cooperation in the present. This point is developed at length in the section on the shadow of the future.

B. STRATEGIES TO ALTER PAYOFF STRUCTURE

If payoff structure affects the likelihood of cooperation, to what extent can states alter situations by modifying payoff structures, and thereby increase the long-term likelihood of cooperation? Many of the tangible and intangible determinants of payoff structure, discussed at the outset of this section, are subject to willful modification through unilateral, bilateral, and multilateral strategies. In "Cooperation under the Security Dilemma," Robert Jervis has offered specific suggestions for altering payoff structures through unilateral strategies. Procurement policy can

---

[18] Haas, Williams, and Babai, *Scientists and World Order: The Uses of Technical Knowledge in International Organizations* (Berkeley: University of California Press, 1977).

affect the prospects for cooperation. If one superpower favors procurement of defensive over offensive weapons, it can reduce its own gains from exploitation through surprise attack (DC) and reduce its adversary's fear of exploitation (CD). Members of alliances have often resorted to the device of deploying troops on troubled frontiers to increase the likelihood of cooperation. A state's use of troops as hostages is designed to diminish the payoff from its own defection—to reduce its gains from exploitation (DC)—and thereby render defensive defection by its partner less likely. Publicizing an agreement diminishes payoffs associated with defection from the agreement, and thereby lessens gains from exploitation. These observations in international relations are paralleled by recent developments in microeconomics. Oliver Williamson has identified unilateral and bilateral techniques used by firms to facilitate interfirm cooperation by diminishing gains from exploitation. He distinguishes between specific and nonspecific costs associated with adherence to agreements. Specific costs, such as specialized training, machine tools, and construction, cannot be recovered in the event of the breakdown of an agreement. When parties to an agreement incur high specific costs, repudiation of commitments will entail substantial losses. Firms can thus reduce their gains from exploitation through the technique of acquiring dedicated assets that serve as hostages to continuing cooperation. Nonspecific assets, such as general-purpose trucks and airplanes, are salvageable if agreements break down; firms can reduce their fear of being exploited by maximizing the use of nonspecific assets, but such assets cannot diminish gains from exploitation by serving as hostages.[19] Unilateral strategies can improve the prospects of cooperation by reducing both the costs of being exploited (CD) and the gains from exploitation (DC). The new literature on interfirm cooperation indirectly raises an old question on the costs of unilateral strategies to promote cooperation in international relations.

In many instances, unilateral actions that limit one's gains from exploitation may have the effect of increasing one's vulnerability to exploitation by others. For example, a state could limit gains from defection from liberal international economic norms by permitting the expansion of sectors of comparative advantage and by permitting liquidation of inefficient sectors. Because a specialized economy is a hostage to international economic cooperation, this strategy would unquestionably increase the credibility of the nation's commitment to liberalism. It also

[19] Williamson (fn. 5).

has the effect, however, of increasing the nation's vulnerability to protection by others. In the troops-as-hostage example, the government that stations troops may promote cooperation by diminishing an ally's fear of abandonment, but in so doing it raises its own fears of exploitation by the ally. In an example from the neoconservative nuclear literature, Paul Nitze, Colin Gray, William Van Cleave, and others assume that missiles will be fired against missiles rather than against industries or cities, and conclude that a shift from counterforce toward countervalue weapons may purchase a reduction in gains from exploitation at the expense of heightened vulnerability to exploitation.[20] Cognitive, domestic, and international structural factors affect payoff structure directly, and also influence perceptions of the benefits and limits of unilateral strategies to alter payoffs.

Unilateral strategies do not exhaust the range of options that states may use to alter payoff structures. Bilateral strategies—most significantly strategies of issue linkage—can be used to alter payoff structures by combining dissimilar games. Because resort to issue linkage generally assumes iteration, analysis of how issue linkage can be used to alter payoffs is presented in the section on the shadow of the future. Furthermore, bilateral "instructional" strategies can aim at altering another country's understanding of cause-and-effect relationships, and result in altered perceptions of interest. For example, American negotiators in SALT I sought to instruct their Soviet counterparts on the logic of mutual assured destruction.[21]

Multilateral strategies, centering on the formation of international regimes, can be used to alter payoff structures in two ways. First, norms generated by regimes may be internalized by states, and thereby alter payoff structure. Second, information generated by regimes may alter states' understanding of their interests. As Ernst Haas argues, new regimes may gather and distribute information that can highlight cause-and-effect relationships not previously understood. Changing perceptions of means-ends hierarchies can, in turn, result in changing perceptions of interest.[22]

[20] See Paul Nitze, "Assuring Strategic Stability in an Era of Detente," *Foreign Affairs* 54 (January 1976), 207-32, for the seminal article in this tradition. Nitze's recommendations hinge on acceptance of the precepts of what has come to be known as nuclear utilization theory. Jervis's recommendations depend on acceptance of the precepts of mutual assured destruction (fn. 5).

[21] See John Newhouse, *Cold Dawn: The Story of SALT I* (New York: Holt, Rinehart & Winston, 1973).

[22] See Haas, "Words Can Hurt You; Or Who Said What to Whom About Regimes," in Krasner (fn. 5).

III. The Shadow of the Future:
Single-Play and Iterated Games

The distinction between cases in which similar transactions among parties are unlikely to be repeated and cases in which the expectation of future interaction can influence decisions in the present is fundamental to the emergence of cooperation among egotists. As the previous section suggests, states confronting strategic situations that resemble single-play Prisoners' Dilemma and, to a lesser extent, single-play Stag Hunt and Chicken, are constantly tempted by immediate gains from unilateral defection, and fearful of immediate losses from unrequited cooperation. How does continuing interaction affect prospects for cooperation? The argument proceeds in four stages. First, why do iterated conditions improve the prospects for cooperation in Prisoners' Dilemma and Stag Hunt while diminishing the prospects for cooperation in Chicken? Second, how do strategies of reciprocity improve the prospects for cooperation under iterated conditions? Third, why does the effectiveness of reciprocity hinge on conditions of play—the ability of actors to distinguish reliably between cooperation and defection by others and to respond in kind? Fourth, through what strategies can states improve conditions of play and lengthen the shadow of the future?[23]

Before turning to these questions, consider the attributes of iterated situations. First, states must expect to continue dealing with each other. This condition is, in practice, not particularly restrictive. With the possible exception of global thermonuclear war, international politics is characterized by the expectaton of future interaction. Second, payoff structures must not change substantially over time. In other words, each round of play should not alter the structure of the game in the future. This condition is, in practice, quite restrictive. For example, states considering surprise attack when offense is dominant are in a situation that has many of the characteristics of a single-play game: attack alters options and payoffs in future rounds of interaction. Conversely, nations considering increases or decreases in their military budgets are in a situation that has many of the characteristics of an iterated game: spending options and associated marginal increases or decreases in military strength are likely to remain fairly stable over future rounds of interaction. In international monetary affairs, governments considering or fearing devaluation under a gold-exchange standard are in a situation that has many of the characteristics of a single-play game: devaluation may diminish the value of another state's foreign currency reserves on a one-

---

[23] This section is derived largely from Axelrod (fn. 7), and Telsor (fn. 6).

time basis, while reductions in holdings of reserves would diminish possible losses on a one-time basis. Conversely, governments considering intervention under a floating system with minimal reserves are in a situation that has many of the characteristics of an iterated game: depreciation or appreciation of a currency would not produce substantial one-time losses or gains. Third, the size of the discount rate applied to the future affects the iterativeness of games. If a government places little value on future payoffs, its situation has many of the characteristics of a single-play game. If it places a high value on future payoffs, its situation may have many of the characteristics of an iterated game. For example, political leaders in their final term are likely to discount the future more substantially than political leaders running for, or certain of, reelection.

A. THE SHADOW OF THE FUTURE AND COOPERATION

How does the shadow of the future affect the likelihood of cooperation? Under single-play conditions without a sovereign, adherence to agreements is often irrational. Consider the single-play Prisoners' Dilemma. Each prisoner is better off squealing, whether or not his partner decides to squeal. In the absence of continuing interaction, defection would emerge as the dominant strategy. Because the prisoners can neither turn to a central authority for enforcement of an agreement to cooperate nor rely on the anticipation of retaliation to deter present defection, cooperation will be unlikely under single-play conditions. If the prisoners expect to be placed in similar situations in the future, the prospects for cooperation improve. Experimental evidence suggests that under iterated Prisoners' Dilemma the incidence of cooperation rises substantially.[24] Even in the absence of centralized authority, tacit agreements to cooperate through mutual stonewalling are frequently reached and maintained. Under iterated Prisoners' Dilemma, a potential defector compares the immediate gain from squealing with the possible sacrifice of future gains that may result from squealing.[25] In single-play Stag

[24] See Anatol Rapoport and Albert Chammah, *Prisoner's Dilemma* (Ann Arbor: University of Michigan Press, 1965), and subsequent essays in *Journal of Conflict Resolution*.
[25] One common objection to this line of argument centers on the irrationality of cooperation if a sequence of Prisoners' Dilemmas has a known last element. On the known last play, the immediate gain from squealing cannot be offset by expectations of future cooperation. On the next-to-last play, the immediate gain from squealing is not offset by expectations of future cooperation, since both actors know that cooperation is irrational on the last move. And so on back toward the initial move. This line of analysis collapses iterated Prisoners' Dilemma into single-play Prisoners' Dilemma. To analysts of international relations, the importance of this objection is limited. In international relations, no experimenter decrees that a series of Prisoners' Dilemmas shall end on the 10th move or at noon. Although any series of transactions will terminate sooner or later, governments do not generally know when the last play will occur. On all rounds of play, the actors' decisions are conditioned

Hunt, each hunter is tempted to defect in order to defend himself against the possibility of defection by others. A reputation for reliability, for resisting temptation, reduces the likelihood of defection. If the hunters are a permanent group, and expect to hunt together again, the immediate gains from unilateral defection relative to unrequited cooperation must be balanced against the cost of diminished cooperation in the future. In both Prisoners' Dilemma and Stag Hunt, defection in the present *decreases* the likelihood of cooperation in the future. In both, therefore, iteration improves the prospects for cooperation.[26] In Chicken, iteration may decrease the prospects for cooperation. Under single-play conditions, the temptation of unilateral defection is balanced by the fear of the collision that follows from mutual defection. How does iteration affect this balance? If the game is repeated indefinitely, then each driver may refrain from swerving in the present to coerce the other driver into swerving in the future. Each driver may seek to acquire a reputation for not swerving to cause the other driver to swerve. In iterated Chicken, one driver's defection in the present may decrease the likelihood of the other driver's defection in the future.[27]

B.   STRATEGIES OF RECIPROCITY AND CONDITIONS OF PLAY

It is at this juncture that strategy enters the explanation. Although the expectation of continuing interaction has varying effects on the likelihood of cooperation in the illustrations above, an iterated environment permits resort to strategies of reciprocity that may improve the prospects of cooperation in Chicken as well as in Prisoners' Dilemma and Stag Hunt. Robert Axelrod argues that strategies of reciprocity have the effect of promoting cooperation by establishing a direct connection between an actor's present behavior and anticipated future benefits. Tit-for-Tat, or conditional cooperation, can increase the likelihood of joint cooperation by shaping the future consequences of present cooperation or defection.

---

by the possibility of future interaction. For a formal analysis of how uncertain time horizons can lead to a resolution of the Prisoners' Dilemma, see Luce and Raiffa (fn. 6), Appendix 8. Discount parameters such as Axelrod's "*w*" may capture the effects of uncertainty. Possible future payoffs may be discounted both because the value placed on future benefits is lower than present benefits and because the stream of future benefits may be interrupted if the structure of the game changes.

[26] This conclusion rests on the assumption that dyadic interactions are moderately independent. For an argument on how defection can provide a benefit (external to a dyadic interaction) by discouraging the entry of other actors, see Shibley Telhami, "Cooperation or Coercion: Tit for Tat and the Realities of International Politics," unpub. (Swarthmore College, January 1985). Note also that cooperation can also encourage (mutually beneficial) entry of other actors.

[27] On iterated Chicken, see Snyder and Diesing (fn. 4), 43-44.

In iterated Prisoners' Dilemma and Stag Hunt, reciprocity underscores the future consequences of present cooperation and defection. The argument presented above—that iteration enhances the prospects for cooperation in these games—rests on the assumption that defection in the present will decrease the likelihood of cooperation in the future. Adoption of an implicit or explicit strategy of matching stonewalling with stonewalling, squealing with squealing, rabbit chasing with rabbit chasing, and cooperative hunting with cooperative hunting validates the assumption. In iterated Chicken, a strategy of reciprocity can offset the perverse effects of reputational considerations on the prospects for cooperation. Recall that in iterated Chicken, each driver may refrain from swerving in the present to coerce the other driver into swerving in the future. Adoption of an implicit or explicit strategy of Tit-for-Tat in iterated games of Chicken alters the future stream of benefits associated with present defection. If a strategy of reciprocity is credible, then the mutual losses associated with future collisions can encourage present swerving. In all three games, a promise to respond to present cooperation with future cooperation and a threat to respond to present defection with future defection can improve the prospects for cooperation.

The effectiveness of strategies of reciprocity hinges on conditions of play—the ability of actors to distinguish reliably between cooperation and defection by others and to respond in kind. In the illustrations provided above, the meaning of "defect" and "cooperate" is unambiguous. Dichotomous choices—between squeal and stonewall, chase the rabbit or capture the stag, continue down the road or swerve—limit the likelihood of misperception. Further, the actions of all are transparent. Given the definitions of the situations, prisoners, hunters, and drivers can reliably detect defection and cooperation by other actors. Finally, the definition of the actors eliminates the possibility of control problems. Unitary prisoners, hunters, and drivers do not suffer from factional, organizational, or bureaucratic dysfunctions that might hinder implementation of strategies of reciprocity.

In international relations, conditions of play can limit the effectiveness of reciprocity. The definition of cooperation and defection may be ambiguous. For example, the Soviet Union and the United States hold to markedly different definitions of "defection" from the terms of détente as presented in the Basic Principles Agreement;[28] the European Community and the United States differ over whether domestic sectoral policies comprise indirect export subsidies. Further, actions may not be

[28] See Alexander L. George, *Managing U.S.-Soviet Rivalry: Problems of Crisis Prevention* (Boulder, CO: Westview, 1983).

transparent. For example, governments may not be able to detect one another's violations of arms control agreements or indirect export subsidies. If defection cannot be reliably detected, the effect of present cooperation on possible future reprisals will erode. Together, ambiguous definitions and a lack of transparency can limit the ability of states to recognize cooperation and defection by others.

Because reciprocity requires flexibility, control is as important as recognition. Internal factional, organizational, and bureaucratic dysfunctions may limit the ability of nations to implement Tit-for-Tat strategies. It may be easier to sell one unvarying line of policy than to sell a strategy of shifting between lines of policy in response to the actions of others. For example, arms suppliers and defense planners tend to resist the cancellation of weapons systems even if the cancellation is a response to the actions of a rival. Import-competing industries tend to resist the removal of barriers to imports, even if trade liberalization is in response to liberalization by another state. At times, national decision makers may be unable to implement strategies of reciprocity. On other occasions, they must invest heavily in selling reciprocity. For these reasons, national decison makers may display a bias against conditional strategies: the domestic costs of pursuing such strategies may partially offset the value of the discounted stream of future benefits that conditional policies are expected to yield.

As Robert Axelrod notes, problems of recognition and control may limit effective resort to reciprocity. In this symposium, such problems are examined in several ways. The essay on "Arms Races and Cooperation" presents a simple simulation designed to assess the sensitivity of Tit-for-Tat strategies to departures from perfect recognition and control. The case studies and the conclusion assess the extent to which problems of recognition and control are, in practice, impediments to effective utilization of strategies of reciprocity.[29]

C.   STRATEGIES TO IMPROVE RECOGNITION AND LENGTHEN THE SHADOW
     OF THE FUTURE

To what extent can governments promote cooperation by creating favorable conditions of play and by lengthening the shadow of the future? The literature on international regimes offers several techniques for creating favorable conditions of play. Explicit codification of norms

---

[29] Axelrod shows that in iterated Prisoners' Dilemma, where actors *can* reliably distinguish between cooperation and defection by others and respond in kind, Tit-for-Tat performs better than do alternative strategies. When recognition and control are perfect, iterated environments strongly favor the emergence of cooperation.

can limit definitional ambiguity. The very act of clarifying standards of conduct, of defining cooperative and uncooperative behavior, can permit more effective resort to strategies of reciprocity. Further, provisions for surveillance—for example, mechanisms for verification in arms control agreements or for sharing information on the nature and effects of domestic sectoral policies—can increase transparency. In practice, the goal of enhancing recognition capabilities is often central to negotiations under anarchy.

The game-theoretic and institutional microeconomic literatures offer several approaches to increasing the iterative character of situations. Thomas Schelling and Robert Axelrod suggest tactics of decomposition over time to lengthen the shadow of the future.[30] For example, the temptation to defect in a deal promising thirty billion dollars for a billion barrels of oil may be reduced if the deal is sliced up into a series of payments and deliveries. Cooperation in arms reduction or in territorial disengagement may be difficult if the reduction or disengagement must be achieved in one jump. If a reduction or disengagement can be sliced up into increments, the problem of cooperation may be rendered more tractable. Finally, strategies of issue linkage can be used to alter payoff structures and to interject elements of iterativeness into single-play situations. Relations among states are rarely limited to one single-play issue of overriding importance. When nations confront a single-play game on one issue, present defection may be deterred by threats of retaliation on other iterated issues. In international monetary affairs, for instance, a government fearing one-time reserve losses if another state devalues its currency may link devaluation to an iterated trade game. By establishing a direct connection between present behavior in a single-play game and future benefits in an iterated game, tacit or explicit cross-issue linkage can lengthen the shadow of the future.[31]

The shadow of the future, strategies of reciprocity, and payoff structure interact in determining the likelihood of cooperation. Incentives to cooperate and to defect are the discounted stream of anticipated payoffs across current and future encounters. The size of the discount rate affects the value of future benefits. A Tit-for-Tat strategy provides a clearer view of how present behavior is likely to affect an adversary's future behavior, and thereby sharpens differences between the anticipated

[30] Schelling (fn. 2), 43-46, and Axelrod (fn. 7), 126-32.

[31] For analyses of issue linkage, see Robert D. Tollison and Thomas D. Willett, "An Economic Theory of Mutually Advantageous Issue Linkages in International Negotiations," *International Organization* 33 (Autumn 1979) 425-49; Oye (fn. 12), chap. 3, "Bargaining: The Logic of Contingent Action"; and Axelrod and Keohane in the concluding essay of this symposium.

stream of payoffs for cooperation and defection. The structure of payoffs in each round of play is the object of the discounting and anticipating.

IV. NUMBER OF PLAYERS:
TWO-PERSON AND N-PERSON GAMES

Up to now, I have discussed the effects of payoff structure and the shadow of the future on the prospects of cooperation in terms of two-person situations. What happens to the prospects for cooperation as the number of significant actors rises? In this section, I explain why the prospects for cooperation diminish as the number of players increases; examine the function of international regimes as a response to the problems created by large numbers; and offer strategies to improve the prospects for cooperation by altering situations to diminish the number of significant players.

The numbers problem is central to many areas of the social sciences. Mancur Olson's theory of collective action focuses on N-person versions of Prisoners' Dilemma. The optimism of our earlier discussions of cooperation under iterated Prisoners' Dilemma gives way to the pessimism of analyses of cooperation in the provision of public goods. Applications of Olsonian theory to problems ranging from cartelization to the provision of public goods in alliances underscore the significance of "free-riding" as an impediment to cooperation.[32] In international relations, the numbers problem has been central to two debates. The longstanding controversy over the stability of bipolar versus multipolar systems reduces to a debate over the impact of the number of significant actors on international conflict.[33] A more recent controversy, between proponents of the theory of hegemonic stability and advocates of international regimes, reduces to a debate over the effects of large numbers on the robustness of cooperation.[34]

[32] See Mancur Olson, Jr., *The Logic of Collective Action: Public Goods and the Theory of Groups* (Cambridge: Harvard University Press, 1965), and Mancur Olson and Richard Zeckhauser, "An Economic Theory of Alliances," *Review of Economics and Statistics* 48 (August 1966), 266-79. For a recent elegant summary and extension of the large literature on dilemmas of collective action, see Russell Hardin, *Collective Action* (Baltimore: Johns Hopkins University Press, 1982).

[33] See Kenneth N. Waltz, "The Stability of a Bipolar World," *Daedalus* 93 (Summer 1964), and Richard N. Rosecrance, "Bipolarity, Multipolarity, and the Future," *Journal of Conflict Resolution* (September 1966), 314-27.

[34] On hegemony, see Robert Gilpin, *U.S. Power and the Multinational Corporation* (New York: Basic Books, 1975), 258-59. On duopoly, see Timothy McKeown, "Hegemonic Stability Theory and 19th-Century Tariff Levels in Europe," *International Organization* 37 (Winter 1983), 73-91. On regimes and cooperation, see Keohane (fn. 11), and Krasner (fn. 5). On two-person games and N-person public-goods problems, see Charles Kindleberger, "Dominance and Leadership in the International Economy: Exploitation, Public Goods, and Free Rides," *International Studies Quarterly* 25 (June 1981), 242-54.

A. NUMBER OF PLAYERS AND COOPERATION

How do numbers affect the likelihood of cooperation? There are at least three important channels of influence.[35] First, cooperation requires recognition of opportunities for the advancement of mutual interests, as well as policy coordination once these opportunities have been identified. As the number of players increases, transactions and information costs rise. In simple terms, the complexity of N-person situations militates against identification and realization of common interests. Avoiding nuclear war during the Cuban missile crisis called for cooperation by the Soviet Union and the United States. The transaction and information costs in this particularly harrowing crisis, though substantial, did not preclude cooperation. By contrast, the problem of identifying significant actors, defining interests, and negotiating agreements that embodied mutual interests in the N-actor case of 1914 was far more difficult. These secondary costs associated with attaining cooperative outcomes in N-actor cases erode the difference between CC and DD. More significantly, the intrinsic difficulty of anticipating the behavior of other players and of weighing the value of the future goes up with the number of players. The complexity of solving N-person games, even in the purely deductive sense, has stunted the development of formal work on the problem. This complexity is even greater in real situations, and operates against multilateral cooperation.

Second, as the number of players increases, the likelihood of autonomous defection and of recognition and control problems increases. Cooperative behavior rests on calculations of expected utility—merging discount rates, payoff structures, and anticipated behavior of other players. Discount rates and approaches to calculation are likely to vary across actors, and the prospects for mutual cooperation may decline as the number of players and the probable heterogeneity of actors increases. The chances of including a state that discounts the future heavily, that is too weak (domestically) to detect, react, or implement a strategy of reciprocity, that cannot distinguish reliably between cooperation and defection by other states, or that departs from even minimal standards of rationality increase with the number of states in a game. For example, many pessimistic analyses of the consequences of nuclear proliferation focus on how breakdowns of deterrence may become more likely as the number of countries with nuclear weapons increases.[36]

Third, as the number of players increases, the feasibility of sanctioning defectors diminishes. Strategies of reciprocity become more difficult to

---

[35] See Keohane (fn. 11), chap. 6, for extensions of these points.
[36] See Lewis A. Dunn, *Controlling the Bomb* (New Haven: Yale University Press, 1982).

implement without triggering a collapse of cooperation. In two-person games, Tit-for-Tat works well because the costs of defection are focused on only one other party. If defection imposes costs on all parties in an N-person game, however, the power of strategies of reciprocity is undermined. The infeasibility of sanctioning defectors creates the possibility of free-riding. What happens if we increase the number of actors in the iterated Prisoners' Dilemma from 2 to 20? Confession by any one of them could lead to the conviction of all on the major charge; therefore, the threat to retaliate against defection in the present with defection in the future will impose costs on all prisoners, and could lead to wholesale defection in subsequent rounds. For example, under the 1914 system of alliances, retaliation against one member of the alliance was the equivalent of retaliation against all. In N-person games, a strategy of conditional defection can have the effect of spreading, rather than containing, defection.

B.   STRATEGIES OF INSTITUTIONALIZATION AND DECOMPOSITION

Given a large number of players, what strategies can states use to increase the likelihood of cooperation? Regime creation can increase the likelihood of cooperation in N-person games.[37] First, conventions provide rules of thumb that can diminish transaction and information costs. Second, collective enforcement mechanisms both decrease the likelihood of autonomous defection and permit selective punishment of violators of norms. These two functions of international regimes directly address problems created by large numbers of players. For example, Japan and the members of NATO profess a mutual interest in limiting flows of militarily useful goods and technology to the Soviet Union. Obviously, all suppliers of militarily useful goods and technology must cooperate to deny the Soviet Union access to such items. Although governments differ in their assessment of the military value of some goods and technologies, there is consensus on a rather lengthy list of prohibited items. By facilitating agreement on the prohibited list, the Coordinating Committee of the Consultative Group of NATO (CoCom) provides a relatively clear definition of what exports would constitute defection. By defining the scope of defection, the CoCom list forestalls the necessity of retaliation against nations that ship technology or goods that do not fall within the consensual definition of defection.[38] Generally, cooper-

[37] In addition to providing a partial solution to the problems of large numbers, regimes may affect the order and intensity of actor preferences as norms are internalized, and may heighten the iterativeness of situations as interaction becomes more frequent.

[38] For a full analysis of intra-alliance cooperation on East-West trade, see Michael Mastanduno, "Strategies of Economic Containment: U.S. Trade Relations with the Soviet

ation is a prerequisite of regime creation. The creation of rules of thumb and mechanisms of collective enforcement and the maintenance and administration of regimes can demand an extraordinary degree of cooperation. This problem may limit the range of situations susceptible to modification through regimist strategies.

What strategies can reduce the number of significant players in a game and thereby render cooperation more likely? When governments are unable to cooperate on a global scale, they often turn to discriminatory strategies to encourage bilateral or regional cooperation. Tactics of decomposition across actors can, at times, improve the prospects for cooperation. Both the possibilities and the limits of strategies to reduce the number of players are evident in the discussions that follow. First, reductions in the number of actors can usually only be purchased at the expense of the magnitude of gains from cooperation. The benefits of regional openness are smaller than the gains from global openness. A bilateral clearing arrangement is less economically efficient than a multilateral clearing arrangement. Strategies to reduce the number of players in a game generally diminish the gains from cooperation while they increase the likelihood and robustness of cooperation.[39] Second, strategies to reduce the number of players generally impose substantial costs on third parties. These externalities may motivate third parties to undermine the limited area of cooperation or may serve as an impetus for a third party to enlarge the zone of cooperation. In the 1930s, for example, wholesale resort to discriminatory trading policies facilitated creation of exclusive zones of commercial openness. When confronted by a shrinking market share, Great Britain adopted a less liberal and more discriminatory commercial policy in order to secure preferential access to its empire and to undermine preferential agreements between other countries. As the American market share diminished, the United States adopted a more liberal and more discriminatory commercial policy to increase its access to export markets. It is not possible, however, to reduce the number of players in all situations. For example, compare the example of limited commercial openness with the example of a limited strategic embargo. To reduce the number of actors in a trade war, market access can simply be offered to only one country and withheld from others. By contrast, defection by only one supplier can permit the target

---

[39] For a pure libertarian argument on private exchange as an alternative to public management, see Conybeare (fn. 12).

of a strategic embargo to obtain a critical technology. These problems may limit the range of situations susceptible to modification through strategies that reduce the number of players in games.

IV. CONCLUSION

As I noted at the outset, the analytic approach presented in this symposium constitutes an implicit attack on the traditional boundary between studies of international political economy and studies of security. The emphasis on cooperation, the reliance on the three circumstantial dimensions, and the analysis of associated strategies to alter circumstances are not specific to either security affairs or political economy. This essay and Duncan Snidal's complementary introduction, "The Game *Theory* of International Politics," define and operationalize the three sets of abstract explanatory and prescriptive propositions, and discuss the uses and abuses of game theory in the empirical study of international politics. The six empirical essays in the main body of this collection provide a limited trial of these propositions by probing diverse situations, strategies, and outcomes in both security and economic affairs.[40]

In the first of the three case studies in security affairs, Robert Jervis explains the incidence, scope, and duration of great-power concerts. He begins by noting that counterhegemonic war appears to be a necessary condition for the emergence of concert, and then offers an explanation of why the Concert of Europe lasted from 1815 to 1854, but attempts at concert following World Wars I and II collapsed. His analysis stresses the effects of an international structural cause—counterhegemonic war—and of concert itself on the preconditions for cooperation.

Stephen Van Evera explains the collapse of a fragile peace in 1914. His analysis stresses the effects of a family of ideas—militarism, nationalism, and social imperialism—on the governing elites' perceptions of their interests and of each other. Van Evera suggests that these ideas undermined each of the three situational preconditions for cooperation, and are necessary to the explanation of the outbreak of the First World War.

George Downs, David Rocke, and Randolph Siverson transcend some of the superficial controversies over strategy that divide analysts of arms control. Their essay identifies conditions that determine when unilateral

---

[40] See Alexander George and Richard Smoke, *Deterrence in American Foreign Policy* (New York: Columbia University Press, 1974) for a seminal example of how an austere theoretical framework and detailed historical cases can promote both development of theory and historical understanding.

action, tacit bargaining, and explicit negotiation are likely to reduce the intensity of arms races. Their analysis of 19th- and 20th-century arms races that did not terminate in war stresses the effects of payoff structure and of problems of recognition and control on the efficacy of arms-control strategies.

In the first of the case studies in political economy, John Conybeare examines factors that may promote and inhibit commercial cooperation. He explains why cooperation was not robust during the perpetual iterations of the Anglo-Hanse conflict, how asymmetries of power initially impeded cooperation in the late 19th-century Franco-Italian case, and how the "publicness" of the Hawley-Smoot tariff impeded cooperation during the 1930s.

Between 1930 and 1936, international monetary relations were marked by the collapse of fixed exchange rates and resort to competitive devaluation, the emergence of bilateral and regional cooperation, and limited monetary coordination under the Tripartite Stabilization Agreement. Kenneth Oye considers circumstantial and strategic determinants of the incidence and scope of monetary cooperation in the 1930s.

In times of financial crisis, individual creditors can derive benefit from limiting their exposure to protect themselves against default. But if many creditors limit their exposure, default is assured. In his essay, Charles Lipson notes that contemporary debt rescheduling requires the cooperation of literally hundreds of creditors, and explains how private sanctions and institutional settings have fostered cooperation (to date).

By juxtaposing a generic analytic framework and two sets of cases organized along traditional subdisciplinary boundaries, the contributors to this collection encourage speculation along several lines. First, to what extent do cases in security affairs and political economy tend to fall into different areas of the space defined by the three situational dimensions? Second, to what extent does readiness to resort to associated sets of strategies appear to differ in security affairs and political economy? Third, what aspects of cooperation in security affairs and political economy are *not* explained by the core approach employed in this volume? Finally, what additional situational and strategic variables might improve the quality of explanation?

In the concluding essay, Robert Axelrod and Robert Keohane consider these questions. They begin by examining the fit between observed cooperation and conflict, and the three sets of situational preconditions. They then review the case studies, assessing the possibilities and limits of strategies to alter payoff structure, to lengthen the shadow of the future and create favorable conditions of play, and to reduce numbers of players, with particular emphasis on reciprocity and regime building. Axelrod and Keohane ultimately move toward a new synthesis. They suggest that international regimes can reinforce and institutionalize reciprocity, and that nations have enhanced the prospects for cooperation by relying on a combination of atomistic reciprocity and regime establishment.

THE GAME *THEORY* OF
INTERNATIONAL POLITICS

By DUNCAN SNIDAL*

THE application of game theory to international politics is hardly new, but there has been a recent increase in the popularity of the approach. This resurgence has been associated with new applications of game models to international political economy in addition to their now standard role in military-political strategic analysis. This is a timely antidote to the exclusive usage of strategic analysis to refer to military affairs. What is fundamental to strategic analysis is not the specific subject matter of military or economic issues, but a basic conception of how we understand politics among states. This conception of nation-states as interdependent, goal-seeking actors lies at the heart of strategic game analysis; it is applicable across different issue areas.

The ultimate promise of game theory lies in expanding the realm of rational-actor models beyond the restrictive confines of the traditional Realist perspective to a more complex world where concern is less exclusively with problems of conflict and as much with problems of cooperation. This expansion will provide a stimulus to the ongoing theoretical project of integrating the military and political-economy sides of international politics. One important aspect of this theoretical inte-gration is the development of models capable of encompassing different issue areas that are usually treated as fundamentally disparate. Individ-ually, the articles in this volume advance that goal by applying game models across a wide range of international political, military, and eco-nomic issues. Collectively, the articles show the value of game theory in a broader theoretical enterprise: understanding different questions of international politics within the same theoretical framework. Thus, as will be elaborated upon throughout this article, the ultimate payoff of game theory is the use of game *models* to understand different aspects of international politics in terms of a unified *theory*.

A second valuable aspect of this resurgence of interest in game theory

* Raymond Duvall has provided a number of important ideas on how to formulate the argument of the paper. I have also benefited greatly from discussions with the other par-ticipants in this symposium, and from comments by Kenneth Oye, Robert Axelrod, and especially Robert Keohane. Chris Achen and John Freeman made valuable comments on earlier drafts, as did participants in the Program on Interdependent Political Economy (PIPE) Workshop at the University of Chicago.

is a greater concern for empirical application of the models. Earlier military-strategic analyses were based on deductive arguments, but remained untested beyond anecdotal embellishment. Perhaps this could be excused by the fortunate fact that there had been insufficient data on the outbreak of nuclear war as the central dependent variable. However, relevant historical evidence on non-nuclear deterrence also has only recently been systematically exploited.[1] One virtue of recent game theory applications to issues of both military and political economy is its attention to the empirical implications and evaluation of the deductive theory. In examining the usefulness of game theory for theorizing about international politics, I will emphasize the requisites for this empirically oriented side of the game-theoretic enterprise.

Applying game theory to a substantive body of knowledge such as international relations raises a host of difficult empirical questions. For example: Who are the relevant actors? What are the rules of the game? What are the choices available to each actor? What are the payoffs in the game? Is the issue best characterized as single-play or repeated-play? In analyzing any particular issue, it is impossible to answer all of these questions with certainty. Game theory often seems to demand more information than can feasibly be obtained. Ironically, it cannot always adequately incorporate other important available information—including relevant historical details about the context of interaction, insights into the personalities and behavior of decision makers, and understandings of the diplomatic or foreign policy process. These shortcomings of game theoretic analysis have led some analysts to conclude that its usefulness as a theoretical guide to the empirical study of international politics is seriously impaired.

This conclusion shows a misunderstanding of the power of (game) theory by treating it as a descriptive and not as an analytical tool. Too many "applications" of game theory have merely been in the spirit of sorting out whether the Cuban missile crisis was really Chicken or Prisoners' Dilemma. Such usage may be helpful for reconstructing and interpreting particular events, but it misinterprets the primary value of game theory as that of redescribing the world, and is therefore limited as a test of game theory. It would be a more appropriate test of a

[1] Among more recent works, see Alan Alexandroff and Richard Rosecrance, "Deterrence in 1939," *World Politics* 29 (April 1977), 404-24; Bruce Bueno de Mesquita, *The War Trap* (New Haven: Yale University Press, 1981); Alexander George and Richard Smoke, *Deterrence in American Foreign Policy* (New York: Columbia University Press, 1974); Robert Jervis, *Perception and Misperception in International Politics* (Princeton: Princeton University Press, 1976); John Mearsheimer, *Conventional Deterrence* (Ithaca, NY: Cornell University Press, 1983); and Glenn Snyder and Paul Diesing, *Conflict Among Nations* (Princeton: Princeton University Press, 1977).

deductive theory to investigate the empirical correctness of its analytical predictions. This requires giving empirical content to it through its assumptions (e.g., about preferences and payoffs) rather than just adapting the theory (or one of its many models) to fit some historical or current event.

The distinction can be illustrated by an example of game theory used as a descriptive rather than an analytical tool. In *Conflict Among Nations*, which is widely regarded as an ambitious application of game theory to international relations, Snyder and Diesing use game models of 16 historical cases to investigate bargaining in international crises. Their technique is to reconstruct the game structure underlying each crisis from a detailed historical analysis of events. They show a sophisticated awareness of the difficulty of such reconstruction and would not be surprised if (as often happens in this sort of analysis) others offered different interpretations of various crises. Such a challenge, however, is only a test of their skill in reconstructing a crisis in game terminology, and not a test of the theory itself. Indeed, because Snyder and Diesing use the totality of the crisis (including the outcome) to generate the descriptive game model, their use of game theory does not produce any predictions that could be empirically falsified. None of the deductive power of game theory is employed. Thus, their work is not an example of the empirical application of game theory even though it illustrates the purely descriptive use of game models.[2]

The real power of game theory, for both empirical and theoretical purposes, emerges when it is used to generate new findings and understandings rather than to reconstruct individual situations. This objective requires treating game theory as a *theory* of international politics in terms of the goal-seeking behavior of states in an interdependent international system. It means that game models will not be useful in predicting outcomes that are largely determined by nonpurposive or nonsystematic behavior. If all or most cases are determined by such factors, then game theory will have little to say about international politics. If the underlying assumption of self-interested action by strategically rational states is correct, however, and preferences, strategies, and payoffs can be modeled accurately, then the theory will generate important testable predictions.

[2] My comments are not intended as criticism of an ambitious and insightful enterprise. The authors' descriptive use of game theory is appropriate, given an ultimate concern with different models of decision making and bargaining rather than with game theory, which is used only in "the limited role ... [of] depicting the structure of a crisis" Snyder and Diesing (fn. 1), 87. Nevertheless, *if* any analytical game theory approach were attributed to the work, a game theorist could reasonably object that it had been emasculated (cf. p. 182).

This position is based on the now widely accepted view that the purpose of any theory—including game theory—is not to reproduce reality, but to increase our understanding of fundamental processes by simplifying it. For this reason, it is not desirable to incorporate all of the details of any individual case. Simplicity and abstraction guide us through a morass of information to focus on more fundamental issues.

While the simplicity of game models leads to a clarity that illuminates social phenomena, the deductive apparatus of game theory allows us to infer new understandings about international politics. The best-known example is Prisoners' Dilemma. Analysis in terms of this 2 x 2 game provides insights on issues such as GATT or SALT, which could never be achieved by, say, archival research alone. Expanding the analysis to N-person Prisoners' Dilemma and the logic of collective action explains why international cooperation sometimes fails even when it is in the interest of all states. Further investigation of the impact of states of different sizes and of hegemonic "leadership" (in terms of privileged groups) shows how various distributions of capability and interest facilitate or impede collectively optimal outcomes.[3] And changed incentives in dynamic games explain why cooperation has been more successful through GATT than through SALT, where mutual suspicions reinforce perceptions of substantial danger if the other side were to renege on cooperation.

These are the fertile directions in which game theory can lead empirical investigation of international politics. In the first section of this paper, I elaborate on game theory as a theoretical approach to international politics by contrasting it with metaphorical and other uses of games. This exercise lays a foundation for discussing the requisites for empirical application of the theory. In the second section, I discuss the overarching theoretical constructs in game models and their implications for applying the theory to specific international issues. These constructs raise a new set of questions that expand our understanding of particular issues. In the third section, I examine theoretical extensions of simple game models that expand the contextual richness of empirical applications by incorporating key features of international political interactions. The discussion in both of these sections makes reference to the technical game literature, but the focus is on the empirical issues of international politics raised by game-theory approaches.[4] In the final section, I sum-

[3] Duncan Snidal, "The Limits of Hegemonic Stability Theory," *International Organization* 39 (Autumn 1985), 579-614.

[4] The articles in this volume presuppose a basic familiarity with game-theoretic approaches. A good introduction is Henry Hamburger, *Games as Models of Social Phenomena* (San Francisco: W.H. Freeman, 1979); Martin Shubik, *Game Theory in the Social Sciences: Concepts*

marize the usefulness and limits of game theory as a theory of international politics and as a guide to empirical research.

I. Game Theory as a Theory of International Politics

The diverse logics of applying game theory to empirical phenomena are highlighted by its different applications as metaphor, analogy, model, or theory. Even though these terms are sometimes used interchangeably, distinguishing among them illuminates the relation of the game approach to empirical evidence. These differences go well beyond hackneyed calls for more rigorous approaches even if some uses are inherently more rigorous than others. Instead, different logics in using game theory reflect different understandings of how to apply it empirically. Most applications of game theory to international politics have been in terms of metaphor and analogy; they are unsatisfactory guides for application in terms of model and theory. Since we are concerned here with empirical application of deductive rather than purely descriptive models, these distinctions are important. Finally, in presenting these categories, the object is not to provide definitive definitions of terms, but to demonstrate the varying implications that the different logics hold for game-theoretic approaches to international politics.

A. METAPHOR

The use of metaphor is pervasive not only in literature, but in science and policy. Mechanical and biological metaphors are common in the social sciences. An applied example is the metaphor of "falling dominoes," which has been significant in postwar U.S. foreign policy. The power of the metaphor rests on its loose and open-ended nature. It invites us to speculate and engages us in creative conjecture. No formal deductive apparatus is involved: an implied comparison of two entities is used to infer further properties or conclusions from one to the other.[5]

Metaphors allow for the creative transfer of ideas across intellectual realms. This explains their heuristic and expository value—especially in exploratory stages of theory construction where their open-ended character is amenable to innovative thinking. However, they are also highly susceptible to misunderstanding and misuse. Open-endedness can de-

and Solutions (Cambridge: MIT Press, 1983) provides a more advanced treatment. Two accessible "classics" are R. Duncan Luce and Howard Raiffa, *Games and Decisions* (New York: Wiley, 1957), and Thomas Schelling, *Strategy of Conflict* (Cambridge: Harvard University Press, 1960).

[5] Martin Landau, "On the Use of Metaphor in Political Analysis," *Social Research* 28 (Autumn 1961), 331-53.

volve into sloppiness or silliness if metaphorical transfer is (mis)applied without thorough attention to the correspondences in the properties and conclusions of the entities being compared. These dangers are well illustrated by the more "vulgar" and misleading applications of biological and mechanical metaphors to understanding society.

Thus the use of metaphors in social science needs to be somewhat guarded; metaphorical richness must be progressively restricted by more precise formulations as research advances. For example, consider the Hobbesian state of nature as a fundamental metaphor for international politics. Although instructive for highlighting the security dilemma among states, it is misleading when it is overinterpreted to the conclusion that any international cooperation requires an international government comparable to the Hobbesian sovereign. This confusion does not arise from a more sophisticated specification of the metaphor, which recognizes salient differences between the two political environments (e.g., states are inherently more secure in the international system than are individuals in the Hobbesian state of nature) that allow for decentralized international cooperation.[6]

Increased rigor of specification is not to be confused with expression in a different form—specifically with mathematical as opposed to purely verbal statement. We do not improve a metaphor simply by translating it into a game matrix. Glib assertions that "Issue X is Prisoners' Dilemma," or that the "Cuban missile crisis was a game of Chicken," efficiently convey a metaphor, but do not make the metaphor more plausible or take much advantage of the power of game theory. Typically, such statements simply restate what we already know—perhaps embellished by means of a particular reconstruction of historical events. Real rigor requires tightening the correspondence between the metaphor and the issue at hand. Analogies and models are to some extent simply more controlled metaphors, although they are further distinguished by their respective logics of inference.[7]

---

[6] The Hobbesian (domestic) state of nature is contrasted with the current international situation in Charles Beitz, *Political Theory and International Relations* (Princeton: Princeton University Press, 1979). Decentralized international cooperation is dealt with from a strategic-actor perspective in Robert O. Keohane, *After Hegemony* (Princeton: Princeton University Press, 1984), and from a more purely game-theoretic perspective in Duncan Snidal, "Interdependence, Regimes and International Cooperation" (Ph.D. diss., Yale University, 1981). See also the related articles in Stephen Krasner, ed., *International Regimes* (Ithaca, NY: Cornell University Press, 1983).

[7] Metaphors are distinguished by the looseness of their correspondence rules, but *not* necessarily by the absence of mathematical sophistication. For an example of a mathematically sophisticated (though ultimately nonfruitful) metaphor, recall Paul Smoker's use of the harmonic motion of springs as a metaphor for arms rivalry, in "The Arms Race as an Open and Closed System," *Peace Research Society (International) Papers* 7 (1967), 41-62. For a

B.   ANALOGY

The key to analogy is the special type of reasoning it invokes. On the basis of certain closely established resemblances between two entities, further similarities are inferred. If X_i represents the ith property of entity X, an analogy between A and B is established by demonstrating a correspondence between a number (say, j) of their properties and/or relations $(A_1 \leftrightarrow B_1, A_2 \leftrightarrow B_2, \ldots, A_j \leftrightarrow B_j)$. On the basis of the analogy, we infer (tentatively) that for properties $A_{j+1}, A_{j+2}, \ldots$ (etc.) known to pertain to A, there exist corresponding properties $B_{j+1}, B_{j+2}, \ldots$ (etc.) in B. This inferential reasoning is external to both entities and resides in the comparison between them. Neither side of the analogy need contain any internal deductive structure (i.e., none of the properties $j+1, j+2 \ldots$ (etc.) can necessarily be logically derived from properties $1, 2, \ldots, j$ for either A or B). The logic of inference is then heavily inductive, resting on observed isomorphisms and, ultimately, on empirical confirmation of derived propositions (i.e., properties $j+1, j+2, \ldots$ etc.).

Analogic inferences are tentative until empirically confirmed. A central task of analogic reasoning is to distinguish *negative* (i.e., incorrect) from *positive* (i.e., correct) analogies. *Neutral* analogies, not yet known to be correct or incorrect, are viewed agnostically until more evidence is available. Therefore, analogy is a guide to empirical observation that points out parallels between properties of different phenomena, rather than a deductive tool whose conclusions about the existence of those properties we can subscribe to without question. Its main difference from the metaphor is the tighter specification of correspondences between properties and the closer evaluation of conclusions to which this leads.

One fashionable way of using analogy has been to relate international politics to neoclassical microeconomic models. Central among these has been the analogy between states in the international political system and firms in an oligopolistic market (and, implicitly, the game-theoretic structure underlying that market). This analogy is constructed from a number of postulated empirical correspondences, including:[8]

---

critical discussion, see Peter Busch, "Mathematical Models of Arms Races," an appendix to Bruce Russett, *What Price Vigilance?* (New Haven: Yale University Press, 1970).

[8] The oligopoly analogy is widespread. The correspondences presented here can be found in Kenneth Waltz, *Theory of International Politics* (Reading, MA: Addison-Wesley, 1979), esp. chap. 7. Other examples of microeconomic analogies are Robert Gilpin, *War and Change in World Politics* (New York: Cambridge University Press, 1981) and Robert O. Keohane, "The Demand for International Regimes," *International Organization* 36 (Spring 1982), 325-55.

economic marketplace ↔ international system
firm ↔ nation-state
firms maximize profits ↔ states maximize survival
oligopolists ↔ great powers
market concentration ↔ concentration of power
price wars ↔ military wars
both are self-help systems
firms and states both act strategically.

These correspondences establish the analogy that allows other inferences from oligopoly theory to the international system. They include the proposition that, since oligopolistic market concentration leads to market stability and fewer price wars, concentration of power in the international system will lead to system stability and less international conflict. The status of this inference is that of a hypothesis whose *a priori* plausibility depends on whether the initial correspondences are compelling. If empirically verified, the positive analogy becomes a new supporting correspondence which, in turn, buttresses the strength of the analogy as further implications are pursued. There may also be negative analogies, however, which must be identified as incorrect inferences. One example is the disanalogy between the role of elimination through competition which plays an important role in the marketplace but is inconsequential in the system of states. Another difference is that economic outcomes are evaluated primarily in terms of systemic properties such as efficiency rather than of the fate of individual firms, while international systems are evaluated fundamentally in terms of the impact they have on individual states.

Although analogy can be a powerful tool for conceptualizing international politics, its limitations are apparent. Disanalogies can be recognized but not eliminated; features of interest that have no corresponding property in the analogy cannot be analyzed. Finally, the logic of inference is primarily inductive, and no direct use is made of deductive logic. Since that is where the power of the game-theoretic approach lies, analogy uses only a portion of this power. A better alternative is to use game-theory models that directly incorporate the most salient features of the international system.[9]

C. MODEL

There is an even stronger concern for a tight correspondence between an entity and its model. Because it can be abstract and "constructed,"

---

[9] On the "economic approach" (of rational, maximizing behavior) versus economics as

a model can be tailored precisely to the problem under investigation. Its key distinguishing characteristic is a formal logic that is both deductive and internal (as opposed to the inductive and external logic of analogy). Using the same notation, let A be a model of B with correspondences $1, 2, \ldots, j$ established. Property A_{j+k} is a conclusion of the model if it can be deduced from some combination of $A_1, A_2, \ldots, A_j$. The corresponding property B_{j+k} is then asserted on the basis that it follows logically from the corresponding combination of $B_1, B_2, \ldots, B_j$. This differs from analogy in that no recourse is made to induction beyond the initial establishment of the isomorphism. Instead, the model simply illuminates a logical relationship among the properties of B, which is more expeditiously demonstrated among the corresponding relations in its model A.

As a result, the model has a more closed form than the analogy. In an analogy, establishing correspondences $A_1 \leftrightarrow B_1, \ldots, A_j \leftrightarrow B_j$ does not guarantee that each A_{j+k} implies a corresponding B_{j+k}. Some analogic inferences may be incorrect (and thus set aside) without significantly harming the analogy—provided that sufficient correspondences are established and that other correct inferences pertain. By contrast, the internal deductive argument of a model that allows us to conclude A_{j+k} based on properties $A_1, A_2, \ldots, A_j$ of A indicates that, *if our correspondences are valid*, then conclusion B_{j+k} *must* also apply. If empirical evaluation shows B_{j+k} does not hold, then the model itself must be reformulated. The result is a more closed form: negative analogies are not permitted to coexist alongside positive analogies. We are forced to revise and reconstruct the model.[10]

The compensating features of (empirically verified) models are that neutral analogies (i.e., untested conclusions) can be accepted until disproven, and that the logical structure of the model suggests new avenues of inquiry. Therefore correspondences must be tighter in a model than in an analogy. A wrong correspondence in an analogy need not impair the (external) logic of inference if sufficient other correspondences still

---

analogy, see Brian Barry, *Sociologists, Economists and Democracy* (Chicago: University of Chicago Press, 1978).

[10] I do not want to convey too pristine a view of how models are developed. Models are always constructed with an eye toward some of their inferences (what assumptions are needed to produce a certain conclusion). Moreover, the *ceteris paribus* clause is often invoked to deal with important correspondences that are *not* contained in the model. However, the logical structure of the model forces our theoretical assumptions and conclusions to be consistent and leads to other wholly unanticipated inferences. The *ceteris paribus* clause should not become a refuge from incorporating further considerations into the model; it should be a stimulus for its progressive refinement.

hold. In a model, a single wrong correspondence may disrupt the (internal) logic of deduction and produce false conclusions. Thus, with stronger requirements for its correspondence rules and stronger deductive powers, a model makes stronger claims about the world.[11]

Understanding and explanation is deepened by the deductive form of the model. The need for tightness in correspondences, and for revision of the model when it is inadequate, requires that our knowledge be more precise. Whereas in analogy it is unclear which correspondences (or how many) are necessary, the model clarifies which ones play a role in the logic of inference (i.e., those that enter into the deductive reasoning). The model thus promotes parsimony and simplicity. It also directs us to evaluate the accuracy of the most important correspondences, and allows us to investigate how changes in correspondences (assumptions) might lead to different conclusions.

Finally, models of processes or of things (i.e., of a specific empirical phenomenon such as a particular arms race) need to be distinguished from models of theories (i.e., of a general category of phenomena such as arms races). The former involve abstraction of an entity's properties to represent them in a simpler set of relations. This sort of model may incorporate a theory, but may also be consistent with many theories. A model of a theory, on the other hand, contains a set of linked law-like statements applicable to a range of phenomena. Game theory poses a healthy tension between these types of models: a game model may be treated as a straightforward representation of a specific phenomenon or as involving a broader theoretical perspective and a more general interpretation of the particular event.[12]

D.   THEORY

Since the same representation can be a model for different theories, interpretation of a model depends on the theory in which it is embedded.[13] The theory contains a deductive structure plus an inter-

[11] Models are *not* primarily distinguished from analogies and metaphors by mathematical sophistication. (See note 7.) For example, physical models and analogue machines (including computer simulations viewed as physical machine representations) are models that are not in explicit mathematical form. Mathematics is simply a particular way of expressing a model. It is useful in forcing us to tighten up correspondences, in exposing weaknesses in a model or metaphor, and in providing a powerful means of pursuing deductive implications.

[12] Again, the distinction between a theory and its model is not always clear. Mary Hesse argues that "almost any model or interpretation carries some surplus meaning. If, however, a model is used in a way that exploits this surplus meaning in prediction and explanation, we shall call it a theoretical model." See Hesse, "Models and Analogy in Science" in Paul Edwards, ed., *The Encyclopedia of Philosophy* (New York: Macmillan and Free Press, 1967), 354-59.

[13] For example, waves provide a model for both water motion and light; similarly, the

pretation of fundamental assumptions and theoretical constructs. This richer interpretive structure (as compared to the tighter correspondences in the model) provides for greater richness of explanation. Through it, the theory maintains a greater open-endedness and a surplus meaning which guides revision and extension of the model. A further source of theoretical richness lies in the multiple models that may be contained within a theory and that emerge according to specific parametric conditions. Through these models, seemingly different phenomena—perhaps varying due to contextual factors—can be understood within the same theoretical framework.

Game theory viewed as a *theory* of intentional behavior illustrates the relation between a theory and its model. The assumption of rationality allows interpretation of solutions in terms of intentional behavior of actors. Specification of different political-institutional environments (e.g., the capitalist market in economic oligopoly theory versus anarchic international society in balance-of-power theory) determines rules of the game that result in different interpretations of models, and ultimately in different models, as the rules are more explicitly introduced into the analysis. Alternatively, different specifications of actors' policy choices and/or preferences may result in different games (e.g., Chicken versus Prisoners' Dilemma) arising within one fundamental theoretical interpretation of the international system. A primary virtue of game theory as theory is the enormous diversity of models contained within it.

For game theory to be a theory of international politics (rather than a general theory of strategic behavior), specific empirical assumptions (correspondences) are required. For example, by assuming that power-maximizing states are the principal actors, game theory subsumes the Realist position. But the game-theoretic approach is not coincident with Realism. While it necessarily treats actors as rational, its empirical assumptions need assert neither that the key actors are states nor that they maximize power. With a different specification of these assumptions, game theory is equally consistent with a modified structural approach.[14]

---

coupled differential equations which can be interpreted as a model of an arms race in international relations may have a very different meaning in thermodynamics. Indeed, it is impossible to speak of a model *of* something—as opposed to a purely logical and empirically uninterpreted model—without theory to guide us on the correspondence rules. Any empirical model must be embedded in a theory. However, the theoretical richness is often tightly circumscribed in the model. A good example is the use of the "as if" assumption to establish a correspondence at a purely observational level without plumbing the deeper implication of the observed behavior. (See note 17.)

[14] Robert O. Keohane, "Theory of World Politics: Structural Realism and Beyond," in Ada Finifter, ed., *Political Science: The State of the Discipline* (Washington, DC: American Political Science Association, 1983).

Thus it brings contending perspectives into the same framework and emphasizes their different empirical assumptions.

As a general theoretical approach to international politics, game theory does assume goal-seeking behavior in the absence of centralized, authoritative institutions. It thereby illuminates the fundamental issues of international anarchy and the implications of different configurations of national interests and political circumstances for international conflict and cooperation. At its best, it uses simplifying assumptions to expand our range of understanding and to provide deeper interpretations of international politics.

Metaphor, analogy, model and theory are complementary in social scientific research; they are each appropriate at various stages. It is often useful to go back and forth among them. As research advances, however, metaphor and analogy are of increasingly limited usefulness. The greater rigor and deductive power of the model, together with the interpretive richness and open-endedness of its corresponding theoretical framework, make that combination ultimately more productive.[15]

International political analysis is ripe for a transition to game theory as a theory of international politics. Game metaphors and analogies already are widely used to illuminate and clarify international issues. To apply the deductive power of game theory directly, we must tighten up correspondences between empirical situations and game models, and separate assumptions from predictions. As we do this, the model and theory will provide a guide to relevant empirical evidence just as the evidence will provide a guide for evaluating and revising the model. Treated this way, game theory becomes more than just a new language in which to rewrite history or to restate our arguments. It becomes a powerful tool for expanding our understanding and for stimulating research. The price we pay for such power lies in the assumptions and work required to link the deductive logic to empirical reality. In the remainder of this paper, I address issues raised in using game theory, both as model and as theory, for the empirical investigation of international politics.

II. Using Game Theory to Build Theory
in International Relations

Concepts of game theory provide a guide for constructing theory in international relations. The most fundamental concepts—strategy, stra-

[15] Here we can agree that "perhaps every science must start with metaphor and end with

tegic rationality, preferences, and payoffs—and their implications for understanding international politics will be discussed in this section. Although I will refer mainly to simple 2 x 2 games, the discussion applies equally to other game models. Those will be more explicitly covered in the section on incorporating contextual features of international issues into game models.

A. STRATEGIES

A strategy is a complete plan for action, covering all contingencies including random exogenous events as well as endogenous behavior by others. For any but the most trivial decisions, this conception is hopelessly complicated and beyond the calculating power of any man, machine, or state bureaucracy. Although it is possible to treat strategies as simplifications of more complex decision processes, it is more fruitful to treat them as simplified representations of general policy stances. In trade policy, for example, it is meaningful to speak—on a broad level—of strategies of "free" versus "restricted" international trade without worrying about the myriad of nuances such as differential treatment of steel versus textiles, or the use of tariff versus nontariff barriers. Similarly, strategies of reducing military spending, of increasing international tensions, or of promoting environmental protection are each meaningful without supposing that someone has compiled an exact listing of how to pursue that policy under every conceivable contingency. The simple 2 x 2 game pursues this to its logical extreme where only two choices (often too persuasively labeled "cooperate" and "not cooperate") are available. Although not without limitations, this assumption is a useful simplification for illuminating the fundamental nature of an issue area.

The notion of a strategy is so comprehensive that it can encompass a wide range of phenomena. This breadth of coverage is a central advantage of game theory. However, the limitations of such breadth need to be understood to ensure that the idea of a strategy is used to clarify rather than to confuse. One example is how a strategy incorporates dynamic considerations by allowing for contingent planning through time in response to changing circumstances. Some of the most powerful game-theoretic results emerge when dynamic problems are treated as static choices of strategies which actors will play through time. As we shall find in Section III, however, dynamic considerations are sometimes

---

algebra; and perhaps without the metaphor there would never have been any algebra"— although by the argument of this section, the word "model" should be substituted for "algebra." See Max Black, *Models and Metaphors* (Ithaca, NY: Cornell University Press, 1962), 242.

obscured when they are subsumed under a static analysis. Even where this is not the case, it will be useful to distinguish simple games that cover a single decision-making period from *sequences* of simple games (i.e., supergames) that represent continued play over a number of periods.

A second concern is over the relationship between having a strategy and behaving rationally. Here the distinction between model and theory is useful. We can agree with Axelrod that, viewed as a model, an "organism does not need a brain to employ a strategy."[16] He demonstrates important results by using game models for a wide range of phenomena where "strategies" have little to do with planning or strategic behavior in the usual sense of the word. For example, game models combined with the assumptions of natural selection offer suggestive explanations for the behavior of bacteria, microbes, and other lower-order life. Similar analyses can be applied to economic and political processes. Thus the models of game theory can be useful for theories not involving rational actors. But, as Axelrod points out, "game-playing becomes richer" in the context of a theoretical understanding where strategies are related to intentional behavior. Explicit use of such strategic rationality in the theory of games captures important aspects of international politics not found in game models divorced from the rationality assumption.[17]

B. STRATEGIC RATIONALITY

The cornerstone of Realism is its treatment of states as rational actors. This requires only that states make logically correct calculations in using available information to pursue well-defined goals. This assumption has been subjected to an onslaught of attacks from advocates of theoretical alternatives including bureaucratic politics, psychological models of decision making, social choice, and complex organizations. The best of these critiques provide significant lessons that the game-theoretic tradition needs to address—as will be discussed in the following subsection on the derivation of game payoffs. Nevertheless, even though claims for its exclusive usefulness are surely exaggerated, the value of the rationality

[16] Robert Axelrod, *The Evolution of Cooperation* (New York: Basic Books, 1984), chap. 5.

[17] This position agrees with Milton Friedman's well-known "as if" argument on one level, but differs from it on another. Friedman's argument is that it does not matter if the actors being modeled actually make (strategic) calculations as long as they act "as if" they did. For him, the proof of the pudding is the accuracy of the predictions that result from the assumption. But if we are to understand and explain behavior in addition to predicting it, his argument will be insufficient. To understand state behavior in international politics, and to avoid *post hoc* reconstruction of behavior as "rational," we must pay attention to the nature and limits of state rationality. See Friedman, "The Methodology of Positive Economics," in Frank Hahn and Martin Hollis, eds., *Philosophy and Economic Theory* (New York: Oxford University Press, 1979), and Mark Blaug, *The Methodology of Economics* (New York: Cambridge University Press, 1980).

assumption for the study of international politics has largely withstood these challenges.

The interdependence perspective, and the game-theoretic tradition more generally, pose a different challenge to the conception of *nonstrategic rationality* that dominates simplistic (but nonetheless distressingly common) views of Realism.[18] Rationality in this Realist world centers on the struggle for power in an anarchic environment. States fend for themselves as they pursue their contradictory interests. Because of the conflictual nature of this "self-help" environment, the situation is mistakenly seen as zero-sum where no cooperation is possible and states can pursue their own best interests without regard for the interests of others. The game-theory perspective reveals that these circumstances prevail only in artificially constructed, two-player parlor games. For real international issues, states' interests will not be properly characterized by assuming such pure opposition of interests. This leads directly to a *strategic rationality* which incorporates the realization that pursuit of egoistic interest requires consideration of interactions of one state's choices with other states' choices. No state can choose its best strategy or attain its best outcome independent of choices made by others. The related substantive implication is that national policy makers need to pursue opportunities for cooperative interactions even as they seek to protect against conflictual interactions.

Two aspects of rationality are especially important for game-theoretic analyses.[19] The first, common to both nonstrategic and strategic conceptions, is the ability to forgo short-run advantages for longer-run considerations. The second, which is the distinguishing trait of strategic rationality, is that actors choose courses of action based on preferences and expectations of how others will behave. Thus, when a state undertakes a certain action, it does not necessarily follow that the immediate result is itself a preferred end for that state. It could be a strategically planned means to some other objective. (An example considered below is the use of Tit-for-Tat strategies to elicit long-run cooperation sometimes at short-run cost.) This possibility requires us to consider how each choice is interrelated with prior and subsequent choices, and to understand national goals independently from observed behavior.

---

[18] Strains of this narrow interpretation of rationality are apparent even among the best proponents of Realism. See, for example, Waltz (fn. 8), 70. Sophisticated versions of Realism—and certainly those that have incorporated game-theoretic notions—have employed an understanding of strategic rationality. For a clear-headed discussion of narrow rationality, see Bueno de Mesquita (fn. 1), 29-33.

[19] See Jon Elster, *Ulysses and the Sirens: Studies in Rationality and Irrationality* (New York: Cambridge University Press, 1979).

The assumption of strategic rationality is fundamental to a game-*theory* interpretation of international politics. Individual actions and collective outcomes are understood in terms of states' strategic pursuit of self-interest. The development of institutional arrangements such as regimes is explained in terms of efforts to overcome problems of collective action by altering the "rules of the game."[20] The prospects for further cooperation as well as the dangers of increased conflict can be investigated in terms of the strategic possibilities facing states. As is often the case in theoretical enterprises, the stronger the (rationality) assumptions made, the richer the interpretation provided by game theory. Conversely, if the rationality assumption is seriously circumscribed by (say) bureaucratic, psychological, or organizational factors, the same models need to be interpreted differently.

Finally, strategic rationality lies at the heart of one of the most attractive features of game theory. By placing the rational choice of state policy at the forefront of the explanation, game theory allows for an autonomy in state choice even as it predicts and explains those choices deterministically through an understanding of the overall strategic interaction. Thus the game model combines purposeful behavior with a specification of the structure of international politics which constrains that behavior. It links systematic macro-theory to voluntaristic decisions. States have choices; but the choices they make are determined to a greater or lesser extent by the exigencies of international politics.[21]

C. PAYOFFS

Rationality assumes that states pursue goals, but those goals are not specified. A game-theoretic perspective requires analyzing states' motivations and how their preferences map into payoffs within a game model. Establishing this correspondence between an issue area and its game model is the toughest problem confronting successful empirical application of game theory. To do so, we must posit national goals that depend on internal values as well as on external circumstances, thereby incorporating other empirical and theoretical understandings of international issues into the model.

For an inductive derivation of payoffs, *what* has happened cannot serve as an explanation of *why* it happened. Simple-minded uses of the "revealed preference" approach, which Sen aptly labels a "robust piece of *evasion*," lead to circular reasoning from the choices made by actors

[20] See Keohane (fn. 6), and Snidal (fn. 6).

[21] Pierre Allan, *Crisis Bargaining and the Arms Race* (Cambridge, MA: Ballinger, 1983), 5-6, and Hahn and Hollis (fn. 17), 15.

back to their preferences.[22] Except for metaphorical and purely descriptive purposes, nothing is gained by this sort of restatement of the situation. To avoid circularity, revealed preference can be applied in a somewhat different way. Choices made by a state in other situations where it faced similar circumstances can be used to infer preferences (and hence payoffs) inductively. Now the evidence used to determine the game payoff structure is independent of the outcome. Further independent evidence about preferences may be available in archives and memoirs, including statements of leaders about their objectives. Such sources require a careful and systematic approach to the collection of evidence; self-serving statements of leaders need to be ruled out, and biased or *ad hoc* collections of anecdotes in support of a postulated payoff structure must be avoided.

But even the most rigorous inductive approaches are problematic for game models because strategic rationality casts doubt on any such interpretation of relevant evidence. Since actors sometimes forgo immediate interest for longer-term gain, observed action may not reflect preferences directly. Furthermore, the essence of strategic behavior is that a state may forgo individually optimal actions to collaborate with others in achieving mutually preferred outcomes (e.g., the observation of "cooperative" behavior in Prisoners' Dilemma should not lead us to the incorrect inference that a state's highest individual payoffs are associated with such behavior). Observed behavior of strategic actors is thus often a biased and unsatisfactory indicator of underlying interests.

Finally, inductive procedures provide only an incomplete map of preferences. With regard to revealed preference, only choices actually made by a state are directly observed; evidence about their evaluation of other possible outcomes is indirect and incomplete. In terms of simple games, direct evidence is available on only one of the four cells. This paucity of information is even more striking because the 2 x 2 game is already a simplified representation of a much richer set of preference mappings. Thus, even if augmented by other sources, purely inductive evidence will generally be inadequate for determining the structure of a game matrix.

Theoretical specification of states' preferences can provide a route out of this empirical quandary. Such "theories of the payoffs" necessarily precede the game model. They enable game theory to be constructively and complementarily linked to other approaches to international politics—even, in some cases, to theories that may be viewed as alternatives

[22] Armatya Sen, "Rational Fools: A Critique of the Behavioral Foundations of Economic Theory," in Hahn and Hollis (fn. 17), 92; emphasis in original.

to rational models. The possibilities for developing a theoretical basis for the derivation of payoffs are best seen by considering alternative ways to accomplish this goal.

When theoretical knowledge of an issue area is substantial, assessing states' preferences is straightforward. This knowledge provides a way to model a situation and derive its payoff structure. Consider the neo-classical theory of international trade. It provides an elaborate framework for deriving the payoffs determined by strategy choices which might include the imposition of tariffs, restrictions on capital flows, or subsi-dization of industries. Such strong theory allows precise specification of the strategic situation between states over a host of important trade questions. A second example is found in the literature on military spend-ing. Theoretical arguments about the impact of military expenditures among allies and rivals, combined with knowledge of prevailing inter-national tensions and alliances, can reveal the underlying strategic struc-ture of these situations.[23]

But states' preferences may not always be tightly linked to objective understandings of an issue area. Perceptions and information processing, as well as organizational or bureaucratic imperatives, may change the relevant payoffs for decision makers. Theoretical understanding of such factors may illuminate additional considerations that influence states' decisions on foreign policy alternatives. Of course, extreme versions which explain behavior largely in terms of the decision process itself will compete with, rather than complement, game models. But less extreme versions which leave a role for intentional behavior will suggest relevant empirical factors that affect strategic behavior. For example, Keohane incorporates "bounded rationality" into decisions to participate in international regimes, while Allan uses the concept of "diplomatic climate" to admit cognitive considerations of past events into rational models. When rational action is circumscribed but not overwhelmed by such factors, theoretical integration of this sort will be productive.[24]

Theoretical considerations are also valuable when partial information restricts the logical possibilities for the payoff structure. For example, if a situation is symmetric or if the nature of common and conflicting interests is understood, then the set of possible 2 x 2 games can be considerably reduced.[25] Alternatively, substantive knowledge that an

[23] Mancur Olson and Richard Zeckhauser, "An Economic Theory of Alliances," *Review of Economics and Statistics* 48 (No. 3, 1966), 226-79; Snidal (fn. 6), chaps. 5-6.

[24] Keohane (fn. 6), chap. 7, and Allan (fn. 21), chap. 4. There are limits to rational theory, however: it cannot always incorporate contending approaches except in a trivializing way. Even some issues that are internal to the theory—especially problems of preference aggre-gation in determining a "national interest"—are far from resolved.

[25] Russell Hardin demonstrates how to narrow the range of relevant games for deterrence

issue area is characterized by relative rather than absolute gains (for instance, mercantilist versus liberal trade policies), or about the way policy choices are interrelated across states (for instance, international transmission of macroeconomic policies among economically integrated states) will help to describe the game structure. Information about the general political-institutional setting for relations among states, about the likelihood of an issue continuing into the future, or about the number and relative size of the states involved—all of which are discussed separately below—will also help to identify the structure of strategic interrelationships.

Theoretically inspired approaches to inferring payoff structures have several advantages over purely inductive approaches. First, by focusing on underlying motivations rather than on observed outcomes, preferences are distinguished from actions, and individual interests from strategic calculations. Theoretical approaches also provide more complete information on the payoffs for outcomes beyond the one that actually occurs (e.g., on all of the "cells" of the 2 x 2 game), which permits an analysis of the complete game structure. Finally, by forcing us to investigate new questions concerning the motivations underlying the behavior of states, they ensure that the analysis is not simply a redescription of the issue in more formal language.

A second advantage of theoretical derivation is that it systematically addresses the question of changing preferences through time and/or changes in the institutional environment of international politics. One requirement of the game-theoretic approach is that actors have reasonably stable preferences and behave consistently when confronted with comparable choices. If preferences change too quickly, the model degenerates to a generalized *post hoc* revealed-preference exercise, where actions are assumed to reflect prevailing fluctuations in preferences. A theoretical approach avoids this circular reasoning by incorporating those factors that affect preferences and payoffs through time (including prior outcomes) directly into the theory of payoffs. Such systematic treatment of changing preferences or evolving institutions allows for a properly dynamic treatment of international issues.

But the greatest advantage of theoretical specification of payoffs is that it unleashes the deductive power of game theory. By combining the game structure defined by preferences and available strategies with game theory solution concepts, we are led to new inferences about the behavior of individual states and about the overall outcome. These (falsifiable)

problems in "Unilateral Versus Mutual Disarmament," *Philosophy and Public Affairs* 12 (Summer 1983), 236-54.

predictions are independent of observed behavior, which provides evidence on the correctness of the assumptions and the usefulness of the game-theoretic approach. If the theory withstands the test, these new deductions expand our knowledge and understanding of international behavior, and the analysis moves beyond metaphor and analogy to models and theory.[26]

A final implication of theoretical derivations for payoffs is that any particular application is not a test of the game-theoretic approach in isolation, but of game theory in combination with the particular theoretical assumptions embodied in the game structure (for instance, the underlying motivations of actors from which the payoffs are derived). If a particular model is inadequate, the theory of the payoffs will be rejected before the game-theoretic approach itself. The general usefulness of the latter will be rejected only if a more plausible payoff theory cannot be constructed. Even then, we will not be sure whether this failing is really due to our own (possibly temporary) shortcomings in understanding and specifying actor motivations. Nevertheless, the theoretical specification of payoffs makes the game model more vulnerable to empirical evidence and leaves it potentially falsifiable. This condition qualifies it as a serious explanation and more than just a tautological redescription of the world. Finally, attempts to revise the theoretical specification in order to accommodate contradictory evidence are likely to lead to innovations in our understanding of international politics.

III. The Context of International Politics and Game Models

One common but misguided criticism of game models is that they are too "simple" to capture the complexity of international politics. Game models may not be able to capture all details of international interactions, but in earlier sections of this paper I have argued that simplicity actually enhances the power of the theory for grasping complexity. I will now expand that argument by looking at extensions of simple game models to capture key contextual factors of international politics. The theoretical use of game models allows us to adapt them directly to the most salient aspects of international politics.

[26] Examples of these deductions include those discussed above. The success of rational-actor approaches in other areas of political science is due to precisely this sort of approach (for example, the assumption that candidates maximize votes leads to conclusions about their behavior). For a discussion of this (and a critique of the trivializing use of revealed preferences by imputing utility to "citizen's duty" to explain voting), see Barry (fn. 9), chap. 2.

A. EXTERNAL GAME ENVIRONMENT AND INTERNATIONAL REGIMES

The goal in specifying a game structure is to capture the essential features of an international situation. Some of these are assumptions (actors, strategies, payoffs) while others are predictions (the outcome). The value of a game representation depends on how successfully it captures significant aspects of the international environment. Game theory also allows for broader interpretations, so that features not explicitly entered into a model may be useful for understanding and interpreting it.

The specification of actors, capabilities, and preferences defines an overall game model of a specific issue. Each state's strategic interconnection with others outlines "structural" constraints that determine its opportunities. This notion of structure is atomistic in viewing structure as simply the sum of the individual units and emphasizes the structure of individual issues rather than that of the overall international system. It is therefore inadequate for examining certain conceptions of world structures.[27] Nevertheless, the international system, with its established patterns of practice and rules, is significant for defining the individual game model and for deriving conclusions from it. In this way, the structure of international politics modeled as the rules of the game is distinguished from the behavior of states within those rules. (Of course, the rules of the game may be altered through establishment of new patterns of behavior, expectations, and norms, which emerge as new rules in the longer term.)

Indeed, even the definition of issues, actors, and choices depends on the preexisting international order. For example, separation of trading issues into the GATT framework, recognition of states as relevant decision makers, and acceptance of restraint from force in deciding trade disputes all reflect theoretical assumptions as to which aspects of the existing trade *regime* can be taken as "given" for analysis of the politics of international trade. The assumptions of one analysis may be the objects of investigation in another. Regimes are not independent of the existing global political structure, but are built upon it and "nested" so that the fabric of one provides the foundation of another. Therefore the rules of the existing international order define the underlying game, even as the game is used to pose further questions about the development of international regimes.

Empirical issues concerning the emergence of regimes are related to

[27] Richard Ashley, "The Poverty of Neo-Realism," *International Organization* 38 (Spring 1984), 236-86.

theoretical issues raised by solutions within game theory. For individual states, these issues include the concept of *maximizing self-interest* (e.g., maximax versus maximin strategy choices), and how this is affected by the norms, conventions, and expectations that emerge in the regime. This leads to the question of *efficiency*, or whether the regime enables states to exploit mutual interests. A third question is whether the outcome is *self-enforcing* (i.e., a stable equilibrium) so that the regime will be maintained by the self-interested behavior of states without centralized enforcement. A final concern is the distribution of benefits and considerations of *fairness* which affect our evaluation of a regime.

These central questions for investigating the role of international institutions in promoting international cooperation provide criteria for predicting and evaluating behavior within the regime as well as transformation of the regime itself. This fuller interpretation of the game model is in terms of the theoretical assumptions of strategic rationality and interdependent decision making that are fundamental to game theory.

B.   PAYOFF MEASUREMENT FOR ANALYZING BARGAINING AND ASYMMETRY

Stronger assumptions about preferences—for example, interval versus ordinal measurement—contain more information for deriving stronger conclusions from game models. The appropriate level of measurement depends on our knowledge of the issue as well as the particular theoretical questions to be investigated. Ordinal measurement is typically the minimal level that provides a sufficiently clear definition of the game structure for fruitful game analysis, but it is not always adequate.[28] Stronger measurement is necessary for analysis of certain central questions. Consider some key examples: the result that repetition of an issue facilitates cooperation is based on interval-level comparison of alternative streams of (discounted) payoffs through time. Cooperation through issue linkage, viewed in terms of "trading" assistance on one issue for assistance on another, depends on interval-level weighing of benefits gained in one issue against costs incurred in the other. Indeed, solutions to bilateral bargaining problems can be shown, in general, to depend on interval-level payoffs. Even a simple 2 x 2 game can be dramatically

[28] Ordinal payoffs correspond to "first," "second," and so forth. Interval measurement requires meaningful "units" (e.g., degrees of temperature or units of payoff) for the "distance" between outcomes (e.g., change in the temperature or in a state's payoff). Cardinal measurement requires a meaningful "zero" (e.g., absolute zero in temperature scales) and is largely irrelevant for game theory. Other levels of measurement may fall between these categories (e.g., partial orderings may give us interval-level comparisons between some outcomes, but no direct comparison between others).

altered by replacing its ordinal payoffs with interval-level payoffs that are consistent with the original ordinal ranking. In brief, interval-level payoffs will be necessary, in addition to the simple order of preferences, whenever intensity matters.

Where interval-level payoffs are not available, partial information about intensity may still be useful. For example, the incentive to defect on a cooperative agreement might be known to be greater in one situation than in another, even if the comparison cannot be made more precise. The greater incentives will tend to make decentralized agreements less effective and decrease the prospects for cooperation. Thus, ordinal payoffs can often be augmented by partial information on preference intensity.[29]

Intensities of preferences differ not only *for* actors but *across* actors. The latter situation raises the thorny issue of "interpersonal" comparisons of utility, whereby relative welfare gains of states are compared. Such considerations are central in normative evaluation of outcomes (for instance, the distributive implications of alternative Law of the Sea proposals), and may thereby influence actions of states (such as granting tariff preferences to less developed countries). Interpersonal comparisons are also important in purely "positive" analysis, however. The ability to do great harm (or confer benefit) to another at a relatively low cost may affect a state's behavior. This is especially true for situations of asymmetry where one state is substantially more vulnerable than another. Less vulnerable states will use their position advantageously to determine the outcome; when both are equally vulnerable, outcomes are more likely to be equal.[30] It is treacherous but essential to make such comparisons— especially where issues are extremely asymmetric. Ordinal game models often make issues appear symmetric (for instance, by treating a very large state and a very small one as equal partners in a Prisoners' Dilemma with the "same" ordinal preferences) even though they are extremely asymmetric under interpersonal comparison and interval measurement (if, say, the issue is vital to the small country but inconsequential to the large one). Since many key problems of international politics revolve around questions of interdependence versus dependence, this consideration is important.

[29] For example, see Robert Jervis, "Cooperation under the Security Dilemma," *World Politics* 30 (January 1978), 167-214, at 174. Nevertheless, ordinal payoffs can carry our analysis very far, and econmists once (erroneously) even believed they were sufficient for virtually all purposes. An interesting account of how measurement is integrally related to the questions we are investigating is Robert Cooter and Peter Rappoport, "Were the Ordinalists Wrong About Welfare Economics?," *Journal of Economic Literature* 22 (June 1984), 507-30. For a thoughtful but more technical discussion of these issues, see Shubik (fn. 4), chaps. 4 and 5.

[30] For examples of the impact of vulnerability, see Jervis (fn. 29), 171-73.

Thus, problems of bargaining (including linkage and cooperation through time) and of asymmetry can be captured in game-theoretic models that include stronger theoretical attention to underlying preferences and stronger measurement of payoffs. Such game models also provide a handle on important normative questions surrounding positive analysis. While these various problems are difficult to deal with, they are not intrinsic to game theory analysis; the latter only serves to illuminate some of the substantive and theoretical shortcomings in our understanding of international politics.

C.   ITERATED AND DYNAMIC GAMES: TWO ACTORS PLAYING THROUGH TIME

International politics is inherently dynamic and involves interactions among states through time. As discussed above, a strategy can encompass dynamic situations within a purely static analysis (that is, where states choose entire future courses of action at once). But compressing all of these possibilities into a single choice may involve unrealistic assumptions about the capacity of states as decision makers, and obscure important aspects of international politics. To understand the impact of evolving international regimes, of changing expectations, of learning and adjustment by states, or of changing national preferences, the concept of "change through time" needs to be clarified.[31]

The term "dynamic" is not as precise as its mathematical connotation implies, and it has many different usages. For international politics it emphasizes (1) the impact of states making multiple decisions through time, and (2) mutual adjustment among states through time. It is of particular importance whether new equilibrium outcomes emerge when the game is played through time, and whether these are stable. These questions (rather than the form of the game) distinguish dynamic analysis.

Treating international issues as dynamic is complicated by the problem of defining the decision-making period. Discrete time models have predominated because they are easier to work with. The standard treatment has been in terms of sequential plays of iterated games where time is divided into decision periods corresponding to a single play of a static game. However, changes in "revealed" preferences or contextual factors between iterations should not be invoked on an *ad hoc* basis to define different game iterations or to fit different game models to an issue at different points in time. Instead, dynamic analysis requires theoretically informed understandings of time-changing empirical patterns. For ex-

[31] Complications of inconsistent time preferences are ignored here. See Elster (fn. 19), chap. 2.

ample, superpower "succession crises" due to machinations within the Soviet Politburo or the American electoral process may explain systematic fluctuations in the politics between them. Alternatively, past interactions may affect present behavior, perhaps by increasing interdependence or by changing expectations and trust among nations. Incorporating such effects allows us to adapt a systematic sequence of static models to the changing circumstances of a dynamic world, but it requires stronger theoretical assumptions about international politics (for instance, of exogenous factors that affect the game structure, or endogenous changes in expectations) than those necessary to construct the individual static game models.

A further application of dynamic analysis arises when current behavior is affected by prospects for future play of the game. Continuation of an issue through time may affect a state's behavior in each "play" of the game and alter the (equilibrium) outcome. The power of this analysis is illustrated by its most exciting result to date: whereas cooperation is not individually rational in single-play Prisoners' Dilemma, it will be rational under certain (specified) conditions in the iterated Prisoners' Dilemma supergame.[32] The reason is that states will forgo short-run incentives to defect when they can thereby achieve longer-run benefits from cooperation through time. This makes international cooperation possible in the absence of centralized enforcement and indicates the importance of dynamic analysis of international politics. It is also a prime example of using the deductive power of game theory to derive new results.

Iteration changes not only the outcome of the game, but the underlying structure of the situation. Whereas in single-play Prisoners' Dilemma there is a dominant strategy to defect, and the actions of others are barely relevant, coordination with other states becomes important in the iterated game. For example, the Tit-for-Tat strategy (i.e., reciprocate the other's last move) is effective only when the other state (in a bilateral situation) or a sufficient number of states (in a multilateral world) have adopted a compatible strategy. Thus the fundamental problem facing the individual state is altered once the Prisoners' Dilemma game is iterated. However, cooperation is not always enhanced by iterated plays of other games. For example, prospects of continued plays of coordi-

---

[32] Cooperation will make sense in anticipation of, and in response to, cooperation by the other party. An early formulation of the impact of iterated Prisoners' Dilemma games is Martin Shubik, "Game Theory and the Paradox of the Prisoner's Dilemma," *Journal of Conflict Resolution* 14 (June 1970), 181-93. The result is worked out formally in Michael Taylor, *Anarchy and Cooperation* (New York: Wiley, 1976) and extended via tournament techniques in Axelrod (fn. 16).

nation games provide incentives to break existing cooperation agreements in order to press for an alternative coordination point that the players prefer. Thus, while Prisoners' Dilemma and the failure of cooperation is not always the proper metaphor for international relations, neither is iterated Prisoners' Dilemma and success in cooperation the proper metaphor. Individual issues need to be modeled separately to understand the impact of iteration.[33]

It is interesting to reflect upon the Prisoners' Dilemma supergame as a "dynamic" game. Since it involves choosing a single strategy for playing the game through time (e.g., play Tit-for-Tat or play Always Defect), it has the formal properties of a static game. It is dynamic only in the sense that strategies are consciously directed toward the problem of how to play in an iterated series of static games. Through this, it provides a systematic analysis of shifts within strategies during a sequence of iterated games (for example, a shift from "cooperate" to "not cooperate" within a Tit-for-Tat strategy). This interpretation of the supergame (plus the fact that it may involve a transformation of the static game as discussed above) gives it dynamic qualities.[34]

The greater power of the supergame requires stronger assumptions that states compare current benefits (for instance, from not cooperating on the current play) with future benefits (for instance, maintaining cooperation through time). Such comparisons necessarily involve interval-level payoffs and more information about preferences (intensities as well as ordering) than do ordinal payoffs. Also, because payoffs from individual iterations are received at different points in time, states must compare them through "discount rates" showing their time preference for immediate versus future benefits. These discount rates depend on domestic circumstances, the situation of the state in the international

[33] The coordination aspects of the two-person Prisoners' Dilemma supergame can be seen in the matrix of supergame strategies in Taylor (fn. 32), 39. For a discussion of the differences between iterated Prisoners' Dilemma and iterated Coordination, see Duncan Snidal, "Coordination Versus Prisoners' Dilemma: Implications for International Cooperation and Regimes," *American Political Science Review* (forthcoming, December 1985).

[34] A further dynamic adjustment process in terms of the evolution of strategies, whereby more successful strategies in one period are more likely (for reasons of survival, imitation, or learning) to occur in subsequent periods, is added by Axelrod (fn. 16). R. Harrison Wagner, "Theory of Games and International Cooperation," *American Political Science Review* 77 (June 1983), 330-46, provides a useful critique of the attempt to embody dynamic assumptions in a single 2 x 2 game through the use of sequential games that deny "players the opportunity to cheat (by assuming that they will cooperate condititonally) . . ." (pp. 332-33). However, he commits a similar error in assuming conditional behavior within the extensive game (p. 344). Iterated game analysis keeps the decision period much cleaner and less subject to artificial insertion of "conditional" cooperation that is based, in effect, on the ability either to predict the future or to recover from an adversary's behavior before payoffs accrue.

system, and uncertainty about continuation of game iteration into the future.[35]

One important factor is the number of iterations in a game. The longer an issue is expected to persist, the greater the impact that future play will have on current choices. Similarly, the more quickly states can adjust their policies, the shorter the time frame of any single game, and hence the more iterations in any fixed period of time. This suggests that states may promote cooperation (in Prisoners' Dilemma) by improving verification in arms control, or by dividing negotiations into larger numbers of smaller sequential steps. These policies will be enhanced by perceptions of other states as reliable partners for future cooperation, but diminished by incentives to take a "final move" and sacrifice future collaboration for immediate advantage.

In addition to providing an insight into incentives to cooperate, iterated game analysis raises questions of how states adjust to new equilibrium outcomes. Axelrod's work explores the evolution of cooperation through the natural superiority of certain strategies, especially Tit-for-Tat, in iterated games. However, while the evolutionary *model* is insightful for understanding the emergence of cooperation, evolutionary *theory* is misleading in its specification of the mechanism of adjustment. This is because the international system has neither the selective elimination (states are rarely eliminated even in war) nor the random variation that evolutionary theory requires. Instead, there is rational adjustment through learning and planning of a sort that is better captured by game theory. Even though its model of behavior is identical (for example, in showing the efficacy of Tit-for-Tat), rational adaptation allows for a more compelling and fruitful theoretical interpretation of international politics and cooperation than does evolutionary theory.[36]

Interpretation of dynamic games in terms of strategic rationality directs research to the incentives underlying the emergence of international regimes that facilitate cooperation. Interactions are understood in terms of the deliberate behavior of states trying to improve their welfare

[35] The formal results for cooperation through time require either that the game continue forever or that there be uncertainty about its termination date. Luce and Raiffa (fn. 4) show that cooperation will not be rational if the termination date is known. Russell Hardin argues in *Collective Action* (Baltimore: Johns Hopkins University Press, 1982) that since this is implausible, future play will provide incentives to cooperate.

[36] This is a case where the same model is a model for two different theories (e.g., evolutionary and rational). Axelrod's discussion (fn. 16) recognizes the alternative interpretation of his model in terms of learning and adaptation, especially in his chapter on cooperation in trench warfare. Nowhere does he provide a vulgar evolutionary view of politics. Nevertheless, it is important to emphasize the very different interpretations of his model of iterated play under rational as opposed to evolutionary theory. See Elster (fn. 19), chap. 1, and Keohane (fn. 14).

through cooperation. Acceptance of the rules and norms of regimes is interpreted in terms of maximizing behavior: regimes are effective and persist only as long as states find it in their interest to maintain them. This rational adjustment mechanism explains cooperative behavior even when there is no threat of elimination and when the environment of international politics is changing too rapidly for evolutionary adjustment to ensure successful adaptation. It also explains why cooperation might emerge on global issues where all nations are affected equally, so that evolutionary selection among them according to their behavior is impossible. At the very least, we should hope that adjustment to cooperation will be rational in a world of nuclear weapons.

D.   A MULTILATERAL WORLD: N-PERSON GAMES

Game models with more than two actors are important since many international issues involve larger numbers of states (for instance, five actors in the classic European balance of power, many participants in the Law of the Sea, and the "Groups" of five, ten, seventy-seven, etc., in contemporary economic regimes). A consideration of N-person game-theory models suggests how such extensions can be helpful for some problems, but are of only limited usefulness for others.[37]

N-person games are complicated and provide few simple "answers," but a number of interrelated assumptions can simplify the analysis of specific situations. The first simplification pertains when the *number of states is large*, so that no state has a substantial impact on any other state. Each can assume that its actions are unnoticed and pursue its interests on the assumption that others will not react. This reduces the problem to narrow rationality—equivalent to the one-player "game against nature"—and poses no problems of strategic complexity. That is not to say that such situations are without interest or are nonproblematic: collective-action problems can lead to collectively suboptimal outcomes.

---

[37] When should a situation be treated as an N-person game? In some cases the answer is obvious because it is technically impossible for the actions of many states to be insulated from one another. For example, in conservation of fish stocks in a "commons," all states fishing that commons will be relevant. The "N-ness" of the problem will depend on the exact nature of the commons. If fish species are nonmigratory and the commons is territorially divided, then only territorial states (perhaps as few as one) need be involved. But if species are migratory and/or the commons is not divided, then any state that fishes those species may be a relevant actor. This determination may be complicated if states act strategically and misrepresent the extent of their interest in the issue, or if the number of participants itself is not exogenous to the regime. For example, in the construction of economic regimes (e.g., trading blocs), deciding the scope of membership may hinge on the expected impact on the regime. An overview of the technical game theory material is available in Anatol Rapoport, *N-Person Game Theory* (Ann Arbor: University of Michigan Press, 1970) and in Shubik (fn. 4).

The large-number assumption, however, is not always fruitful for international politics because issues often involve intermediate numbers of states with the capacity for monitoring and reacting to each others' actions—especially if there is the possibility of discrimination as discussed below.

A related simplification is the assumption of *symmetry*. This pertains when states face similar opportunities, have similar interests, and are of approximately equal impact in an issue area. In such cases, the relation of each state to every other is roughly the same; multilateral relations can be understood in terms of the strategic relation of any one state to all of the others. Schelling's and Hardin's analyses of "k-groups," and many problems of public-good provision are examples.[38] These symmetrical models can sometimes even be modified to incorporate certain asymmetries within them (for instance, the introduction of different distributions of interest into a symmetric problem of public-good provision).[39]

A final simplification concerns the ability of states to *discriminate* their actions with respect to other states. For example, states differentiate their tariff schedules (e.g., common markets or the Generalized System of Preferences) and use military force to defend allies while threatening enemies. To be effective, discrimination must be linked to strategy choices of other states so that it can be made contingent on their behavior. In this respect, perfect discrimination is the opposite situation from that of large numbers. When discrimination is perfect, each state can adopt a separate policy toward every other state, and the N-person game can be analyzed as a set of *linked* two-person games. Axelrod's analysis of the evolution of cooperation relies on this assumption since actors are assumed to be capable of cooperating with some actors while not cooperating with others. By using the discrimination assumption, he derives a compelling account of the emergence of cooperation among "N" actors while relying largely on two-actor game theory.[40]

Discrimination is not always a reasonable assumption. It may be difficult on technical grounds having to do with the nature of the issue or the capacities of states. For example, problems in the provision of

[38] Hardin (fn. 35); Thomas Schelling, *Micromotives and Macrobehavior* (New York: Norton, 1978).
[39] Snidal (fn. 3).
[40] Axelrod's analysis has every actor playing the same strategy (e.g., Tit-for-Tat) against every other actor; but that may mean behaving differently vis-à-vis different states on any particular move (according to how they behaved on the previous turn). However, the linked nature of the 2 x 2 games is central to his analysis since the evolutionary survival of actors depends on comparisons of how each fares (on average) against all the others. Axelrod (fn. 16), chap. 3.

international public goods arise precisely because states cannot isolate their actions toward one state from those toward another (e.g., restraint in the size of fishing catches from international waters). Even if feasible, discrimination may be hard to enforce. Thus, discriminatory trading arrangements are susceptible to evasion through transshipping, and it is usually difficult to threaten one state militarily without making others nervous. Even where discrimination is technically feasible, political arrangements such as the norm of nondiscrimination in trade may make it impossible. In other cases, political institutions such as alliances or trading communities are designed to facilitate discrimination. When it pertains, discrimination allows analysis of N-person games in terms of simpler models.

Many N-person situations will not fall under the related assumptions of large numbers, symmetry, or discrimination.[41] What can be done to analyze these important situations in international politics? First, there are a few general conclusions from N-person game theory that can increase our understanding of international politics. Although N-person game theory often disappoints by providing a multiplicity of solutions instead of a single one to any particular game, this multiplicity itself provides insight into the nature of strategic problems.[42] Differences among solutions highlight important aspects of the strategic structure for understanding politics among nations. For example, conflict between the criteria of efficiency (Pareto-optimality) and of maximizing national self-interest highlights the inherent conflict between collective and individual rationality in the problem of collective action. Similarly, analysis of the existence of the "core" solution may indicate problems for cooperation that are likely to arise whenever there are multiple strong and overlapping subcoalitions in a population of states.

Second, more specific applications of N-person game results may be possible through modeling specific international issues. The oligopoly literature has already provided inspiration for international political research; its rich body of theoretical and empirical knowledge undoubtedly contains further insights. However, this knowledge should not be incorporated by analogy (as in Waltz), but by its example of how to

[41] The hardest issues to analyze will be nonsymmetric ones involving intermediate numbers of states with limited capacities to discriminate their actions. That category, of course, covers much of the ground in international politics.

[42] This problem is not unique to N-person games; it also crops up in two-person games (e.g., in the differences between outcomes predicted between maximax versus minimax strategies). While solution concepts sometimes converge in N-person games, they often do not, and the complexity of the strategic structure makes it harder to compare or choose among them than in two-person games. See Rapoport (fn. 37), and Shubik (fn. 4).

construct models and theory. Tailoring models directly to international politics will capture the richness of international politics better than even the most heroic attempts to patch up the analogy between firms and states. For example, the literature on balance of power contains tremendous insights on strategic interrelations among different numbers of states—but much of this work remains inchoate, expressed in terms of descriptive rules of behavior instead of a more formally articulated model in terms of the goals of states. Other work that takes the important step of attempting to model the goals of states directly fails to take into account the strategic interrelationship among them.[43] Integration of these two approaches holds great potential for a more complete theoretical understanding of political-military relations.

Nevertheless, there are few easy results from N-person game theory, and it is far from a panacea. In general, the theory will be inadequate if our goal is to recreate specific situations in our models. This will be especially true for the more complicated N-person dynamic games that have not been discussed here. But insofar as our goal is understanding general problems of international cooperation as the number of states increases, the simplifying assumptions and general conclusions of game theory will be valuable.

IV. CONCLUSION:
GAME THEORY AND INTERNATIONAL COOPERATION

The ultimate criterion for evaluating game theory is whether it expands our understanding of substantive issues such as those analyzed in the case studies of international cooperation in the essays that follow. The theory is very general and does not provide specific predictions without additional, auxiliary assumptions. Its usefulness therefore depends on whether it poses interesting questions about the politics of international issues and suggests fruitful directions for empirical elaboration, rather than on whether it provides correct answers in any narrow sense. The case studies provide a test of the explanatory power of this empirical elaboration of the theory. Of course, the test is not of specific predictions of behavior in particular circumstances—theories don't make those sorts of predictions—but of general explanations of behavior in issue areas. If explanations in particular case studies are not empirically compelling, it may be either because the general theoretical approach is

[43] Two relevant works to build upon are Morton Kaplan, *System and Process in International Politics* (New York: Wiley, 1957) and Bueno de Mesquita (fn. 1).

deficient or because there are problems in the particular empirical elaboration. Thus the test of the theory is ultimately whether the case studies, taken as a whole, demonstrate that a game theory approach provides new insights to international politics.

Game theory as a theory of international politics has a richness that makes it amenable to such broad empirical application. The theoretical constructs are flexible and can be adapted to different substantive problems. The tremendous variety of models contained within the theory allows for a systematic incorporation of the most salient contextual features pertaining to different issues. In the simple 2 x 2 game, this is reflected in the different game structures (for example, Prisoners' Dilemma versus Chicken) that can be distinguished through the careful modeling of payoffs and of the international environment. Extensions to N-person and dynamic games allow other important dimensions to be addressed. Diverse international issues can be handled within a common game-theoretical framework which does not suppress that diversity, but builds upon it to explore the implications of various contextual differences. In this way, the theory emphasizes the importance of context without becoming lost in it.

This versatility of game models can be a vice rather than a virtue when used improperly. Metaphorical and analogical approaches are valuable for descriptive and expository purposes, but are too flexible to provide falsifiable propositions. The same is true of models applied in a *post hoc* fashion. Only models embedded in theoretical arguments, and carefully tailored to the relevant empirical correspondences (e.g., for payoffs or number of iterations) in an issue area will provide interesting and (potentially) falsifiable empirical claims. Moreover, the deductive power of these models will help to keep inferences separate from assumptions even as they produce new predictions.

It is as a theory of state behavior that games hold their greatest promise for understanding international relations. As a general theory, game theory brings the contending "interdependence" and "Realist" positions together in a common framework. While limited by the correctness of its assumptions about strategic rationality, game theory is sufficiently flexibile to incorporate many differing assumptions about world politics and individual issues. Self-interested behavior of states is not prejudged as necessarily leading to either cooperation or conflict. Nor is the emergence of stronger international institutions, formal or informal, seen as either inevitable or utopian. Instead, these conditions are simply among the diverse possibilities that might be predicted depending on the concrete circumstances of different issues. The theory pushes us to fill in the appropriate empirical correspondence for investigating such possibilities. In this way, a "game *theory* of international politics" will help us to elucidate and renovate the broader metaphors of "Hobbesian anarchy" and "international organization" that have divided and obscured our understanding of international politics.

FROM BALANCE TO CONCERT:
A Study of International
Security Cooperation

By ROBERT JERVIS*

INTERNATIONAL anarchy and the security dilemma make co-operation among sovereign states difficult. Indeed, when international politics is viewed from this perspective, the central question is not, "Why do wars occur?" but "Why do wars not occur more often?"[1] We should therefore explore the conditions under which the major states try to gain security through joint efforts. What is important here is that these conditions can be derived from the theory of cooperation under the security dilemma.[2]

The first point is quite obvious. There are no cases of world government, world federation, or even a worldwide pluralistic security community. The closest thing is the concert system, which has occurred only three times in modern history—from 1815 to 1854 (although in its strongest form it only lasted until 1822), 1919 to 1920, and 1945 to 1946. The term "Concert of Europe" is often applied to late 19th-century international politics, but the pursuit of self-interest was not sufficiently transformed to justify this label. The two 20th-century concerts were very brief, and one can argue that they did not really come into existence

* I am grateful for comments by Robert Art, Alexander George, Joanne Gowa, Deborah Larson, Paul Lauren, Glenn Snyder, Stephen Walt, Kenneth Waltz, and the other contributors to this volume.

[1] For the concept of the security dilemma, see John Herz, "Idealist Internationalism and the Security Dilemma," *World Politics* 2 (January 1950), 157-80; Herbert Butterfield, *History and Human Relations* (London: Collins, 1951); Arnold Wolfers, *Discord and Collaboration* (Baltimore: Johns Hopkins University Press, 1962), 83-90. In *Man, the State, and War* (New York: Columbia University Press, 1959), Kenneth Waltz noted that using anarchy as the starting point implies that it is peace, not war, that needs to be explained.

[2] For general discussions of the problems of cooperation in the absence of supranational sovereignty, see Robert Jervis, "Cooperation under the Security Dilemma," *World Politics* 30 (January 1978), 167-214; Robert Axelrod, *The Evolution of Cooperation* (New York: Basic Books, 1984); Robert O. Keohane, *After Hegemony* (Princeton: Princeton University Press, 1984). For treatments of this problem from the perspective of international law, see Gerhard Niemeyer, *Law Without Force* (Princeton: Princeton University Press, 1941); Michael Barkun, *Law Without Sanctions* (New Haven: Yale University Press); Terry Nardin, *Law, Morality, and the Relations of States* (Princeton: Princeton University Press, 1984); and Friedrich Kratochwil, "Following Rules," unpub. (Columbia University, 1984).

at all. At a minimum, there was a short period of extensive cooperation, and many statesmen and observers had at least some hopes for a longer-lasting concert.

The best example we have comes from the years immediately after 1815. In essence, the concert was characterized by an unusually high and self-conscious level of cooperation among the major European powers. The states did not play the game as hard as they could; they did not take advantage of others' short-run vulnerabilities. In repeated plays of the Prisoners' Dilemma, then, each state cooperated in the expectation that the others would do the same. Multilateral and self-restrained methods of handling their problems were preferred to the more common unilateral and less restrained methods.[3]

More frequently, states are restrained only externally, by what others are doing, or by the anticipation of what others will do if they act against the others' interests. This pattern characterizes the balance of power. Under the balance of power, a number of restraints are evinced: no state gains dominance, wars do not become total, unconditional surrenders are rare, the territory of losing states is not divided up among the winners, and usually the loser is soon reintegrated into the system. These restraints arise from the clashing self-interests of the individual states. They will work together to prevent any state from dominating; but because today's enemy may be tomorrow's ally and vice versa, it does not make sense to be too harsh with the defeated state. Indeed, since each member of the winning coalition worries about excessive growth in its partners' power and fears that they may be planning a separate peace with the adversary, there may be competition among the allies to see who can be most reasonable toward the loser. Although the results of these competitive dynamics are restrained as states block each other's ambitions in order to maintain their own power, it is hard to see this situation as mutual cooperation and an escape from anarchy and the security dilemma. In fact, the latter are the very forces that drive the system.

[3] Jervis, "Security Regimes," *International Organization* 36 (Spring 1982), 362-68; Richard B. Elrod, "The Concert of Europe: A Fresh Look at an International System," *World Politics* 28 (January 1976), 159-74; Paul Gordon Lauren, "Crisis Prevention in Nineteenth-Century Diplomacy," in Alexander George, with others, *Managing U.S.-Soviet Rivalry* (Boulder, CO: Westview Press, 1983), 31-64. Paul Schroeder argues that, contrary to the commonly held view, Metternich did not fit the description of a concert statesman. See Schroeder, *Metternich's Diplomacy at its Zenith* (New York: Greenwood Press, 1969), 251-66 and throughout. Matthew Anderson argues that Alexander I is the best model of such a statesman who had "a real sense of European responsibilities and a willingness to make sacrifices to meet them." See Anderson, "Russia and the Eastern Question, 1821-41," in Alan Sked, ed., *Europe's Balance of Power, 1815-1848* (London: Macmillan, 1979), 82.

I. Assumptions of the Balance of Power and the Concert

The balance of power normally maintains itself. The fortunes of individual states rise and fall, but the system usually continues. Why does this continuity sometimes fail, and why does a concert system arise? The most obvious clue is provided by the timing of the concerts. They occur after, and only after, a major war fought to contain a potential hegemon. That is not a coincidence; such a war undermines the assumptions of a balance of power system and alters the perceived payoffs in a way that facilitates cooperation.

Although scholars disagree about many aspects of the balance of power, most would concur that the following four assumptions are crucial to its operation.[4] First, there must be several actors of relatively equal power. The minimum number is two (although perhaps one large power can be balanced against several smaller ones). Second, all states must want to survive. They may seek expansion, and usually some of them do. But the condition that is necessary—and usually easy to meet— is that they are not anxious to form a confederation with one another.[5] (These two assumptions do not enter into the rest of the analysis and so can be set aside.) Third, states must be able to ally with each other on the basis of short-run interests. To use Liska's term, there must not be many strong "alliance handicaps."[6] The states cannot be so constrained by ideologies, personal rivalries, and national hatreds that they are unable to align and realign on the basis of what is necessary to maintain their security. Finally, war must be a legitimate instrument of statecraft. That is not to say that it is welcome, but that states believe they can resort to the use of armed force if they believe it to be helpful.

Concert systems form after, and only after, a large war against a potential hegemon because such a conflict alters the last two assumptions and increases the incentives to cooperate. The war weakens the assumption of the absence of alliance handicaps in two ways. First, it leads to unusually close bonds among the states of the counter-hegemonic coalition, even though disputes and hostility within the coalition never disappear. It is hard to form such a coalition in the first place, and even

[4] For a somewhat different list of criteria, see Inis Claude, *Power and International Relations* (New York: Random House, 1962), 90-91.

[5] The frequent argument that the balance of power assumes that states seek to maximize their power is unnecessary and leads to confusion. See Kenneth Waltz, *Theory of International Politics* (Reading, MA: Addison-Wesley, 1979), 118, 126, and Robert O. Keohane, "Theory of World Politics: Structural Realism and Beyond," in Ada Finifter, ed., *Political Science: The State of the Discipline* (Washington, DC: American Political Science Association, 1983), 514-15.

[6] George Liska, *Nations in Alliance* (Baltimore: Johns Hopkins University Press, 1962).

the shared experience of fighting a winning war does not remove all sources of friction. But it does tend to produce significant ties among allies. Probably more important in undermining the assumption of no alliance handicaps—and a factor contributing to the bonds among the allies—is the belief that the defeated hegemon is not a normal state. Under the balance of power, all states are potentially fit alliance partners; none is seen as much more evil than any other. But a war against a potential hegemon alters this belief. France after the Napoleonic wars and Germany after the two World Wars were not seen as similar to other states. Instead, they were thought to be ineradicably aggressive. The supposed causes for this aberrant behavior varied; reasons have been sought in national character and climate, in the importance of an authoritarian family structure, or in geography. Whatever the cause, the consequence is that the defeated state is seen as a potential danger in the future. Thus, even though the victors may reintegrate the losing state into the international system—as the powers did after the Napoleonic wars—a significant part of the purpose of doing so is to continue to restrain it.

The balance-of-power assumption that war is available as a normal policy instrument is also undermined by the conflict with a hegemon. Such a war will be long and destructive because it is fought against a powerful and strongly motivated state, and requires something close to total victory. After such an experience, the winners will be highly sensitive to the costs of war and will therefore be hesitant to resort to armed force unless their most vital interests are at stake. That is particularly true because in most cases the war against the hegemon will have been accompanied by, or will have led to, large-scale social unrest.

Concert systems decay, and indeed only the first of them lasted a significant length of time. Different factors were at work in each of the three periods, but in general the passage of time alters the unusual postwar situation and reestablishes the balance-of-power assumptions. As the memories of the war fade, the bonds erode that helped to hold the blocking coalition together. Friction tends to build as each state believes that it is sacrificing more for unity than are the others. Because of perceptual dynamics, each will remember the cases in which it has been restrained, and ignore or interpret differently cases in which others believe they acted for the common good. Fear of the state that had earlier sought hegemony is also likely to decline over time. Unless it gives continued evidence of unreasonable behavior, the others may well decide that it is not particularly evil or aggressive after all. The painful memories of the enormous costs of war also become dimmer as time passes, and a new generation, with no first-hand experience of the war, comes to power.

II. Concert Systems and the Security Dilemma

The factors that explain the transformation of a balance-of-power system to a concert and back again can be seen in terms of variables that heighten or ameliorate the security dilemma. Four kinds of factors are important here: changes in the relations between offensive and defensive strategies, changes in the payoffs, changes in the ability to determine what others are doing and to make appropriate responses (transparency and timely warning), and changes in the estimates and predictions of what others will do.

A. OFFENSE-DEFENSE BALANCE

The virulence of the security dilemma is influenced by whether offensive weapons and strategies can be distinguished from defensive ones, and whether the offense is more potent than the defense.[7] Even when the states want to cooperate, they may not be able to when offensive and defensive motivations lead to the same threatening behavior, and when actors believe that it is better for them to take the offensive and strike the first blow rather than to let the other side strike first. Under such conditions, there is no way for states to increase their security without menacing others. When these conditions are reversed, however, mutual security is possible.

This argument has usually been applied to military systems,[8] but the logic holds in the political arena as well. Under the balance of power, offensive and defensive strategies are likely to be similar, and the offense often has the advantage as states can capitalize on the temporary weaknesses of others. Because many wars are short and decisive, there is an emphasis on making immediate gains and avoiding immediate losses. The obvious fear is that the latter will pyramid, and the obvious hope is that the former will set off a positive feedback. On the tactical level

---

[7] Jervis (fn. 2), 186-214; George Quester, *Offense and Defense in the International System* (New York: Wiley, 1977).

[8] Stephen Van Evera, "The Cult of the Offensive and the Origins of the First World War," *International Security* 9 (Summer 1984), 58-107; Jack Snyder, "Civil-Military Relations and the Cult of the Offensive, 1914 and 1984," *International Security* 9 (Summer 1984), 108-46; Snyder, *The Ideology of the Offensive: Military Decision-making and the Disasters of 1914* (Ithaca, NY: Cornell University Press, 1984); Jack Levy, "The Offensive/Defensive Balance of Military Technology: A Theoretical and Historical Analysis," *International Studies Quarterly* 28 (June 1984), 219-38; Barry Posen, *The Sources of Military Doctrine: France, Britain, and Germany Between the Two World Wars* (Ithaca, NY: Cornell University Press, 1984).

as well, offensive strategies are often appropriate. Taking others by surprise is perfectly legitimate, and likely to be efficacious.

Under the concert, the situation is quite different. The expectation that the system of mutual restraint will last means that there is less stress on making short-run gains and less fear of short-run losses. Because states are less likely to take advantage of temporary imbalances, they need not act quickly in the anticipation that if they do not, others will take advantage of them. Indeed, taking advantage of others (that is, failing to cooperate with them when they are cooperating with you) is likely to be self-defeating. It endangers the system and may well be met by negative sanctions from the other members. Under the balance-of-power system, others will oppose this type of behavior only if they believe that doing so is in their immediate self-interest. Under the concert, these calculations are diluted by the states' interest in maintaining a high level of cooperation. Thus, states that are too ambitious and seek excessive gains are likely to be opposed by a broader coalition acting to maintain the concert. In this situation, defensive political strategies are likely to be different from as well as more attractive than offensive ones.

Because a large counter-hegemonic war undermines the balance-of-power assumption that wars are a normal tool of statecraft, defensive strategies gain a further advantage. If war is seen as likely in the near future (as it often is under the balance of power), incentives may be high to undertake a preventive or a preemptive war. The alternative to going to war *now* may not be the maintenance of peace and the status quo, but being attacked later. If conditions are propitious, if the state's alliance structure is intact, if the temporary distribution of power is favorable, then a war is likely in a balance-of-power system, irrespective of the state's general intentions; the state need not seek expansion in order to initiate a war. By contrast, when states think that war can be avoided for a long period of time, even conditions conducive to war are less likely to lead to fighting because the payoffs for not initiating conflict are higher than they are when war is used as a normal policy instrument. Thus, if states are willing to live with the status quo, they are freer to follow defensive policies.

When defensive policies are more effective than offensive ones, states that support the status quo need not seek protection through expansion; when offensive goals are sought by policies that differ from those used to reach defensive ones, it is easier for status quo powers to identify each other. By and large, these expectations are borne out by international politics in the period between the Napoleonic and the Crimean wars. It seems that at that time, two common problems inhibiting cooperation among status quo states were less pressing. Only infrequently did states have to gain their own security at the expense of that of others, and identification errors were relatively rare—in part because of the differentiation between offensive and defensive postures. These conditions facilitated cooperation both by reducing the number of cases in which status quo powers mistook each other for aggressors and by making states less fearful of the danger that what was intended as mutual cooperation would be seen as appeasement.

B.   CHANGES IN PAYOFFS

The development of a concert system is supported by changes in the payoffs. Games that are structured as Prisoners' Dilemma will vary in the likelihood of leading to mutual cooperation according to the cardinal value of the utility of the various outcomes. Prisoners' Dilemmas in which the payoffs for CC are relatively high and those for CD, DC, and DD are relatively low are more likely to yield cooperative solutions.[9] In other words, cooperation is more probable when mutual cooperation is only slightly less attractive than exploiting the other, when being exploited is only slightly worse than mutual competition, and when the latter outcome is much worse than mutual cooperation. The concert arises largely because the payoffs fit this configuration.

INCREASED COSTS OF NON-COOPERATION

In discussing the post-1815 period, Medlicott argues that "it was peace that maintained the Concert, and not the Concert that maintained peace."[10] There is something to this—the high perceived cost of war was an important factor. But the point should not be pushed too far. Knowing that statesmen want to preserve the peace does not tell us how they would go about trying to reach this goal, or whether they would succeed. Indeed, the standard problem in the security dilemma is that although all actors desire security, the interaction of their efforts produces general insecurity. Nevertheless, their strong motivation to avoid war is probably a necessary condition for the maintenance of a concert. Thus it is important that a war against a hegemon increases the costs of mutual non-cooperation. The former allies know that if they get into heated squabbles with each other, the defeated enemy will take advantage of

---

[9] Jervis (fn. 2), 167-86. Note that this is not the same as saying that the chances for cooperation increase as the payoffs for cooperation increase and those for defection decrease. It is equally important that payoffs for outcomes in which one side defects and the other cooperates be moderate—that the former not gain too much or the latter suffer too greatly.

[10] W. N. Medlicott, *Bismarck, Gladstone, and the Concert of Europe* (New York: Greenwood Press, 1969), 18.

the splits. Although they are not unwilling to use the former enemy against their former allies (Britain did so with France soon after the Napoleonic wars), disagreements are muted by the fear that if they are carried too far, the war against the hegemon may have to be fought all over again. However, conflict is not entirely out of the question.[11] The very fact that each state knows that the others see war as too costly to be a viable option allows each to use the common interest of avoiding catastrophe as a lever to extract competitive gains. But because the costs of war are high, states have incentives to reduce conflict, and are willing to run substantial risks of being exploited in order to decrease the chance that their policies will lead to unnecessary competition.

Costs of anarchy and revolutions. To the extent that statesmen believe that the previous war was caused in part by anarchy in general, and by economic rivalries in particular, there are additional incentives for co-operation. The views of Woodrow Wilson fit into the first category. Wilson saw the balance-of-power system as one of the main causes of World War I; he concluded that, in order to avoid future wars, greater international cooperation—in the form of the League of Nations—was necessary. Similarly, many Americans believed that the Depression and the economic rivalries of the interwar period were significantly responsible for the rise of Hitler and World War II. U.S. decision makers therefore felt that economic cooperation was important not only for the economic gains it would bring, but also to reduce the chances of a future war.

After the Napoleonic Wars, the incentives for unity were increased by the conviction that wars and revolutions were linked. Each could lead to the other, and so both were dangerous. There were differences of opinion and of interest among the powers on this point: the liberal powers—Britain and France—were both less threatened by unrest and less worried that revolutions would automatically spread. They (especially Britain) opposed the use of the concert to sanction counter-revolutionary interventions because they saw such actions as mere covers for narrow national interests, and because they perceived many revolutions as good, or at least as not evil. Nevertheless, even they feared radicalism in its most extreme forms; this fear produced more of a common basis of understanding than is usual in international politics.

[11] Serious threats of war were made on several occasions. See, for example, the incidents and attitudes discussed in Roger Bullen, *Palmerston, Guizot, and the Collapse of the Entente Cordiale* (London: Athlone, 1974), 54; Harold Temperley, *The Foreign Policy of Canning, 1822-1827* (London: Cass, 1966), 81-83, 371; Gordon Craig, "The System of Alliances and the Balance of Power," in J.T.P. Bury, ed., *New Cambridge Modern History*, X, *The Zenith of European Power, 1830-70* (New York: Cambridge University Press, 1960), 254-57.

States have often welcomed unrest within their rivals' and neighbors' territories because it weakened them.[12] But if the revolutions were likely to spread, they would be a menace to all. As late as 1854, the King of Prussia wrote: "I shall not allow Austria, the incovenient, intriguing Austria, to be attacked by Revolution, without drawing the sword on her behalf, and this from pure love of Prussia, from self-preservation."[13] At that time, states were interdependent in their internal security, which limited their foreign policy goals and means. It limited their goals because the chance of revolution would be increased if they were to defeat another regime too completely, to humiliate it, or even to deny it a share of international influence on which its domestic legitimacy rested in part. A too narrow conception of self-interest would therefore be self-defeating, not because the other would retaliate, but because the other might suffer a revolt. The shared fear of unrest also limited the means of statecraft, in that statesmen in this period largely forswore the tool of fomenting revolutions to undermine unfriendly regimes abroad. The absence in the concert of this common tactic in the balance of power is striking, and contributed to mutual cooperation. Indeed, in one case in which a statesman was believed to have made a threat of creating unrest, others reacted very strongly, arguing that this behavior was both dangerous and a breach of the way the great powers had pledged to act.[14]

Opposition to revolution also facilitated cooperation by forming three bases for reintegrating France into the system. First, the hegemon that had been such a threat could be seen in part not as France, but as *revolutionary* France. Combatting the latter was not inconsistent with establishing good relations with the former. Indeed, the new French regime was as much the enemy of revolutionary France as were the members of the grand coalition. (This logic would also seem to apply to Germany after the two World Wars. Nascent efforts to define the enemy as the old regime failed in 1918 largely because of the pressure of public opinion—a factor that lies outside the structural explanations offered here. They succeeded after 1945, but in a context of competition between the two main powers, a point to which we will return.) Second, France could hope to overturn the Vienna system only by engaging in a large war. Such an effort would require the mobilization of enormous domestic resources, which in turn would call for a revolutionary regime. But that would have been as much of a menace to France's rulers as it

[12] Geoffrey Blainey, *The Causes of War* (New York: Free Press, 1973).
[13] Quoted in F. H. Hinsley, *Power and the Pursuit of Peace* (Cambridge: Cambridge University Press, 1963), 221.
[14] Temperley (fn. 11), 383-84.

would have been to the neighboring states. Thus, France was to a significant extent self-deterred, and could therefore be trusted—at least to a degree. Third, renewed revolution in France was less likely if France was treated fairly in the international arena. It was therefore important for the other countries to establish the legitimacy and efficacy of the new regime in the eyes of its people.

INCREASED GAINS FROM COOPERATION

The other side of this coin is that fighting a potential hegemon leads to higher postwar payoffs for cooperation among the former allies. First of all, the vital goal of ensuring that the past enemy will not again seek dominance can be reached only by maintaining cooperation. To the extent that this interest leads to cooperation on other issues—for example, trade, scientific and cultural exchanges, joint efforts to deal with common problems—states are likely to have heightened expectations of the benefits of working together on a broad front. Common goals give each state a stake in the well-being of the others: to the extent that they expect to cooperate in the future, they want all to be strong, especially if they think they may again have to contain the former enemy. Far from states' values being negatively interdependent (as is often the case in world politics), they are positively linked: each gains if the other is satisfied, and willing and able to carry out its international obligations.

Furthermore, the experience of fighting the hegemon can produce at least a slight degree of altruism. During the war each of the allies may come to value its partners' well-being—not only for the greater contribution to the common good, but as an end in itself. If this altruism carries over into the postwar period, each state will see added benefits in cooperating because of the expectation that all would gain. There may be a similar effect at the elite level: decision makers in each country may develop sufficient ties with their opposite numbers so that each wants the others to stay in power—a goal to which cooperating with the other states is likely to contribute.

Differences in the potential gains from cooperation help to explain why a lasting concert could be formed after the Napoleonic Wars, but not after World Wars I and II. Because Germany was divided after 1945, maintenance of the coalition was not necessary to ensure that it would not seek dominance again. Indeed, reducing the danger from Germany was the purpose of the Morgenthau Plan originally endorsed by Roosevelt, and is at least partly responsible for the fact that few statesmen in either East or West have given more than lip service to the goal of reunification. In large part, of course, the division of Germany grew out of the separate occupation zones because of the general dispute between the United States and the Soviet Union. Had the Allies been able to cooperate on other issues more safely, Germany might have been reassembled. Furthermore, dividing Germany was a way of managing the superpower conflict. Trying to reach joint decisions that would govern the entire country would have been a source of much greater tension and dispute than allowing each side to control its sector. Still, by keeping Germany divided, and thus less of a menace, the Allies removed one of their major incentives for postwar cooperation.[15] The main dangers that Germany continued to pose—such as the acquisition of nuclear weapons by either half, or attempts to reunite—could best be managed by each superpower acting independently.

Bipolarity and the development of nuclear weapons allowed the superpowers to limit the danger of war, without a concert. Unilateral and competitive (rather than joint and cooperative) policies were effective in safeguarding the American and Soviet core values. After 1815, by contrast, there was no way any one of the great powers, with the possible exception of Great Britain, could have maintained its security by acting alone.

After World War I, Germany remained whole; neither bipolarity nor nuclear weapons existed to allow the victorious powers to gain security without cooperation. And yet, a stable concert could not persist, in seeming contradiction to our theory. Part of the explanation is that the withdrawal of two of the major states (for idiosyncratic, domestic reasons) meant that it was far from certain that the two remaining powers could maintain the peace even if they cooperated. Had the United States and Russia remained in the coalition, the pressures would have increased on Britain and France to work together. Indeed, many of he postwar disputes sprang from the fact that Britain would not guarantee France's security, thus forcing the latter to take strong unilateral measures against Germany. Britain's offer of such a pact had been conditional on American participation, which was not forthcoming. Cooperation was therefore inhibited by factors of domestic politics, and these lie outside the realm of the theory elaborated here, which is structural.[16]

---

[15] As early as May 1946 the British Foreign Secretary, Ernest Bevin, understood this. He noted that one cost of keeping Germany divided was that "we should have lost the one factor which *might* hold us and the Russians together, viz. the existence of a single Germany which would be in the interest of us both to hold down." Quoted in Alan Bullock, *Ernest Bevin, Foreign Secretary* (London: Oxford University Press, 1985), 268; emphasis in original. French strength after 1815 as a source of cohesion of the concert is discussed in Roy Bridge, "Allied Diplomacy in Peacetime: The Failure of the Congress 'System,' 1815-23," in Sked (fn. 3), 34-53.

[16] For discussions of how American domestic constraints affected the chances of Soviet-

DECREASED FEAR OF EXPLOITATION

In many cases, the factor most responsible for the lack of cooperation is each state's fear that it will be exploited if it cooperates. After a counter-hegemonic war, these fears are lowered by the transformation of the system. Because all members of the coalition value the maintenance of the concert, there is a good chance that they will defend it. This means that they will provide at least some support and assistance to a state that has been double-crossed. For instance, if State B reacts to State A's cooperation by exploiting it, States D, E, and F can be expected to help A, or, at minimum, not to increase its distress. Thus, there is a "safety net" under the states. Although exploitation is possible, its consequences are likely to be kept within manageable bounds by the reactions of others.

If this type of cooperation is to work, however, there must be more than two major states in the system. The fact that this was not the case after World War II may have contributed to the quick breakdown of cooperation. Even if Waltz's arguments about the greater stability of a bipolar system are correct,[17] it may be harder to maintain a high level of cooperation when there are only two main actors in the system. Although each can use the threat of all-out war to protect its vital interests, the fact that other states cannot do much to decrease the costs of superpower defection increases the two sides' fear of exploitation, and so makes cooperation more difficult to establish and maintain.

Changes in vulnerability. The costs of exploitation decrease as states' vulnerabilities decrease. The security dilemma is especially severe if one defection can destroy a state (for instance, by a surprise attack). If states are strong enough so that a few defections cannot cripple them, they can better afford to take chances on cooperation. The effect of a major war on the costs of later defections is mixed. On the one hand, such a war is likely to exhaust the participants and produce prodigious internal strains; to the extent that states believe that they are too weak to survive if they are forced into a conflict under unfavorable circumstances, the fear of defection and the pressures for preventive war may grow. On

---

American cooperation after World War II, see Robert Dallek, *Franklin D. Roosevelt and American Foreign Policy, 1932-1945* (New York: Oxford University Press, 1979); John Gaddis, *The United States and the Origins of the Cold War, 1941-1947* (New York: Columbia University Press, 1972); and Alexander George, "Domestic Constraints on Regime Change in U.S. Foreign Policy: The Need for Policy Legitimacy," in Ole Holsti, Randolph Siverson, and Alexander George, eds., *Change in the International System* (Boulder, CO: Westview Press, 1980), 233-62.

[17] Kenneth Waltz, "The Stability of a Bipolar World," *Daedalus* 93 (Summer 1964), and Waltz (fn. 5).

the other hand, if the experience of a successful war against a hegemon gives the states a sense of confidence that they can meet challenges, they will be more relaxed about the danger of defections. One reason why a lasting concert could be formed after 1815 but not after 1945 was the weakness of many of the important participants in the latter period. Most of the European states—which were stakes in the game more than they were players—had been broken by the war, and the United States feared that they could easily fall under Soviet influence. Even more important, the Soviet Union was so weak that it could not afford the sort of cooperative arrangements that would open it to Western influence while subjecting it to the danger of a powerful defection.

In many cases, a postwar settlement will make cooperation easier by reducing the states' vulnerabilities. Borders are often changed to correspond with salient ethnic and geographic lines. To the extent that states become more ethnically homogeneous and establish their borders along the lines of natural fortifications like rivers and mountain ranges, they can defend themselves more easily, thereby reducing the costs of defection.

DECREASED GAINS FROM EXPLOITATION

If the states are sometimes pushed to defect because of the fear of the deleterious consequences that will follow if their cooperation is met by the defection of others, they can also be pulled to defect by the positive gains that such a policy can provide. And, in the same way in which the configuration of the postwar world reduces the costs a state will pay if another defects, it reduces the gains that will accrue to the state if it defects itself. The state will have to expect that its defection will meet opposition not only from the particular state it is harming, but also from others in the old coalition. Even if the use of threats and force produces short-run gains, the long- and medium-run effects are likely to be less favorable than they would be under the balance-of-power system. Because of the general commitment to the maintenance of the concert, "bandwagoning" is less likely than it would be under the balance of power.[18]

To the extent that states gain increased security through defection, the transformation that leads to the concert reduces the need to defect because it provides an alternative route to that goal. If members believe that the coalition will remain together and that it can keep them secure,

[18] Ibid., 125-26; Stephen Walt, "Alliance Formation and the Balance of World Power," International Security 9 (Spring 1985), 3-43, and Walt, The Origins of Alliances (Ithaca, NY: Cornell University Press, forthcoming).

they need not pursue unilateral and competitive measures to improve their own security at the expense of others. Indeed, if states have reason to believe that safety lies in the health of the concert, increasing their security by supporting the concert system does not make others less secure, but has the opposite effect. This incentive was clearly operating after 1815. Although states did not completely trust the concert to provide for their security, they did act on the assumption that one of the best guarantees of their individual interests was the well-being of the established cooperative arrangements.

Another important value to be gained by defection is a change in the status quo. After an anti-hegemonic war, this, too, is less attractive than usual. The winners are likely to be relatively satisfied because they are able to write the peace terms. For the losers, of course, the situation is different. After 1815, France was not wildly dissatisfied because the peace settlement was a moderate one. But that was not the case after 1918, in part because of the increased role of allied public opinion, which demanded a harsh peace. For Germany, the resulting incentives to defect not only made it less willing to join a concert, but also increased tensions among the Allies because of disagreements on how to deal with the situation.[19]

The fact that after 1815 the states had been quite satisfied with the status quo gave the concert great legitimacy in the eyes of the statesmen. They saw it as facilitating the achievement of their most important values. The sorts of cooperative behavior that characterized it therefore became imbued with more than instrumental worth, and the concert and its norms took on a moral value, which in turn increased compliance and self-restraint.

Mechanisms for controlling exploitation. Because of three procedural norms, states found it more difficult or less advantageous than usual to try to exploit others under the concert of 1815. The first was the provision for frequent meetings, which had the further function of increasing transparency. The Quadruple Alliance, which was signed upon the defeat of Napoleon, called for periodic conferences of the states' leaders "for the purpose of consulting upon their common interests, and for the consideration of the measures which ... shall be considered the most salutary for the repose and prosperity of Nations, and for the mainte-

---

[19] Factors beyond our structural model have to be taken into account for a complete explanation of the difference between the British and French positions. On this topic, one of the earliest discussions still remains unsurpassed: Arnold Wolfers, *Britain and France Between Two Wars* (New York: Harcourt, Brace, 1940). For a discussion of the extent to which France was a revisionist state after 1815, see Roger Bullen, "France and Europe, 1815-48: The Problem of Defeat and Recovery," in Sked (fn. 3), 112-44.

nance of the peace of Europe."[20] Because such conferences could be used to coerce some of the members and to provide the cover of legitimacy for narrowly national activities, Britain often refused to participate. (Recall Canning's famous quip: "conferences are useless or dangerous; useless if we are in agreement, dangerous if we are not."[21]) But, even from the English perspective, the conferences were a symbolic affirmation of the importance of European interests and European unity, and constituted a barrier to defection. The fact that the states had pledged to discuss all major issues jointly made it harder for any one of them to seek outcomes that were unacceptable to others. Changes in the status quo were not considered legitimate unless and until the great powers had assented to them, often by holding a conference. Form and substance are not unrelated: if states are committed to gaining widespread ratification for crucial actions, they must accept limits on the extent to which they can hope to make competitive gains.[22]

Related to the system of conferences was the great powers' habit of negotiating jointly with third parties (especially Turkey). One purpose was to increase the pressure on the powers with which they were dealing, a practice that was especially helpful with a recalcitrant and skilled target such as Turkey. But the increased ability of each of the great powers to see that the others were not taking advantage of them and their concomitant willingness to limit their own potential gains was at least as important. Paul Schroeder has shown that alliances can be a tool of control.[23] This restriction is not necessarily one-sided: formal alliances and informal understandings that states will act together can limit the freedom of action of all the parties. By working together, the powers ensured that none could steal a march on the others.[24]

The third way in which great powers limited the potential advantages of exploiting each other was by formal and mutual self-denying ordi-

[20] Quoted in René Albrecht-Carrié, ed., *The Concert of Europe* (New York: Walker, 1968), 32.

[21] Quoted in Temperley (fn. 11), 135.

[22] Thus, in late July 1914, French statesmen were disturbed to learn that Austria and Germany rejected a role for the other European powers in the dispute between Austria and Serbia; this indicated a non-cooperative approach and a desire to inflict a settlement that others would find objectionable. See John Keiger, *France and the Origins of the First World War* (London: Macmillan, 1984), 153. For a discussion of the relationship between cooperative processes and cooperative outcomes, see Morton Deutsch, "Fifty Years of Conflict," in Leon Festinger, ed., *Retrospection on Social Psychology* (New York: Oxford University Press, 1980).

[23] Schroeder, "Alliances, 1815-1914: Weapons of Power and Tools of Management," in Klaus Knorr, ed., *Historical Dimensions of National Security Problems* (Lawrence: University Press of Kansas, 1976), 227-62.

[24] This is not to deny Hinsley's argument that the British realized that their Continental partners' habit of demanding too extensive collaboration would make the concert impractical. Only a somewhat looser arrangement, the British felt, would allow the concert to succeed. See Hinsley (fn. 13), 202-12.

nances. Many of the treaties signed between 1815 and 1854—especially those involving the relations between great powers and smaller ones—contained a provision by which each of the former forswore any unilateral advantage. Article V of the treaty by which Britain, France, and Russia coordinated their efforts to force Turkey to grant independence to Greece was typical: "The Contracting Powers will not seek, in these arrangements, any augmentation of territory, any exclusive influence, or any commercial advantage for their Subjects, which those of every other Nation may not equally obtain."[25] Similarly, when the powers guaranteed the independence of Belgium, the treaty registered that

> They were unanimously of opinion that the five Powers owe to the interest, well understood,—to their own union, to the tranquility of Europe, and to the accomplishment of [Belgian independence], a solemn avowal, and a striking proof of their firm determination not to seek in the arrangements relative to Belgium, under whatever circumstances they may present themselves, any augmentation of territory, any exclusive influence,—any isolated advantages. . . .[26]

Such words do not totally prevent unregulated competition, and they were repeated so often that perhaps they became ritualistic. But they constituted commitments that could not be broken lightly, and they summarized the spirit of the concert.

C.   INCREASED TRANSPARENCY AND TIMELY WARNING

Cooperation is made more likely not only by changes in payoffs, but also by increases in the states' ability to recognize what others are doing—called "transparency" in the literature on regimes. Coupled with the ability to act on this information, transparency can produce a situation in which, in effect, the choices of CD and DC are effectively ruled out. Short periods of defection or exploitation may occur; but if they can be detected and countered, the only real alternatives are CC and DD. Inspection and verification are therefore essential even in the absence of formal agreements.

Concert systems are fairly transparent in part because of a relatively high level of communication among the actors. By and large, these communications are also fuller, franker, and less deceptive than those that characterize normal international politics. Indeed, deception is made more difficult by the increase in the volume and diversity of information exchanged.[27] Extensive communication makes it easier for states to explain how and why they are behaving as they are, and to understand

---

[25] Quoted in Albrecht-Carrié (fn. 20), 109.
[26] *Ibid*, 69.
[27] R. V. Jones, *Most Secret War* (London: Hamish Hamilton, 1978), 23-26.

what others are doing. This reduces—although it does not eliminate—misunderstandings that can cause a breakdown; consequently, states have greater confidence that others are not planning to exploit them. For example, many analysts believe that the establishment of the Standing Consultative Commission (S.C.C.) has been one of the most useful outcomes of SALT.[28] Although a few have argued that this forum has been used by the Soviets to abet their deceptions, most believe that a number of potentially disruptive issues were successfully handled through the confidential and relatively frank exchange of technical information. In some instances, one side halted or modified activities that constituted, or could be seen as constituting, a violation of the agreements. In other cases, the United States or the Soviet Union was persuaded that activities it viewed as suspicious were actually permissible.

Under some circumstances—and this may have happened after 1815 but apparently did not with the S.C.C.—all sides gain a useful understanding of the other states' general interests and perspectives. For three interrelated reasons, defection thus becomes less likely. First, if decision makers can determine when and whether others are exploiting them, they will not defect in the mistaken belief that they are responding to others' defections. Second, if they can not only determine what the others have done, but why they are doing so, their confidence in their ability to predict the others' future behavior increases. Third, because they realize that others have a similar ability to detect and understand their behavior, they do not fear that others will defect in the mistaken belief that they themselves have already done so; nor will they defect in the hope that they can escape detection.

After 1815, statesmen realized that a relatively high level of full and honest communication could increase the chances of maintaining cooperation. To this end, they were often willing to forgo the advantages of surprise, and to inform others of what they planned to do even if they knew that the latter would not approve of the action. This was one function of the frequent meetings of the great powers. If each state had a good idea of the others' plans, all could avoid the common trap of exaggerating the threat they believed others to be posing. Furthermore, it could be in a state's interest to give a warning and learn what the response of others would be if it were to act on its intentions. The participants could thus look ahead several plays of the game; if the outcome was worse than mutual cooperation, the first state could decide

[28] Robert Buchheim and Dan Caldwell, *The US-USSR Standing Consultative Commission: Description and Appraisal* (Providence, RI: Center for Foreign Policy Development, Brown University, May 1983), Working Paper No. 2.

to refrain from taking its disruptive action. Such arrangements are not foolproof, of course; not only does the state lose the possibility of taking others by surprise, but it runs the risk that others will exploit it by bluffing or by adopting undesired commitments.[29]

Among states with a relatively high degree of common interests, these costs are outweighed by the facilitation of cooperation that results. Indeed, such a system of warnings can be advantageous even among adversaries. As Van Evera has noted, the pre-World War I German strategy of *faits accomplis*, culminating in a posture in which, unbeknownst to the others, mobilization meant war, deprived both German and Entente statesmen of the ability to make the timely threats that might have avoided war.[30] While German (and Austrian) statesmen were preoccupied with the advantages of taking their enemies by surprise, they overlooked the fact that such tactics also meant that they would learn too late whether or not their actions would lead to world war.

In some cases, transparency mainly means determining what specific actions others are taking. That is not always easy, as the current discussion of whether the Soviets are violating the SALT agreements reminds us; but it is usually easier than deciding whether the others' actions constitute cooperation or defection. The model developed by Downs and his colleagues shows the problems that misinterpretations create for a strategy of strict reciprocity. An examination of many cases reveals that states tend to underestimate the extent to which others are cooperating, the extent to which their adversaries will perceive that they have defected, and the extent to which a disinterested observer would share this judgment.[31] These problems do not disappear during the concert; indeed, their presence is one reason why cooperation tends to dissipate. But, with a high level of communication, it becomes more likely that statesmen will gain an understanding of the others' perspectives, which can help them to interpret the behavior of others and to design at least some of their own behavior so that it is less likely to be incorrectly seen as defection.

Transparency can facilitate cooperation only if the information it provides can be used to avoid or mitigate the consequences of the other's defection. That is the notion of "timely warning" which is invoked in

[29] For instances of deception, especially on Metternich's part, see Schroeder (fn. 3), 46, 82-83, 207, 212, 219.

[30] Van Evera (fn. 8).

[31] See Downs and others, "Arms Races and Cooperation," pp. 118-46 of this collection; Robert Jervis, *Perception and Misperception in International Politics* (Princeton: Princeton University Press, 1976), 67-83, 354-55.

arms control arrangements like the Nuclear Non-Proliferation Treaty. The verification provisions of such agreements cannot prevent states from taking the forbidden actions, but they can let others know that a violation is occurring, so that they can take effective countermeasures.

The arrangements of the concert cannot completely meet this requirement but, by providing guidelines for behavior, they help statesmen determine whether or not others are cooperating. Living up to agreements is a somewhat artificial definition of cooperation, but it is a useful one, especially when compared to the even vaguer alternative of trying to determine whether the other's actions have the effect—or were motivated by the intention—of doing harm. Furthermore, agreements provide at least a basis for a common understanding, even though there is almost always room to argue about what they mean and what constitutes behaving in accord with them. States thus have a bit more confidence that they will be able to determine relatively quickly whether others are defecting, which gives them more time to react. Cooperation would also be facilitated if states were able to react in ways that would protect them from defections without simultaneously menacing others—in other words, if a strictly defensive response was effective. Although I argued earlier that defensive strategies were often possible under the concert, many contextual factors that cannot be related to the presence or absence of the concert are also important.

D. CHANGED ESTIMATES OF THE BEHAVIOR OF OTHERS

Whether or not a statesman will cooperate is strongly influenced by his beliefs about whether others will cooperate. Assuming that he wishes to maintain good relations and does not think he can defect without triggering retaliation, he will do what he thinks others will do—that is, defect if he thinks they will defect and cooperate if he thinks they will cooperate. The changes we have been discussing widen the chances of cooperation by increasing the decision makers' estimates of the likelihood that others will cooperate. The experience of fighting a potential hegemon affects the payoffs of others in the same way that it affects the state's own preferences. Each decision maker knows that all the reasons why his state is likely to seek cooperative solutions also apply to others in the system. Furthermore, he knows that the others realize that he prefers cooperation, thus again reducing the danger that each side will defect in the fear that the other will do so. Thus, there is the possibility of a benign circle and a self-fulfilling prophecy of cooperation.

Expectations about the behavior of others are also important in a different way. Although a state will cooperate only if it thinks the other will, it may defect if it thinks the other has no choice but to cooperate. In the absence of the constraint imposed by the other's threat to reply in kind, the state will be strongly tempted to cheat and to exploit the other. For example, the United States probably did not encourage Soviet restraint when it reduced its spending on strategic weapons between the mid-1960s and the mid-1970s. Not only was the U.S. far ahead of the U.S.S.R. on most measures of strategic power during most of this era, but the Soviets probably believed that Washington had no choice but to hold down its deployments—first because of the costs of the war in Vietnam, and later because of public opposition. Thus they saw no reason to attribute the American behavior to a commitment to mutual restraint or to believe that American behavior would depend on their own.

To the extent that the transformation we have been discussing has any systematic effect on this dimension, it may be to make cooperation *less* likely. States in the concert system may believe that their partners have to cooperate, that the constraints against going off on their own are so strong that even if the state engages in occasional exploitation, the others will not respond in kind. One reason that good relations between Britain and France did not withstand the strain imposed by a serious dispute over influence in Spain in the late 1840s was that the French Prime Minister assumed that the British elite was not "prepared to contemplate a permanent rupture . . . and that if he took independent action in Spain he would have at most a temporary coolness to contend with." Many Englishmen shared the view of their ambassador to Spain that "the *entente* [was] strong enough to weather a temporary storm and . . . that the French would soon reconcile themselves to the loss of influence in Spain."[32] Similarly, Donald Kagan sees the alliance between Athens and Sparta as part of the reason why the peace treaty between the two states brought only a temporary respite in the Peloponnesian Wars: "It allowed Sparta to continue to ignore its obligations under the peace treaty" in the belief that Athens was unconditionally committed to keeping the peace.[33] The perception that others are cooperating not because they think the state will cooperate but because they have no choice is a common one, and the knowledge that others are strongly motivated to cooperate will reinforce this belief. In showing others that defection is possible, the state must be careful not to lead them to infer

[32] Bullen (fn. 11), 81, 93; also see Craig (fn. 11), 257.
[33] Donald Kagan, *The Peace of Nicias and the Sicilian Expedition* (Ithaca, NY: Cornell University Press, 1981), 30.

that it is determined to defect no matter what they do. It is difficult but necessary to establish relations that are conditional, and to convince the other side that they will continue to be so.

III. CONCLUSIONS

Anarchy and the security dilemma do not prevent a relatively high level of cooperation in the form of a concert system. Such systems are rare, however. Usually, a balance of power prevails. The epitome of the operation of the balance of power is a war fought against a potential hegemon. Ironically, such a conflict undermines two of the crucial assumptions that maintain the system: the lack of alliance handicaps and the availability of war as a normal instrument of policy. The transformation of a balance of power into a concert confirms the theoretical arguments about the conditions that facilitate and inhibit cooperation in anarchy. After wars against potential hegemons, the incentives for the former allies to maintain good relations are unusually high. Even if mutual cooperation is the states' second choice and they would all prefer a situation in which they themselves defected while the others cooperated, the gap between the value of their first and second choices is relatively small. What they would lose if the system broke down into mutual defection and competition, furthermore, is very great because such a configuration could lead to the renewed threat from the potential hegemon, or to a very costly war. Because these outcomes are extremely bad, it is rational for states to run some risk of being exploited in order to avoid them.

Under the concert, not only do the payoffs from two symmetrical outcomes (that is, mutual cooperation and mutual defection) encourage cooperation, but so do the two asymmetrical ones. A state may defect either because it is attracted by the possibility of being able to do so while the others continue to cooperate, or because it is repelled by the fear that its cooperation will be met by the defection of others. The latter danger is reduced both by the state's ability to observe what others are doing and by the nascent collective security system that provides some expectation of support from third parties and so reduces the state's vulnerability to defection. The other side of this coin is that the gains a state can expect to make by defecting are smaller under the concert than they are under the balance of power. If there is a concert, others will be quicker to oppose the state if it defects. Even if its efforts to defect succeed in the short run, they will be self-defeating if they result in the destruction of the system of cooperation. It is also important that all states realize that these incentives operate for others as well as for themselves, leading to the possibility of sustained mutual cooperation. The chance of bringing this theoretical possibility to fruition is increased by the relatively high level of communication among the states and the concomitantly increased ability of each to determine how others have acted and are likely to act in the future. None of this means that cooperation is easy or automatic, but it does show that when balance-of-power assumptions no longer hold, the incentives shift so that anarchy and the security dilemma no longer provide a powerful stimulus to undesired conflict.

WHY COOPERATION FAILED
IN 1914

By STEPHEN VAN EVERA*

T HE essays in this volume explore how three sets of factors affect the degree of cooperation or non-cooperation between states. The first set comprises the "structures of payoffs" that states receive in return for adopting cooperative or noncooperative policies; payoff structures are signified by the rewards and penalties accruing to each state from mutual cooperation (CC); cooperation by one state and "defection" by another (CD and DC); and mutual defection (DD). The second set comprises the "strategic setting" of the international "game"—that is, the rules and conditions under which international relations are conducted. Two aspects of the strategic setting are considered: the size of the "shadow of the future," and the ability of the players to "recognize" past cooperators and defectors, and to distinguish between them.[1] The third set is the number of players in the game, and the influence these numbers have on the way the game is played.

In this essay, I will ask whether these three sets of factors can help explain the non-cooperative national policies that culminated in the outbreak of the First World War. Cooperation broke down in several ways: European states adopted expansionist policies that fostered territorial conflict, engaged in arms races with one another, developed mobilization plans whose scope and inflexibility made crises hard to control and wars hard to localize, favored bellicose and secretive diplomatic tactics that rendered diplomacy more difficult, risked war by mobilizing their armies during the July crisis, and ultimately declared war and attacked one another. All these moves contributed to the outbreak of the war; as instances of non-cooperation, all are subjects of this essay. I will address the following questions:

* I would like to thank Robert Art, Charles Glaser, Lori Gronich, Fen Hampson, Lesley Karsten, Steven Miller, Jane Sharp, Jack Snyder, Kenneth Waltz, and the other contributors to this volume for their thoughtful comments on earlier drafts of this paper. I also wish to express my deep appreciation to Michael Salman for his insights and assistance.
[1] On these concepts, see Robert Axelrod, *The Evolution of Cooperation* (New York: Basic Books, 1984), 126-32, 139-41. In his introduction to the present volume, Kenneth Oye emphasizes the size of the "shadow of the future" over "recognition" as the key element in a strategic setting because recognition has less relevance to most of our cases. Recognition was a crucial part of the 1914 story, however; so I give it equal billing with the shadow of the future under the general category of strategic setting.

—Were these non-cooperative policies caused by the factors explored in this volume—perverse payoff structures, small shadows of the future, weak national "recognition" abilities, and relatively large numbers of players?

—If so, why did these factors appear, and how did they produce their malignant effects?

—Could they have been averted, and might this have prevented World War I?

I will argue that World War I arose from a web of six remarkable misperceptions that were prevalent in Europe during the years before the war. Although all six ideas were especially popular in Germany, they flourished throughout the continent. First, Europeans were mesmerized by what one observer called the "cult of the offensive"[2]— a highly exaggerated faith in the efficacy of offensive military strategies and tactics. Second, Europeans commonly overestimated the hostility of neighboring states; this paranoia eventually produced its own reality by justifying aggressive policies that provoked genuine hostility. Third, European leaders falsely imagined a bandwagoning world in which strength and bellicosity would cow opponents and fracture opposing alliances; in fact, however, belligerent policies provoked countervailing coalitions and spirals of conflict. Fourth, Europeans exaggerated the economic and social rewards that territorial expansion could provide. Fifth, many Europeans viewed war itself as beneficial, and believed that international confrontation would promote domestic tranquility; as it turned out, World War I caused great suffering, the fall of governments, and revolution. Finally, each major power taught its people a mythical nationalistic history that emphasized the righteousness of its own conduct, and falsely cast itself as the innocent victim in past conflicts.

These misperceptions harmed cooperation and fostered war through all three mechanisms discussed in this volume. Most importantly, they twisted payoff structures to increase the apparent penalties of cooperative conduct and the rewards of non-cooperative conduct. The cult of the offensive made territorial expansion and preemptive attack appear both feasible and necessary, thereby spurring aggression. It also generated policies of secrecy that made cooperation more difficult. Exaggeration of other states' hostility fed fears of aggression, and engendered aggressive plans to forestall it. Bandwagon notions argued for expansionist policies and belligerent tactics by emphasizing the value of possessing

---

[2] Captain de Thomasson, quoted in Jay Luvaas, *The Military Legacy of the Civil War: The European Inheritance* (Chicago: University of Chicago Press, 1959), 165.

and brandishing superior power. Inflated estimates of the economic value of empire further supported expansionist ideas. Faith in the virtue and in the domestic political utility of war narrowed the gap that people saw between the benefits of general peace and general war, encouraging warlike policies. Nationalist historical mythmaking made concessions seem damaging and firm policies more likely to succeed. In each case, these mistaken beliefs made the rewards of non-cooperative policies seem larger, or their penalties seem smaller.

Second, Europe's misperceptions created a strategic setting that was inimical to international cooperation. The shadow of the future was short because many Europeans expected that the final control of Europe would soon be decided, either by war or by peaceful shifts in the balance of power. This prospect reflected the effects of the cult of the offensive, the bandwagon notions, and the tendency to exaggerate the hostility of others, which together suggested that decisive wars or decisive arms races lay in the near future. At the same time, the recognition abilities of individual European states were weakened by the chauvinism with which they taught themselves history—a chauvinism that muddled the question of responsibility for past conflicts.

Third, these misperceptions rendered the multipolar distribution of power in Europe ever more dangerous by magnifying the risks it created. Multipolarity raised transaction and information costs, thereby encouraging military and political blunders; the cult of the offensive then enlarged the dangers of conducting diplomacy in such a world by rendering these blunders less reversible. The cult, and bandwagon thinking, also encouraged the organization of Europe's powers into a dangerous system of unconditional, offensive alliances. This alliance system made it more difficult to fashion discriminating sanctions that punished aggressors while avoiding harm to the aggressor's allies; retaliatory sanctions thus tended to spread rather than to dampen conflicts. As a result, aggressors were emboldened by knowing that any retaliation they provoked could spark the whole alliance into action on their behalf. Both the nature and the pernicious effects of this alliance system reflected the combined influence of the relatively large number of great powers in Europe and the cult of the offensive.

Contributors to this volume were invited to discuss whether Robert Axelrod's Tit-for-Tat strategy could have promoted international cooperation in the cases discussed. I will suggest that Tit-for-Tat strategies would have failed in 1914 unless they had been combined with a remedy to correct Europe's misperceptions. As Axelrod notes, Tit-for-Tat strategies require congenial conditions for their success.[3] In particular, payoff structures and strategic setting cannot be unduly perverse. In 1914, the European worldview engendered payoff structures and strategic settings that were too perverse to allow Tit-for-Tat to work. That is not an argument against Tit-for-Tat strategies, but a warning that such strategies should include programs of action—including programs to combat misperceptions—to create the congenial conditions they require.

In the following section, I outline the distorted worldview of the European elites and general publics in 1914 and discuss possible sources of misperceptions. In Section II, I explain how these misperceptions twisted payoff structures in perverse directions, fostered an adverse setting for cooperation, and worsened problems created by Europe's multipolar distribution of power. I also discuss why Tit-for-Tat strategies fail under such conditions. Conclusions and implications are suggested in Section III.

I. Misperceptions in Europe before 1914

A. THE CULT OF THE OFFENSIVE

Before World War I, military technology actually favored the defense over the offense: the development of rifles and repeating small arms, the machine gun, barbed wire, and the railroads gave defenders a large and growing advantage. Nevertheless, misled by their militaries, most Europeans assumed that attack was the stronger form of war, and governments premised their foreign and defense policies on the assumption that conquest was easy and security was scarce.[4]

The German military glorified the offense in strident terms, and infused German society with similar views. General Alfred von Schlieffen, author of the German war plan of 1914, declared that "attack is the best defense"; General Friedrich von Bernhardi, a prominent military writer, proclaimed that "the offensive mode of action is by far superior to the defensive mode," and that new technology favored the attacker: "the superiority of offensive warfare under modern conditions

---

[3] See Axelrod (fn. 1), 59, 128-29, 134, 139, 207. Axelrod does not recommend pure Tit-for-Tat strategies, but rather a more forgiving variant—nine-tenths of a tit for a tat—to diminish the requirement for these conditions. See *ibid.*, 138, 186-87.

[4] For more on the cult of the offensive, see Jack Lewis Snyder, *The Ideology of the Offensive: Military Decision Making and the Disasters of 1914* (Ithaca, NY: Cornell University Press, 1984); Snyder, "Civil-Military Relations and the Cult of the Offensive, 1914 and 1984," *International Security* 9 (Summer 1984), 108-46; and Stephen Van Evera, "Cult of the Offensive and the Origins of the First World War," *International Security* 9 (Summer 1984), 58-107.

is greater than formerly." In August 1914, the Kaiser told departing troops, "You will be home before the leaves have fallen from the trees," and one of his generals predicted that the German army would sweep through Europe: "In two weeks we shall defeat France, then we shall turn round, defeat Russia and then we shall march to the Balkans and establish order there."[5] These assumptions guided the Schlieffen Plan, which envisioned rapid and decisive attacks on Belgium, France, and Russia.

Other European states displayed milder symptoms of the same virus. The common view in Europe was summarized by a member of the French Chamber of Deputies in 1912: "The first great battle will decide the whole war, and wars will be short. The idea of the offense must penetrate the spirit of our nation."[6] In Britain, the army rejected defensive strategies despite the lessons of the Boer War. General W. G. Knox declared in 1913, "The defensive is never an acceptable role to the Briton, and he makes little or no study of it," and in 1914 General R.C.B. Haking argued that the offensive "will win as sure as there is a sun in the heavens."[7] The Russian army adopted an impossibly ambitious offensive strategy, envisaging simultaneous attacks against both Germany and Austria.[8] The offensive found proponents even in Belgium: when Germany attacked Belgium in August 1914, one high Belgian officer argued that Belgium should respond by invading Germany.[9]

Thus Europeans badly misread the balance between offense and defense, completely misconstruing military technologies that actually gave the defense an unprecedented advantage.

---

[5] See Gerhard Ritter, *The Schlieffen Plan: Critique of a Myth*, trans. Andrew and Eva Wilson (London: Oswald Wolff, 1958; reprint ed., Westport, CT: Greenwood Press, 1979), 100; Friedrich von Bernhardi, *How Germany Makes War* (New York: George H. Doran Co., 1914), 153, 155; Barbara Tuchman, *The Guns of August* (New York: Dell, 1962), 142; General von Loebell, quoted in Fritz Fischer, *War of Illusions: German Policies from 1911 to 1914*, trans. Marian Jackson (New York: W. W. Norton, 1975), 543.

[6] Emile Driant, quoted in John M. Cairns, "International Politics and the Military Mind: The Case of the French Republic, 1911-1914," *Journal of Modern History* 25 (September 1953), 273-85, at 282.

[7] Quoted in T.H.E. Travers, "Technology, Tactics, and Morale: Jean de Bloch, the Boer War, and British Military Theory, 1900-1914," *Journal of Modern History* 51 (June 1979), 264-86, at 275.

[8] On the evolution of Russian doctrine, see Snyder, *Ideology of the Offensive* (fn. 4), 157-98. Summarizing the doctrines of all three powers is Theodore Ropp, *War in the Modern World*, rev. ed. (New York: Collier, 1962), 222-30.

[9] General de Ryckel, Sub-Chief of the Belgian Army General Staff. He reportedly advised the Belgian King on August 2 or 3, 1914, that the Belgian army should "take the offensive, penetrate into the Rhine province, and march on Cologne. ..." See Luigi Albertini, *The Origins of the War of 1914*, 3 vols., trans and ed. Isabella M. Massey (London: Oxford University Press, 1952-57; reprint ed., Westport, CT: Greenwood Press, 1980), III, 461. See also Tuchman (fn. 5), 127-31.

B.   "OTHERS ARE HOSTILE, WAR IS INEVITABLE"

Before 1914, most Europeans exaggerated the aggressiveness of their neighbors, and generally assumed that war loomed in the near future. The European militaries led the way in fueling such perceptions. German generals portrayed their country as surrounded by rapacious enemies who were only waiting for the right moment to pounce, and declared war to be inevitable. Von Schlieffen warned in 1909 that Russia was guided by an "inherited antipathy of Slavs for Germanic peoples," that England was an "implacable enemy," and that France made "the idea of *revanche* ... the pivot of her whole policy."[10] In 1911, Major-General Wandel of the Prussian Ministry of War agreed that Germany was "surrounded by enemies," and General Bernhardi stated that Germany was "menaced" by "Slavonic waves."[11]

Militaries elsewhere also exaggerated the malevolence of other states. Britain's First Lord of the Admiralty recommended a preventive attack on France in 1898 because "the row would have to come, it might just as well come now as later."[12] The Russian General Danilov drew plans based on the worst-case assumption that Sweden, Rumania, Turkey, Japan, and China would all join the Central Powers in a war against Russia; "he left out only the Martians," one postwar critic declared.[13]

Warnings like these were echoed by academic allies of the military, and by nationalistic scholars and propagandists. Guided by the German navy's propaganda office, the German "fleet professors" warned that Germany was being surrounded and strangled by an insatiable and malevolent Britain. Professors Hermann Oncken and Otto Hintze as-

[10] Quoted in Ritter (fn. 5), 100-101. A more reliable summary of the Entente's intentions is in Imanuel Geiss, ed., *July 1914: The Outbreak of the First World War: Selected Documents* (New York: W. W. Norton, 1967), 26-33.

[11] Quoted in Fischer (fn. 5), 118; Friedrich von Bernhardi, *Germany and the Next War*, trans. Allen H. Powles (New York: Longmans, Green, 1914), 76; see also 92. Similarly, Admiral Tirpitz warned in 1912 that the Anglo-French Entente "*de facto* has the character of an offensive alliance," and General Moltke declared in 1913 that general war was unavoidable: "war with France is inevitable" and "war must come ... between Germandom and Slavdom." Tirpitz, quoted in Fischer (fn. 5), 125; Moltke, *ibid.*, 227, and in Isabel V. Hull, *The Entourage of Kaiser Wilhelm II, 1888-1918* (New York: Cambridge University Press, 1982), 241.

For more examples, see Imanuel Geiss, *German Foreign Policy 1871-1914* (Boston: Routledge & Kegan Paul, 1976), 122, 152; Wallace Notestein and Elmer E. Stoll, eds., *Conquest and Kultur: Aims of the Germans in Their Own Words* (Washington: U.S. Government Printing Office, 1917), 99, 115, 119; and Paul M. Kennedy, "Tirpitz, England and the Second Navy Law of 1900: A Strategic Critique," *Militaergeschichtliche Mitteilungen* (No. 2, 1970), 33-57, at 39.

[12] Quoted in Alfred Vagts, *Defense and Diplomacy* (New York: Kings Crown Press, 1956), 297.

[13] A. A. Kersnovskii, quoted in Snyder, *Ideology of the Offensive* (fn. 4), 168. See also William C. Fuller, Jr., "The Russian Empire and Its Potential Enemies 1909-1914," unpub. manuscript (1980), 17-18, 33.

serted that Britain's real aim was to keep Europe in turmoil so that
Britain could conquer the world;[14] and historian Houston Stewart
Chamberlain (a zealous naturalized German) warned Germans in 1914
that his visits to England in 1907 and 1908 had uncovered "a positively
terrifying blind hatred for Germany, and impatient longing for a war
of annihilation."[15] Wilhelmine German schoolchildren were taught that
Britain had always tried to keep Germany as weak, disrupted, and small
as possible, and that "Germany is a land entirely surrounded by enemies."[16] The German press conveyed the same message to its readers:
"Our enemies have long lain in wait for a suitable moment to attack
us"; "Russia is arming for war against Germany"; Germany's neighbors
"want to ... trample us down from all sides ..."; and Germany faces
"enemies all around—permanent danger of war from all sides."[17]

These images ultimately gripped the minds of the German elites, and
to a lesser extent those of other states. As early as 1901, the Kaiser saw
his country as "surrounded by enemies"; in 1913, he maintained that
"war between East and West was in the long run inevitable. ..."[18] A
Russian statesman noted that "the conflict may be postponed, but that
it will come some day we must remember every hour, and every hour
we must arm ourselves for it."[19] Some British leaders saw themselves

[14] Charles E. McClelland, *The German Historians and England: A Study in Nineteenth-
Century Views* (Cambridge: Cambridge University Press, 1971), 208.

[15] Quoted in William Archer, ed., *501 Gems of German Thought* (T. Fisher Unwin Ltd.:
London, 1916), 113. For more examples, see Abraham Ascher, "Professors as Propagandists:
The Politics of the Kathedersozialisten," *Journal of Central European Affairs* 23 (October
1963), 282-302, at 293; McClelland (fn. 14), 182, 203, 209; Archer (fn. 15), 115; and Louis
L. Snyder, *German Nationalism: The Tragedy of a People* (Harrisburg, PA: The Stackpole
Company, 1952), 146.

[16] Walter Consuelo Langsam, "Nationalism and History in the Prussian Elementary
Schools," in Edward Mead Earle, ed., *Nationalism and Internationlism: Essays Inscribed to
Carlton J. H. Hayes* (New York: Columbia University Press, 1950), 241-60, at 259; Edward
H. Reisner, *Nationalism and Education since 1789* (New York: Macmillan Company, 1922),
209.

[17] *Hamburger Nachrichten* (December 31, 1912), *Kölnische Zeitung* (March 2, 1914), and
Das neue Deutschland (August 1, 1914), quoted in Fischer (fn. 5), 94, 374, 244; *Der Tag*
(April 1913), quoted in Volker R. Berghahn, *Germany and the Approach of War in 1914*
(London: Macmillan, 1973), 170. I. F. Clarke, in *Voices Prophecying War, 1763-1984* (London:
Oxford University Press, 1966), 49, 122, 143, and throughout, reported that European
bookshelves were flooded with novels that conveyed a Darwinistic image of international
relations.

[18] Anon. (probably William Roscoe Thayer), ed., *Out of Their Own Mouths: Utterances of
German Rulers, Statesmen, Savants, Publicists, Journalists, Poets, Businessmen, Party Leaders
and Soldiers* (New York: Appleton, 1917), 3; Fischer (fn. 5), 221. For similar statements, see
Bernadotte E. Schmitt, *The Coming of the War, 1914*, 2 vols. (New York: Charles Scribner's
Sons, 1930), I, 102; Geiss (fn. 11), 121; and James Joll, "1914: The Unspoken Assumptions,"
in H. W. Koch, ed., *The Origins of the First World War: Great Power Rivalry and German
War Aims* (London: Macmillan, 1972), 307-328, at 322.

[19] Izvolsky, December 20, 1911, quoted in Schmitt (fn. 18), I, 55. For more examples, see
ibid., 370, and D.C.B. Lieven, *Russia and the Origins of the First World War* (New York: St.
Martin's, 1983), 96.

as isolated and besieged: Lord Roseberry in 1899 described Britain as only a "little island ... so lonely in these northern seas, viewed with so much jealousy, and with such hostility, with such jarred ambitions by the great empires of the world, so friendless among nations...." Another Briton wrote of Anglo-German relations in 1898 that "an actual state of war against England began some time ago."[20]

In sum, Europeans in general, and Germans in particular, imagined a world of states so belligerent that the coming of war was merely a matter of time.

C. BELIEF IN "BANDWAGONING" AND IN THE EFFICACY OF "WAVING THE BIG STICK"

Before 1914, Europeans widely assumed that states usually chose allies by "bandwagoning" with the stronger side rather than "balancing" against it, and that intimidation would elicit more cooperation from other states than would conciliation.[21] States sometimes do bandwagon, and intimidation can succeed; but because Europeans exaggerated the frequency of both, they overestimated the feasibility of expansion for themselves as well as for their adversaries, and consequently both the practicability and the necessity of expansionist policies. Such beliefs also encouraged bellicose diplomatic tactics which fed spirals of hostility that grew successively worse as big-stick tactics were used in a futile attempt to address hostility produced by the previous application of the big stick.

Germany was the principal locus of bandwagon and wave-the-big-stick thinking; such notions were used by the military to justify the expansion of the German fleet and the development of offensive Germany army war plans. Admiral Tirpitz sold the idea of the grand fleet with a "risk theory" that asserted that a large German fleet could frighten Britain into accepting German continental expansion. Schlieffen held that even if Britain fought to contain Germany, she would abandon the war in discouragement once the German army had defeated France.[22]

Faith in intimidation also colored German civilian thought, as illustrated by Max Weber's aphorism: "Let them hate us, as long as they fear us."[23] Such ideas fed hopes that Germany could expand by threat-

[20] Quoted in Brian Porter, *The Lion's Share: A Short History of British Imperialism 1850-1970* (New York: Longman, 1975), 124; Frederick Greenwood, *ibid.*, 125.

[21] On "bandwagoning" versus "balancing," see Stephen Walt, "Alliance Formation and the Balance of World Power," *International Security* 9 (Spring 1985), 3-43; Walt, "The Origins of Alliances" (Ph.D. diss., University of California, Berkeley, 1983); Kenneth N. Waltz, *Theory of International Politics* (Reading, MA: Addison-Wesley, 1979), 125-27.

[22] Ropp (fn. 8), 212; Ritter (fn. 5), 163.

[23] Ludwig Dehio, *Germany and World Politics in the Twentieth Century*, trans. Dieter Pevsner (New York: W. W. Norton, 1967), 20.

ening her neighbors, and led Germans to exaggerate the political benefits
their country would enjoy if it enhanced its power through expansion.
Pan-German leaders argued in October 1913 that a policy of peaceful
expansion-by-intimidation could succeed once Germany showed her
"mailed fist"; there would be "no one on the Continent (and probably
not even Britain) who would not give in."[24] Likewise—evidently influenced by Tirpitz's risk theory—German Secretary of State Gottlieb von
Jagow believed that, despite British warnings to the contrary, Germany
could browbeat Britain into neutrality in a future conflict.[25]

Germans adopted bellicose tactics in the crises of 1905, 1911, and 1914,
partly in the hope that they could split the opposing alliance by intim-
idating or humiliating its member states.[26] Bandwagon ideas also led
Germans to inflate the value of the empire they sought to acquire, by
suggesting that a larger, stronger Germany would face less hostility.
One German newspaper foresaw that "through a world war ... the
German people will acquire a position in Mitteleuropa which will make
a repetition of such a general war against us impossible."[27] Another
German writer foresaw that if Germany could conquer France and
Austria, "the natural pressure of this new German Empire will be so
great that ... the surrounding little Germanic States will have to attach
themselves to it under conditions which we set."[28] Conversely, some
expressed fear that other states could strip away Germany's sphere of
influence by intimidation, unless she proved more intimidating, or controlled these states directly.[29] Bandwagon notions thus contributed to
both the hopes and fears that underlay German expansionism.

[24] Geiss (fn. 11), 136-37.
[25] In February 1914, von Jagow declared: "We have not built our fleet in vain, and in
my opinion, people in England will seriously ask themselves whether it will be just that
simple and without danger to play the role of France's guardian angel against us." Geiss,
(fn. 10) 25. Chancellor Bethmann-Hollweg later confessed that he had believed before the
war that Germany could intimidate Britain into abandoning her traditional commitment
to maintain the continental balance of power. Fischer (fn. 5), 69. Moltke expressed similar
views; see *ibid.*, 227.
   For more examples, see Wayne C. Thompson, *In the Eye of the Storm: Kurt Riezler and
the Crises of Modern Germany* (Iowa City: University of Iowa Press, 1980), 50; Fischer (fn.
5), 133.
[26] During the July crisis, von Jagow argued that "the more determined Austria shows
herself, the more energetically we support her, so much the more quiet will Russia remain."
Geiss (fn. 10), 123. Bethmann-Hollweg believed that the Austrian attack on Serbia might
shatter the Entente by forcing Russia or France publicly to abandon the ally. See Geiss
(fn. 11), 166, and Schmitt (fn. 18), I, 399.
[27] *Die Post*, December, 1912, interpreting a Bethmann-Hollweg speech, quoted in Fischer
(fn. 5), 241.
[28] Joseph L. Reimer, in 1905, quoted in Notestein and Stoll (fn. 11), 57.
[29] Karl von Winterstetten warned in 1914 that Austria, the Scandinavian states, Rumania,
Bulgaria, and Turkey would all be lost to Germany "if Russia should gain control over one

D. "EMPIRES ARE VALUABLE"

Before 1914, Europeans tended to exaggerate the political and economic benefits that accrued from conquests. This misconception was common throughout Europe, but, like many other misperceptions, it was most pronounced in Germany and among the armed forces.

Military officers often warned that national economic survival depended on the acquisition of more territory. In 1896, Admiral von Müller, for instance, saw Germany locked in a "great battle for economic survival"; without new territories, "the artificial [German] economic edifice would start to crumble and existence therein would become very unpleasant indeed."[30] Bernhardi declared that "flourishing nations ... require a continual expansion of their frontiers, they require new territory for the accommodation of their surplus population"; in France, Marshal Foch spoke in similar terms.[31]

Such views were also widely held by civilians, especially in Germany, where many warned that economic and demographic imperatives required expansion. During the Moroccan crisis, the acquisition of economic rights in Morocco was asserted to be "essential" to the German economy, and "a question of life and death" to German industry.[32] Germany required new territories to contain its growing population, which might otherwise starve, or emigrate and lose its sense of Germany nationality. One author wrote in 1911 that Germany "must expand if she does not want to be suffocated by her surplus population."[33] Another had warned in 1896 that Germany was "forced by our geographical situation, by poor soil ... by the amazing increase in our population ... to spread and to gain space for us and for our sons."[34] These ideas fed

---

of them, and thus be able to exert pressure on the others"; hence Germany should seek to control the whole bloc. Quoted in Notestein and Stoll (fn. 11), 60. For another example, see Thayer (fn. 18), 74.

[30] Memorandum to the Kaiser's brother, quoted in J.C.G. Rohl, ed., *From Bismarck to Hitler: The Problem of Continuity in German History* (London: Longman, 1970), 56-57, 59.

[31] Bernhardi (fn. 11), 21; see also 82-83. Ferdinand Foch, *The Principles of War*, trans. de Morinni (New York: Fly, 1918), 36-37.

[32] *Centralverband deutscher Industrieller*, and Emil Kirdorf, quoted in Fischer (fn. 5), 75, 81. Alexander Wirth forecast that, "if we do not soon acquire new territory, a frightful catastrophe is inevitable." Archer (fn. 15), 53. Similar views were also expressed elsewhere in Europe: in 1888 Joseph Chamberlain warned the British that "if we were to cut adrift from the great dependencies which now look to us for protection and which are the natural markets for our trade ... half at least of our population would be starved." Porter (fn. 20), 80.

[33] Basserman, quoted in Berghahn (fn. 17), 95.

[34] Theodor Schiemann, quoted in Fischer (fn. 5), 39. More examples are in Jonathan Steinberg, *Yesterday's Deterrent: Tirpitz and the Birth of the German Battle Fleet* (London: Macdonald, 1965), 57, and in Notestein and Stoll (fn. 11), 89, 136.

the belief that expansion was imperative for national development: "We
have only one choice: to grow or to waste away."[35]

E.   "WAR IS CHEAP, HEALTHFUL, BENEFICIAL, UPLIFTING, NOBLE . . ."

Before 1914, most Europeans glorified war as a relatively harmless
and even beneficial enterprise. This belief took several forms, some of
them related to other misperceptions. For instance, many discounted
the cost of the next war because they embraced the cult of the offensive
which suggested that any great war would be decided in a matter of
weeks.

Members of the European political and economic elite also believed
that foreign wars would strengthen their domestic political position
against democrats and socialists. They expected that foreign threats
would unify the nation, and a successful war would enhance the prestige
and standing of incumbent regimes and elites. Thus, while war might
bleed the country, it would benefit those who ruled. Again, these "social
imperial" ideas were most popular in Germany, where one newspaper
outlined the benefits of a confrontational and expansionist policy: "We
shall never improve matters at home until we have got into severe foreign
complications—perhaps even into war—and have been compelled by
such convulsions to bring ourselves together"; another paper expressed
the view that a war could ensure "the restoration to health of many
political and social institutions."[36] German soldiers and statesmen often
echoed this theory.[37]

Finally, many Europeans believed war to be beneficial to the whole
society: a healthful, happy, glorious activity, valuable for its own sake.
In 1913, the *Jungdeutschland Post*, a propaganda organ of the German
Army League, painted a picture of joyous combat and happy death for
fallen warriors in German wars of the future:

> For us as well the great and glorious hour of battle will one day strike.
> . . . Yes, that will be a great and happy hour, which we all may secretly
> look forward to . . . quiet and deep in German hearts the joy of war and

[35] Arthur Dix, 1912, as quoted in Fischer (fn. 5), 31.

[36] *Hamburger Nachrichten*, June 1910, quoted in Notestein and Stoll (fn. 11), 113; and *Die
Post*, August 1911, quoted in Fischer (fn. 5), 83.

[37] According to Hofmarschall Zedlitz-Trüzschler, Moritz von Lynker, the chief of the
military cabinet, favored war in 1909 because he saw "war as desirable in order to escape
from difficulties at home and abroad." Hull (fn. 11), 259, quoting Zedlitz-Trüzschler;
Bernhardi held that "a great war will unify and elevate the people and destroy the diseases
which threaten the national health." Notestein and Stoll (fn. 11), 38.

This idea also had detractors high in the German government, however, and emphasis
placed on it should be qualified accordingly. For examples, see Berghahn (fn. 17), 82, 97,
and throughout; Geiss (fn. 11), 125-26; L.C.F. Turner, *Origins of the First World War* (London:
Edward Arnold, 1970), 76; and David E. Kaiser, "Germany and the Origins of the First

a longing for it must live, for we have had enough of the enemy, and victory will only be given to a people who go to war with joy in their hearts as if to a feast ... let us laugh as loud as we can at the old women in men's trousers who are afraid of war and therefore complain that it is ghastly or ugly. No, war is beautiful. Its greatness lifts a man's heart high above earthly things, above the daily round. Such an hour awaits us. We must wait for it with the manly knowledge that when it has struck it will be more beautiful and wonderful to live for ever among the heroes on a war memorial in a church than to die an empty death in bed, nameless ... let that be heaven for young Germany. Thus we wish to knock at our God's door.[38]

In the same spirit, General Bernhardi in 1914 admonished his many readers to recognize war as a "powerful promoter of civilization" and "a political necessity ... fought in the interest of biological, social and moral progress."[39] War promoted civilization by weeding out the unfit: "a biological necessity of the first importance, a regulative element in the life of mankind which cannot be dispensed with. ... Without war, inferior or decaying races would easily choke the growth of healthy, budding elements, and a universal decadence would follow."[40]

Academics, the press, and other publicists also painted a glorified image of war. German newspapers told their readers that "we Teutons in particular must no longer look upon war as our destroyer ... at last we must see it once more as the saviour, the physician"; that "it has been established beyond doubt that regular war is not only the broadest and noblest solution imaginable, but also the periodically indispensable solution to the preservation of State and society"; and that war promised the "renewal and purification of the German people."[41] One German newspaper told its readers on Christmas Eve that war was "part of a

World War," *Journal of Modern History* 55 (September 1983), 442-74, at 470. Discussing this idea further is Berghahn (fn. 17), passim. See also Arno J. Mayer, "Domestic Causes of the First World War," in Leonard Krieger and Fritz Stern, eds., *The Responsibility of Power* (London: Macmillan, 1968), 286-300, esp. 297.

[38] Quoted in Martin Kitchen, *The German Officer Corps, 1890-1914* (Oxford: Clarendon Press, 1968), 141.

[39] Bernhardi, quoted in Notestein and Stoll (fn. 11), 43.

[40] Bernhardi (fn. 11), 18, 20. Other examples are *ibid.*, 23, 37; Kitchen (fn. 38), 96. Bernhardi also believed that even defeat in war could be a healthful experience, bearing "a rich harvest" for the defeated. "[Defeat] often, indeed, passes an irrevocable sentence on weakness and misery, but often, too, it leads to a healthy revival, and lays the foundation of a new and vigorous constitution." *Ibid.*, 28. Bernhardi further argued that the Boer people had benefited from their encounter with British arms in the Boer War: they had made "inestimable moral gains" and won "glorious victories," by which they had "accumulated a store of fame and national consciousness." *Ibid.*, 44.

[41] Dr. Otto Schmidt-Gibichenfels, publisher of the *Politisch-Anthropologische Revue*, November 8, 1912, quoted in Fischer (fn. 5), 194; *Alldeutsche Blätter*, in 1911, quoted in Snyder (fn. 15), 241; *Das neue Deutschland*, August 1, 1914, quoted in Fischer (fn. 5), 244.

divine world order" which ensured the preservation of "all that is good, beautiful, great and noble in nature and in true civilization."[42]

Elsewhere in Europe a similar image of war took hold, although less strongly. In Britain, Hilaire Belloc declared: "How I long for the Great War! It will sweep Europe like a broom, it will make kings jump like coffee beans on the roaster."[43] Professor of history J. A. Cramb felt that war could purify and challenge growing nations, and "universal peace appears less as a dream than as a nightmare."[44] In France, one general argued in 1911 that "it is manifest that war has its role in the economy of societies and that it responds to a moral law. ...."[45]

These opinions were reflected in the ecstasy with which many Europeans greeted the outbreak of war in 1914. The English poet Edmund Gosse saw a "beautiful result" in the "union of hearts" produced by the war, and the Russian composer Igor Stravinsky welcomed the conflict as "necessary for human progress."[46] Friedrich Meinecke, the liberal German historian, later remembered August 1914 as "one of the great moments of my life which suddenly filled my soul with the deepest confidence in our people and the profoundest joy."[47]

---

[42] *Berliner Neueste Nachrichten*, December 24, 1912, quoted in Fischer (fn. 5), 194. Another observer wrote in 1907 that "War is the great chiming of the world clock ... the expulsion of stagnation by progress; the struggle of the stronger and more vigorous, with the chance to create new cultural values of a richer existence; a necessity that cannot be eliminated." Philipp Stauff, quoted in Roger Chickering, *Imperial Germany and a World Without War: The Peace Movement and German Society, 1892-1914* (Princeton: Princeton University Press, 1975), 395. The historian Heinrich Treitschke held that "war is both justifiable and moral," and "the ideal of perpetual peace is not only impossible but immoral as well," and that the "corroding influence of peace" should be deplored. *Ibid.*, 395; Notestein and Stoll (fn. 11), 41.

For more examples, see Chickering 394-95; Archer (fn. 15), 60, 62, 69; Fischer (fn. 5), 33; Notestein and Stoll (fn. 11), 34, 39, 41; Louis L. Snyder, *From Bismarck to Hitler: The Background of Modern German Nationalism* (Williamsport, PA: Bayard Press, 1935), 28; Paul M. Kennedy, "The Decline of Nationalistic History in the West, 1900-1970," *Journal of Contemporary History* 8 (January 1973), 77-100, at 79.

[43] Quted in Roland N. Stromberg, *Redemption by War: The Intellectuals and 1914* (Lawrence: The Regents Press of Kansas, 1982), 180.

[44] Quoted in Kennedy (fn. 42), 82. Sidney Low wrote that wars are "bracing tonics to the national health"; and Lord Lansdowne declared that warfare would benefit society by "strengthening the moral fibre of the nation." Porter (fn. 20), 129; Bernard Brodie, *War and Politics* (New York: Macmillan, 1973), 266. See also Michael Howard, "Empire, Race and War in pre-1914 Britain," in Hugh Lloyd-Jones, Valerie Pearl, and Blair Worden, eds., *History and Imagination: Essays in Honour of H. R. Trevor-Roper* (Duckworth: 1981), 340-55.

[45] General Cherfils, quoted in Cairns (fn. 6), 283.

[46] Quoted in Stromberg (fn. 43), 43, 51. Max Weber wrote that "No matter what the outcome will be, this war is great and wonderful." *Ibid.*, 52. One poet declared that the war had "swept like a purifying storm into our close and fetid atmosphere ..." Ludwig Schueller, quoted in Leon W. Fuller, "The War of 1914 as Interpreted by German Intellectuals," *Journal of Modern History* 14 (June 1942), 145-160, at 152.

[47] Quoted in Joll (fn. 18), 318.

F. SELF-GLORIFYING NATIONALIST MYTHS

Before World War I, a great tidal wave of hypernationalism swept over Europe. Each state taught itself a mythical history of its own and others' national past, and glorified its own national character while denigrating that of others. The schools, the universities, the press, and the politicians all joined in this orgy of mythmaking and self-glorification. As Gilbert Murray described it,

> In every nation of Europe from England and France to Russia and Turkey ... the same whisper from below the threshold sounds incessantly in men's ears. "We are the pick and flower of nations; the only nation that is really generous and brave and just. We are above all things qualified for governing others; we know how to keep them exactly in their place without weakness and without cruelty."[48]

This chauvinist mythmaking poisoned international relations by convincing each state of the legitimacy of its own claims, the rightness of its own cause, and the wrongfulness and maliciousness of the grievances of others. Unaware that its own past conduct had often provoked the hostility it faced, each nation ascribed it to the boundless and innate aggressiveness of others—an aggressiveness that, accordingly, could not be appeased, and required a harsh response. This logic engendered belligerent policies on all sides, creating a climate for war.

In 1905, Kaiser Wilhelm declared that the Germans were "the salt of the earth ..."; in 1914, he told his armies, "you are the chosen people."[49] Chancellor von Bülow declared that "of all the nations of the world the Germans are the people that have most rarely set out to attack and conquer," and "without boastfulness or exaggeration, we may say that never in the course of history has any Power possessing such superior military strength as the Germans, served the cause of peace in an equal measure."[50] Cecil Rhodes proclaimed the British to be "the best people

---

[48] Kennedy (fn. 42), 90.   [49] Quoted in Thayer (fn. 18), 4-5.

[50] Bernhard von Bülow, *Imperial Germany*, trans. Marie A. Lewenz (New York: Dodd, Mead, 1915), 46-48. The writer Richard Dehmel is quoted as stating, "We Germans *are* more humane than the other nations: we *do have* better blood and breeding, more soul, more heart, and more imagination." Klaus Schröter, "Chauvinism and Its Tradition: German Writers and the Outbreak of the First World War," *The Germanic Review* 43 (March 1968), 120-35, at 126; emphasis in original. General Bernhardi proclaimed that the German people are "the greatest civilized people known to history"; that Germans "have always been the standard-bearers of free thought" and "free from prejudice"; and that "No nation on the face of the globe is so able to grasp and appropriate all the elements of culture, to add to them from the stores of its own spiritual endowment, and to give back to mankind richer gifts than it received." Bernhardi (fn. 11), 14, 72; Snyder (fn. 42), 70.

Price Collier, a foreign observer of this self-congratulatory celebration, wrote in 1913 that he "found this pounding in of patriotism on every side distinctly nauseating." Quoted in Konrad Jarausch, *Students, Society, and Politics in Imperial Germany* (Princeton: Princeton University Press, 1982), 333.

in the world, with the highest ideals of decency and justice and liberty and peace, and the more of the world we inhabit, the better for humanity." Joseph Chamberlain concurred "that the British race is the greatest of governing races that the world has ever seen."[51] In France and Russia, scholars and publicists praised the glories of their own national past and national character in similar terms.

In order to justify its own aggressive policies, and to shine more brightly in comparison with others, each state also impugned the humanity and civilization of its neighbors and victims. Kaiser Wilhelm noted that "the Slavs were not born to rule but to serve, this they must be taught." A German described a Russia "barbarous beyond compare," and an England with "only practical talents but no 'culture'."[52] Such thinking justified a master-race mentality, and fed each nation's sense of its own right to conquer and to rule.

The principal agencies for promulgating the chauvinist myths were the state-run schools, where mythical history was inculcated in the young as a matter of government policy, to build public support for the incumbent regime and the existing social and economic order. The elites recognized that people would better support the established system if they believed that their government was always just and wise; they used the schools to instill such beliefs in the young. Boyd Shafer has aptly summarized the common tenor of the education that these policies produced:

> Text and teacher alike, with a few notable exceptions, taught the student that his own country was high-minded, great, and glorious. If his nation went to war, it was for defense, while the foe was the aggressor. If his nation won its wars, that was because his countrymen were braver and God was on their side. If his nation was defeated, that was due only to the enemy's overwhelmingly superior forces and treachery. If his country lost territory, as the French lost Alsace-Lorraine in 1870, that was a crime; whatever it gained was for the good of humanity and but its rightful due. The enemy was "harsh," "cruel," "backward." His own people "kind," "civilized," "progressive."[53]

Professional academic historians were another source of chauvist myth: their writings conveyed to their fellow-countrymen "that only their own nation was great, only their own nation was inventive, in short only their own nation had much history worth knowing."[54] In

---

[51] Quoted in Porter (fn. 20), 134-35. Lord Curzon suggested that the British Empire is "under Providence, the greatest instrument for good that the world has seen." *Ibid.*, 135.

[52] Quoted in Fischer (fn. 5), 222; Richard Dehmel, quoted in Schröter (fn. 50), 125.

[53] Shafer, *Nationalism: Myth and Reality* (New York: Harcourt, Brace, 1955), 185. Also see Carlton J. H. Hayes, *Essays on Nationalism* (New York: Macmillan, 1926), esp. 88-89.

[54] Shafer (fn. 53), 188.

Britain, Macaulay wrote that the British were "the greatest and most highly civilized people that ever the world saw ... [which] have been the acknowledged leaders of the human race in the causes of political improvement."[55] In France, Maurice Barrès asserted that France does not make war "for the sake of spoil, but as a champion of the cause of God, as a knight upholding justice."[56] In Germany, the economist Werner Sombart wrote that the Germans were "the chosen people of this century," and the historian Heinrich von Sybel blamed Denmark, Austria, and France for the wars of German unification.[57] According to H. E. Barnes, Russian historians "glorified [Russian] rulers as national heroes."[58] Thus, the educational institutions of each European state served official efforts to create a false past designed to stimulate public patriotism and chauvinism.

G.   ORIGINS OF EUROPEAN MISPERCEPTIONS

These beliefs apparently stemmed from two principal causes: the extraordinary influence of European professional militaries on civilian opinion, and the social stratification of European societies. Before 1914, the European militaries influenced elite and public opinion to a degree that has been unequaled since, and their propaganda message was heavily laden with all six misperceptions outlined above. At the same time, the political, economic, and social stratification of European societies made the elites fearful of social upheaval, spurring them on to whip up national chauvinism and to pursue bellicose policies in efforts to bolster their domestic political positions.

[55] Quoted in Kennedy (fn. 42), 81. H. Morse Stephens noted that "many English historians were fanatically nationalist and supremely insular in their conviction of the superiority of their own over every other nation." "Nationality and History," *American Historical Review* 21 (January 1916), 225-36, at 233.
[56] Quoted in Harry Elmer Barnes, *A History of Historical Writing*, 2d rev. ed. (New York: Dover, 1962), 216-17. Stephens (fn. 55), 232, found that the French historian Jules Michelet "was almost dithyrambic in his portraiture of the French nation which had become to him a personal hero."
[57] Quoted in Hans Kohn, *The Mind of Germany: The Education of a Nation* (New York: Charles Scribner's Sons, 1960), 300-301; and in Snyder (fn. 15), 141. See also Antoine Guilland, *Modern Germany and Her Historians* (New York: McBride, Nast, 1915).
Responding to this propagandistic German education, the British classicist Alfred Zimmern noted during the war that "Our real opponent is the [German] system of training and education, out of which both German culture and German militarism spring." Stromberg (fn. 43), 146.
[58] Barnes (fn. 56), 224. Such poisonous historical writing led one American historian to reflect on the responsibility of professional historians for causing the war:
   Woe unto us! professional historians, professional historical students, professional teachers of history, if we cannot see written in blood, in the dying civilization of Europe, the dreadful result of exaggerated nationalism as set forth in the patriotic histories of some of the most eloquent historians of the nineteenth century.
Stephens (fn. 55), 236.

The intellectual influence of the military was most powerful in Germany, where the navy organized a Navy League that conducted a vast propaganda effort to sell the navy's program to the German public, and the army used its extensive reserve officer system to indoctrinate middle-class Germany with expansionist and militaristic ideas.[59] Contemporary observers often noted the prevalence and success of this propaganda. An American journalist commented that the German "press is so largely influenced by Admiral von Tirpitz and his corps of press-agents and writers, that it is even difficult to procure the publication of a protest or a reply" to navalist publicity.[60] In 1916, another observer wrote that "Prussia is not a country which has an army; it is an army which possesses a country."[61] The London *Times* declared, "In Prussia the Army is supreme and, through Prussia, the Army rules Germany."[62]

In short, the German army had become "a state within the state,"[63] largely independent of civilian control, playing a major role in shaping German civilian thought. A milder version of the same civil-military

[59] Max Weber, who became an enthusiastic propagandist for militaristic ideas in mid-life, was reportedly converted to the cause by his duty as a reserve officer: his widow wrote that the experience nurtured "a warlike and patriotic attitude which made him hope that one day he would be able to go into the field at the head of his company." Kitchen (fn. 38), 34. Reflecting later on the effects of their service, other German reserve officers noted, "it is surprising how the uniform changes one's politics," and marveled at "the reserve of reliable support for state policy" created by reserve officer service. Jarausch (fn. 50), 344.

Summaries of the activities of the German Navy League are in J.C.G. Rohl, *Germany Without Bismarck: The Crisis of Government in the Second Reich, 1890-1900* (London: B. T. Batsford, 1967), 251-58, and Oron J. Hale, *Publicity and Diplomacy: With Special Reference to England and Germany, 1890-1914* (New York: Appleton Century, 1940), 158-64, 217-20. On the Navy League's "fleet professors," see Charles E. McClelland, "The Berlin Historians and German Politics," *Journal of Contemporary History* 8 (July 1973), 3-33, at 12-21. Longer English-language studies on these subjects, and on the activities of the German Army League, are badly needed.

[60] Price Collier, *Germany and the Germans: An American Point of View* (New York: Charles Scribner's Sons, 1913), 529.

[61] J. Ellis Barker, quoted in Snyder (fn. 15), 254n.

[62] January 14, 1914, quoted in Berghahn (fn. 17), 179. Friedrich Meinecke believed that the Prussian army "produced a curiously penetrating militarism which affected the whole of civilian life"; quoted in Volker R. Berghahn, *Militarism: The History of an International Debate 1861-1979* (New York: St. Martin's Press, 1982), 50. Other contemporaries observed that "the microbe of militarism has been inoculated into the German people," and saw "the predominance of the military spirit" throughout the nation. Charles Sarolea, in Georges Bourdon, *The German Enigma*, trans. Beatrice Marshall (London: J. M. Dent & Sons, 1914), viii; Otto Harnack, in 1908, quoted in Fischer (fn. 5), 27. Admiral von Müller later explained German prewar bellicosity by noting that "a great part of the German people ... had been whipped into a high-grade chauvinism by Navalists and Pan-Germans." Quoted in Fritz Stern, *The Failure of Illiberalism* (London: George Allen & Unwin, 1972), 94.

In 1917 one German official, exasperated at the control of the military over German policy, wrote that "the few perceptive persons in Germany secretly have one war aim: the destruction of Prussian militarism ... No one can say it, however, because it is also an English war aim." Kurt Riezler, quoted in Thompson (fn. 25), 126.

[63] Gordon A. Craig, *The Politics of the Prussian Army 1640-1945* (New York: Oxford University Press, 1955), 252.

pathology was evident in other European states. The Serbian and Austrian militaries moved policy in bellicose directions,[64] and Turkish military leaders were said to be "actively preaching a doctrine of war in which even Bernhardi would have delighted."[65] Even in Britain, "the militarist mind had become too generally the mass mind."[66] The militaries across Europe thus bore important responsibility for the European worldview of 1914.

The militaries did not intend their propaganda to cause war. Rather, they aimed to protect their oganizational interests, which were much the same as those of other organizations—large size, wealth, autonomy, "essence," and prestige. These interests were protected by inculcating civilian society with the six misconceptions outlined above. In the offense-dominant world depicted by cultists of the offensive, the militaries would have more prestige and could claim bigger budgets because national survival would be more precarious, and because they could solve more foreign policy problems by using force offensively.[67] If states exaggerate their neighbors' hostility, their military requirements grow, and militaries can claim a larger portion of national resources. If statesmen believe that bandwagoning behavior prevails and that big-stick-waving tactics usually succeed, the advantages of military superiority and the disadvantages of military weakness seem greater. In turn, this strengthens arguments for larger forces and bolsters the prestige of the military. If empires appear to be economically or socially valuable, the military forces that acquire and defend empires also appear to be more valuable. If war is considered a beneficial, positive activity, force becomes a cheaper way to solve a wider range of problems; the result is a corresponding increase

[64] See Gale Stokes, "The Serbian Documents from 1914: A Preview," *Journal of Modern History* 48 (September 1976), on-demand supplement, 69-83, at 78-81; Arthur J. May, *The Hapsburg Monarchy, 1867-1914* (New York: W.W. Norton, 1968), 399.

[65] A. J. Grant and Harold Temperley, *Europe in the Nineteenth Century, 1789-1914* (New York: Longmans, Green, 1927), 534.

[66] Caroline E. Playne, *The Pre-War Mind in Britain* (London: George Allen & Unwin, 1928), 162.

[67] Military interest in purveying offense-oriented ideas was further magnified by involvement in French and German domestic political and class conflicts, which gave the militaries of these countries an even greater stake in purveying notions that enhanced their prestige, since that would strengthen them against their domestic opponents. Offense-oriented doctrines also provided the militaries with an excuse to maintain their social purity, since they argued successfully that only a socially pristine professional army could wage offensive warfare. On these and other sources of military offense-mindedness before World War I, see Snyder, *Ideology of the Offensive*, and "Civil-Military Relations and the Cult of the Offensive" (both fn. 4), throughout. More general discussions on the origins of military offense-mindedness are in Barry R. Posen, *The Sources of Military Doctrine: France, Britain and Germany Between the World Wars* (Ithaca, NY: Cornell University Press, 1984), 47-51, 67-74, and Stephen Van Evera, "Causes of War," Ph.D. diss. (University of California, Berkeley, 1984), 206-14, 250-54, 280-324.

in the standing and prestige of the professional militaries. Finally, the militaries profit from the patriotic chauvinism fostered by self-glorifying national myths, since rabidly nationalistic citizens are more willing to back national defense programs with their taxes and political support.

Thus, the militaries devised and purveyed their propaganda more to protect their own organizational welfare than to promote international strife. Whatever its purpose, however, this propaganda had calamitous effects on European international relations, making cooperation among states extremely difficult, and war very likely.

The second cause of the European worldview in 1914 lay in the stratification of prewar European societies, and in the fears of democracy and revolution that this stratification fostered among European elites. Such fears increased sharply during the 19th century because industrialization had weakened important instruments of social control by the elite. Specifically, the mass production and proliferation of small firearms had undercut the elite's monopoly of force, and the spread of literacy and the rural migrations to the cities had broken the elite's monopoly of information, giving the lower and middle classes better access to egalitarian ideas. These changes impelled the elites to seek new instruments of social control, leading them to strategies of rule by persuasion and public deception. Such strategies emphasized the purveyance of political myths crafted to persuade the public to accept the established social order. Fear of upheaval also led the elites to explore the social-imperial idea that the loyalty of citizens could be bolstered by foreign wars. Elites were thus drawn toward bellicose policies and moved to purvey myths that could persuade the public to support such policies.

Public loyalty had once been secured by raw coercion and by exploiting public ignorance; now it was increasingly won by infusing the public with positive loyalties, by alarming it with foreign threats, and by impressing it with foreign conquests. To further these aims, European elites purveyed several of the misperceptions mentioned earlier: "self-glorifying nationalist myths," and perhaps "others are hostile" and "empires are valuable." They also lowered their estimates of the costs of war as they came to believe that international conflict could ease their domestic political problems.

This explanation accords with the rise of nationalist mythmaking during the decades following the Napoleonic Wars and the revolutions of 1848, and with its decline after World War II, as the stratification of European society diminished. It also corresponds with the prevalence of expansionist and social-imperial ideas during the decades before World

War I. Finally, it suggests that these ideas were deeply rooted in the European social order: and, while they flourished, they were relatively impervious to attack.

II. Misperception and the Causes of Non-cooperation in 1914

The ideas outlined above created a climate that was hostile to all kinds of international cooperation, and primed Europe for war. In this section, I will trace the effects of these ideas on payoff structures, the size of the shadow of the future, recognition abilities, and the consequences of the numbers of players, and then discuss how they precluded an effective resort to Tit-for-Tat strategies for eliciting cooperation.

A. PAYOFF STRUCTURES AND THE ORIGINS OF WORLD WAR I

The misperceptions of European societies distorted payoff structures in four ways. First, by enlarging both the rewards of DC outcomes and the penalties of CD outcomes, they increased the attractiveness of opportunistic defection (to achieve rewarding DC outcomes) and defensive defection (to avoid disastrous CD outcomes.) Second, by narrowing differences between CC and DD outcomes, they diminished the attractiveness of mutual cooperation. Third, by raising fears that others would answer cooperation with defection, these beliefs made defection appear more attractive in situations where each player had a greater incentive to defect if the other did so. Fourth, by raising hopes that others would answer defection with cooperation, they made defection appear more attractive by suggesting that others would accept an exploitive DC outcome.[68]

1. *The cult of the offensive and payoff structures.* The cult of the offensive

---

[68] These third and fourth effects of European misperceptions—the tendencies to expect that cooperation would elicit defection, and that defection would elicit cooperation—affected only national estimates of the relative probability of CC, CD, DC, and DD outcomes, without affecting estimates of the rewards and penalties of these outcomes. Technically, this puts them outside the definition of payoff structure suggested by Kenneth Oye in his introduction to this volume, which referred exclusively to the rewards and penalties of CC, CD, DC, and DD, without consideration of their probability of occurrence. The probabilities of outcomes, however, affect the rewards and penalties that certain moves will produce, so these probabilities may be included as elements of payoff structure. Furthermore, players do not always deduce the probabilities of outcomes from the rewards and penalties they believe other players to perceive: sometimes they derive their predictions inductively (for instance, from others' observed past behavior). As a result, perceived probabilities are partially independent of the structure of rewards and penalties provided by CC, CD, DC, and DD, and cannot simply be inferred from this structure. A definition of "payoff structure" should capture these perceptions. Accordingly, I use "payoff structure" to include the rewards and penalties of CC, CD, DC, and DD, as well as the probability of their occurrence.

was the most pernicious of Europe's misconceptions, inducing a wide range of non-cooperative conduct, both direct and indirect:[69] states acted directly against one another's basic interests, and they adopted policies that damaged requisite conditions for cooperation, thereby making it harder for both sides to resolve their differences peacefully.

(a) *Expansion and resistance*. The cult of the offensive encouraged the German and Austrian expansionism that led to the crisis of July 1914 and to the war. The Germans probably preferred the status quo to a world war against the entire Entente, and they would not have fomented the July 1914 crisis had they known that a world war would result. In my judgment, however, the Germans *did* want a confined continental war of expansion against France and Russia; and many among the German elite supported the instigation of the July crisis in hopes of provoking just such a war.[70] Moreover, German leaders recognized and accepted the risk that this might entail a wider war against Britain and Belgium.[71]

German expansionism was driven partly by the cult of the offensive, which made wider empire appear both necessary and feasible. In 1913, expansionists pictured a Germany "badly protected by its unfavorable geographic frontiers," and hence in need of wider borders—which, they argued, could easily be gained by a short, victorious war.[72] Had the cult of the offensive not been as strong, these expansionists would have encountered stronger opposition in the form of arguments that expansion was neither necessary nor achievable—that Germany was already secure, and that a wider empire could not be won.

The cult of the offensive also fueled opportunistic expansionism in

[69] For more on the consequences, see Van Evera (fn. 4).

[70] I am satisfied that the "Fischer school" has proved its argument that German prewar intentions were very aggressive. On the controversy over the Fischer school, a useful introduction is John A. Moses, *The Politics of Illusion: The Fischer Controversy in German Historiography* (London: George Prior, 1975).

[71] The dominant factions in the German government seem to have had the following hierarchy of preferences: (1) Entente acquiescence to Austria's destruction of Serbia, giving the Central Powers a peaceful victory in the crisis; (2) continental war against France and Russia; (3) the pre-crisis status quo; (4) world war against Russia, France, Britain, and Belgium. While peaceful expansion was the Germans' first preference, they recognized that the Entente would probably stand firm in a Balkan crisis, which would therefore probably end in war. They instigated the crisis anyhow, because they preferred a continental war (but not a world war) to the status quo, and because they thought they could confine the war to the continent, avoiding a world war. Viewed in toto, 1914 was thus *not* an example of a symmetric or asymmetric "Deadlock" payoff structure, since all players preferred a CC outcome (the prewar status quo) to DD (world war), although Germany preferred CC to DD only narrowly.

[72] Crown Prince Wilhelm, quoted in Notestein and Stoll (fn. 11), 44. Illustrating this confidence, Count Lerchenfeld, the Bavarian representative in Berlin, reported during the July crisis that the German General Staff "looks ahead to war with France with great confidence, expects to defeat France in four weeks. . . ." Quoted in Fischer (fn. 5), 503.

Serbia, Austria, and perhaps in France. In addition, it stiffened the resistance of the Entente powers to German expansionism by reinforcing arguments that any growth in German strength would upset the balance of power and thereby threaten the security of Europe. Hence, it engendered both the impulse to acquire and the impulse to defend, doubly increasing the intensity of the political collision between Germany and the Entente. If we imagine the European states playing a "territorial expansion game" whose players had to decide whether or not to compete for territory and spheres of influence, the effect of the cult was to increase the rewards of DC outcomes (expansion at others' expense) and the penalties of CD (others expand at one's own expense), thereby enlarging the overall incentive to defect.

(b) *Preemption and "windows."* The cult of the offensive helped spark and sustain the spiral of military mobilization of the week of July 25-31, 1914, by encouraging Russia and France to mobilize preemptively, and by spurring others to respond in kind. European leaders were convinced that either side could parlay a small material advantage on the battlefield into a large territorial gain, and that therefore preemptive action which provided even a small material advantage was worthwhile. They naturally concluded that it paid to mobilize first, even if the headstart gained was brief.[73] They also felt unable to leave one another's mobilization unanswered, since a one-sided mobilization would soon give the mobilizing side a decisive offensive capacity. As a result, all European states mobilized once any one state began to mobilize. The cult of the offensive had primed Europe for war: any crisis could quickly explode in a chain reaction of preemptive and reactive mobilizations. Thus, if we imagine Europe playing a "mobilization game" whose players had to decide whether or not to mobilize, the effect of the cult was to enlarge the rewards of DC (an unanswered mobilization achieved against others) and the penalties of CD (others achieve an unanswered mobilization).

The cult also helped to nurture the widespread perception of strategic "windows" of opportunity and vulnerability, which spurred German and Austrian decisions for war in 1914. German warhawks contended that Russia's military strength was growing, and that Germany would eventually be overwhelmed if she allowed it to increase unchecked.[74]

[73] Bethmann-Hollweg declared on August 1, 1914, that "East Prussia, West Prussia, and perhaps also Posen and Silesia [would be] at the mercy of the Russians" if mobilization were delayed; Kraft zu Hohenlohe-Ingelfingen had warned in 1898 that "a delay of a single day [in mobilizing] ... can scarcely ever be rectified." Schmitt (fn. 18), II, 264; Ropp (fn. 8), 203.
[74] On July 18, 1914, Secretary of State von Jagow expressed the common German view:

Similar views prevailed in Austria, whose war minister argued in early July that "it would be better to go to war immediately, rather than at some later period, because the balance of power must in the course of time change to our disadvantage."[75] Without the cult of the offensive, such arguments would have carried less force, since windows would have seemed smaller. Indeed, windows only seemed large because the cult led statesmen to exaggerate the military value of the shifts in force ratios produced by the arms race.[76] If we imagine Europe in a "preventive war" game whose players had to decide whether to attack at moments of material advantage, the cult enlarged both the penalties of CD (others attack when they have the material advantage) and the rewards of DC (one attacks others at a moment of one's own material advantage).

(c) *Russian and German mobilization plans.* Before 1914, Russia and Germany had adopted rigid military mobilization plans that required mobilization and attack in all directions if a local crisis developed. This made any serious crisis very difficult to control. In their broad design, these plans anticipated the preemptive and preventive incentives to mobilize and attack that had been produced by the cult of the offensive.

The Russian plans mandated that, if the army mobilized against Austria, it would also mobilize against Germany—which meant that Germany would mobilize, leading directly to war. Any Austro-Russian conflict would therefore automatically ignite a Russo-German conflagration. Russia's rationale for the plan was dictated by the cult of the offensive: Germany would probably join any Austro-Russian war, partly to shut the window the Russians knew the Germans perceived them to be opening by their military buildup, and partly to avert the grave threat to German security that the Germans feared might arise if Russia destroyed Austria. Therefore the Russians believed that it was better to forestall the Germans at the beginning of any Austro-Russian war by mobilizing, ideally in some secrecy, on the German frontier. In essence, the Russians planned to mobilize preemptively to forestall a preventive German strike against Russia.[77]

Russia will be ready to fight in a few years. Then she will crush us by the number of her soldiers; then she will have built her Baltic fleet and her strategic railways. Our group in the meantime will have become steadily weaker.... I do not desire a preventive war, but if the conflict should offer itself, we ought not to shirk it.
Quoted in Schmitt (fn. 18), I, 321.

[75] Geiss (fn. 10), 84.

[76] The cult of the offensive also helped to cause the arms race that gave rise to these "windows." The logic of defense buildups on all sides rested on arguments that national security was threatened, which presumed that the offense was relatively powerful. Windows of opportunity and vulnerability opened when competitive buildups were not closely synchronized; hence the cult bore some responsibility for both the appearance and the consequence of windows.

[77] For an example of such logic, see Albertini (fn. 9), II, 559.

Meanwhile, the German mobilization plan required mobilization against France—even if the conflict was solely with Russia, and France neither mobilized nor declared war. Again, window reasons were important: the Germans assumed that France would eventually seize the opportunity to attack Germany that was offered by a Russo-German war, and they needed to forestall the possibility that French invaders would conquer their crucial industrial areas in the Rhine Valley.[78] This argument reflected cult-of-the-offensive thinking, since the actual dominance of the defense would have allowed Germany to defend her western territories against France with a small, well-fortified force, even while the main German army was engaged in the east.

German mobilization plans also mandated that "mobilization meant war," because the German army planned to mount a surprise attack on Belgium at the outset of mobilization, with the initial aim of seizing the crucial railroad junction at Liège. There simply was no plan for mobilizing and then peacefully standing by; Germany only had plans for simultaneous mobilization and attack. The purpose of this attack was to seize the advantage of surprise at Liège, and to exploit the brief "window" opened by quicker German mobilization. These ideas, too, were based on the assumption that the offense had the battlefield advantage: the benefits of seizing Liège or exploiting a fleeting post-mobilization numerical advantage would have seemed small if the planners had known that the defense would dominate.[79]

(d) *Secrecy*. The decisions to expand, to mobilize, to attack preemptively and preventively, and to adopt plans incorporating these decisions, led directly to war. But the cult of the offensive also helped to cause the war in a less direct manner: by encouraging secrecy, it fostered blunders and made negotiations more difficult. The German military cloaked their surprise attack at Liège in total secrecy—apparently Chancellor Bethmann-Hollweg, Admiral Tirpitz, and perhaps even the Kaiser were unaware of it[80]—presumably in order to conceal the scheme from the Belgians, who otherwise could have taken steps to ensure that it failed. As a result, statesmen in other countries did not fully realize that

[78] Moltke favored a westward strike because "Germany could not afford to expose herself to the danger of attack by strong French forces in the direction of the Lower Rhine." Geiss (fn. 10), 357.

[79] If we imagine Europe playing a "war plans" game whose players had to decide whether to adopt war-widening or war-limiting mobilization plans, the effect of the cult was to enlarge both the penalties of CD (one adopts restrained plans that others exploit) and the rewards of DC (one adopts violent plans that entail unprovoked mobilization and attack against others.)

[80] See Albertini (fn. 9), II, 581; III, 195, 250, 391; Gerhard Ritter, *The Sword and the Scepter: The Problem of Militarism in Germany*, 4 vols., trans. Heinz Norden (Coral Gables, FL: University of Miami Press, 1969-73), II, 266; Sidney B. Fay, *The Origins of the World War*, 2 vols., 2d ed. rev. (New York: Free Press, 1966), I, 41-42.

mobilization meant war: being unaware that German mobilization plans mandated the attack on Liège, they also were unaware of an important reason *why* mobilization meant war. Russian civilians approved Russian mobilization measures without fully realizing that this made war inevitable;[81] and British diplomats failed to try to halt the Russian measures, apparently also unaware that if Russia's actions sparked German mobilization, war was unavoidable.[82] Thus Russia lit the fuse to war, and Britain let it burn, partly because German military secrecy concealed the mechanism by which the war would break out, which in turn concealed from Russian and British leaders the actions they had to avoid or prevent in order to preserve the peace.

The Russian military also concealed important plans from top Russian civilians.[83] This policy encouraged the disastrous blundering of top Russian civilians, who during the July crisis announced a partial, south-only mobilization against Austria—apparently without realizing that a south-only mobilization would ruin a future northern Russian mobilization against Germany, if this became necessary.[84] By the time they discovered their error, the Russians faced an all-or-nothing choice: to back down in humiliation or to order full mobilization. They did the latter. Had these civilians understood the implications of the mobilizations they ordered, they might have refrained from such an awesome step.

Military secrecy in turn reflected the competitive international climate that the cult of the offensive helped to produce. By making the security of states seem precarious, the cult put a premium on all assets that provided security—including information. Since a breach of security was likely to spell the difference between victory and defeat, states enshrouded their military plans in secrecy.[85]

Prewar secrecy also took a political form, embodied in the *fait accompli* strategy adopted by Germany and Austria, who secretly planned and prepared the crisis and then suddenly sprang their surprise ultimatum to Serbia on the Entente on July 23. The British and the Belgians thus had no opportunity to warn Germany that they would fight if Germany launched a continental war. German leaders therefore held illusions that

---

[81] Albertini (fn. 9), II, 309, 515, 541, 551, 574, 579-81; III, 56, 60-65, 105.

[82] Albertini (fn. 9), II, 330-36; Schmitt (fn. 18), II, 41n.

[83] See Fuller (fn. 13), 4-6, noting this policy and "the mutual incomprehension of soldiers and civilians in late Imperial Russia" that it belied.

[84] Albertini (fn. 9), II, 295-96.

[85] If we imagine Europe playing an "information game" whose players had to decide whether to adopt open or secret information policies, the effect of the cult was to enlarge both the rewards of DC (others adopt an open information policy that one exploits without reciprocating), and the penalties of CD (one adopts an open information policy that others exploit without reciprocating).

Belgium would permit the German army to cross its territory, and that Britain would stand by and let Germany attempt to conquer the continent.[86] Germany and Austria presumably kept their plans secret to prevent the Entente from preparing an effective, unified response to their attack on Serbia, and (assuming that Germany *sought* a continental war) to give the French and Russians less time to tighten their ties with Belgium and Britain before the war began. The German scheme was modeled on the wars of 1866 and 1870, in which Prussia successfully presented Europe with *faits accomplis* before statesmen had time to react and contain Prussian gains.

The prevalence and consequences of secrecy in 1914 raise an important theoretical point, illustrating that, while perverse payoff structures can induce defection which directly harms the other player, they also can induce defection which *harms conditions that promote cooperative play*. For example, games of Prisoners' Dilemma can be played more cooperatively under conditions of transparency—that is, when both sides have full real-time information on the other's actions and intentions, and thus can take steps to prevent defection by deterring, appeasing, or persuading the potential defector to cooperate instead.[87] But perverse payoff structures can undermine transparency by rewarding secrecy. For instance, if the state that strikes first stands to gain an important military advantage, all states have an incentive to conceal their grievances against one another, because complaints could provoke a preemptive strike by alerting the other side that the conflict is serious. This reluctance to complain confuses diplomacy and negotiation, and promotes miscalculation. In 1950, for example, the United States failed to recognize that China would attack if American armies approached the Yalu, partly because China failed to warn the U.S. with an ultimatum—presumably because this would have deprived the Chinese armies of the surprise they would need if the Americans ignored their warning.[88] Likewise, when the offense has the advantage, competition for information grows more intense; states therefore tend to conceal their political and military plans, as they did before 1914.

[86] See, for instance, Schmitt (fn. 18), II, 390n; Albertini (fn. 9), II, 429, 514-27; Tuchman (fn. 5), 143; Geiss (fn. 10), 25; Fischer (fn. 5), 133, 227.

[87] See Robert Jervis, "Cooperation under the Security Dilemma," *World Politics* 30 (January 1978), 167-214, at 181.

[88] The Chinese did issue warnings in late September and early October, but they did not repeat these warnings after the Chinese and American armies approached each other in November (producing a battlefield first-strike advantage); they issued no ultimatum before attacking on November 26.

On this episode, see Alan Whiting, *China Crosses the Yalu* (Stanford, CA: Stanford University Press, 1960), 92-150, and Alexander George and Richard Smoke, *Deterrence and American Foreign Policy* (New York: Columbia University Press, 1974), 184-234.

These examples illustrate "peace/victory dilemmas" which force states to choose between strategies that enhance cooperation and those that enhance the likelihood of winning the competition. Such dilemmas show that perverse payoff structures encourage non-cooperation both directly and indirectly, leading players to harm one another's core interests, *and* to damage conditions under which cooperation would be able to overcome these perverse incentives.

2. *Other misperceptions and payoff structures.* The effects of other misperceptions on payoff structures were as dangerous as those of the cult of the offensive, though less multifarious. Belief in bandwagoning led Europeans to compete harder for any advantage that was thought to be cumulative. In bandwagon thinking, winning one round increases one's power in the next; a player can therefore force the other's cooperation in subsequent rounds of play by winning early rounds. This "slippery slope" assumption heightened the apparent penalties of CD outcomes and the rewards of DC outcomes in instances where cumulative resources seemed to be at stake, pulling the players toward defection. German expansionist policies and the German naval buildup represented defections of this sort.

The belief that "wave-the-big-stick" tactics were efficacious represented a forecast of how the other player's conduct would be affected by one's own, suggesting that "if we defect, they won't." Such a prediction recommended defection by suggesting that a defecting player could force a DC outcome on the other player, while avoiding DD and CD. Defection thus seemed very attractive. This logic underlay the bellicose German conduct in the crises of 1905, 1911, and 1914.

The conviction that others were inflexibly hostile offered the inverse proposition—"even if we don't defect, they will"—with the same effect. It made cooperation more difficult, this time by convincing statesmen that other states would exploit rather than reciprocate cooperative behavior, trapping cooperators in CD outcomes. Playing cooperatively made no sense in such a world, even if both players stood to gain from mutual cooperation, because the other player would not reciprocate. But players could at least forestall a CD outcome (which otherwise was certain) by playing uncooperatively; defecting was therefore logical even though the subsequent DD outcome was inferior to all outcomes except CD. Many uncooperative actions before World War I are explained by this line of thinking, including decisions on all sides to adopt expansionist aims, to develop inflexibly aggressive mobilization plans, and to mobilize during the July crisis. In each case, the rationalization for the move followed some form of the argument that "whatever we do, they will do their worst to us, so we had better do our worst to them"; in other words, "they will defect, so we must."

Taken together, these two beliefs added up to the proposition that defection causes others to cooperate while cooperation causes others to defect. Clearly, such beliefs produce an explosive world by simultaneously removing all incentives to cooperate and providing large inducements to defect.

The tendency to exaggerate the economic and social value of empire had the same effect as exaggerations of its security value that were induced by the cult of the offensive: Europeans competed harder for territory, as reflected in German, Austrian, Russian, Serbian, and French expansionism. In essence, they overestimated the economic and social rewards of DC outcomes in contests for territory and spheres of influence; hence, they exaggerated the benefits of defecting on territorial questions.

The tendency to glorify war and to underestimate its costs led states to risk war more willingly. In essence, such beliefs narrowed the perceived gap between CC and DD outcomes in instances where DD results involved war or the risk of war, encouraging the powers in the reckless policies they adopted in 1914.

Finally, self-glorifying nationalist mythologies spawned four related ideas that twisted payoff structures in perverse directions. First, myth-ridden states more quickly assumed of their opponents that "they know they are wrong and we are right, so they are only testing us, and will back down if we stand firm and demonstrate that we know we are right." These states also assumed that "our opponents' credibility will not suffer much harm if they back down because they are not defending legitimate interests, hence they can concede quite easily." In short, the states deduced that firm tactics would work—that, by defecting, they could force others to cooperate—because their false history suggested that the balance of interest and resolve lay on their side. In turn, this suggested that the other side would concede to threats, knowing that otherwise it would face endless DD outcomes. Such thinking rendered both sides less willing to cooperate, and set them on a collision course.

Second, myth-ridden states more quickly concluded that "we are defending our legitimate interests; if we concede, we show everyone that we can be blackmailed to abandon any interest." By exaggerating the legitimacy of their own claims, they exaggerated the scope of the precedent their own concessions would set, so they firmly resisted concessions.[89] In other words, cooperation grew less attractive because the penalties of CD outcomes appeared larger.

Third, the cultural arrogance engendered by nationalist mythmaking nurtured a contemptuous estimate of the abilities and tenacity of others, fueling false expectations of easy military victory.[90] As a result, Europeans exaggerated the benefits and underestimated costs of war, thus underestimating the penalties of DD in encounters where DD outcomes involved the risk of war.

Fourth, such mythmaking diminished the ethical pain of conquering and killing other people. Believing their cause to be just, their imperial rule generous, and their victims culturally backward or even subhuman, Europeans assumed that subjugating or killing others was no great sin. The ethical cost of uncooperative conduct was thus diminished. In other words, the penalties of DC and DD outcomes decreased relative to those of CD and CC in instances where DC and DD involved war and conquest.

B. STRATEGIC SETTING AND THE ORIGINS OF THE WAR

The case of 1914 thus illustrates the power of perceived payoff structures and the importance of structuring payoffs to reward cooperative conduct. In the following section, I will discuss how Europe's misperceptions also impeded cooperation by shortening the shadow of the future and by undermining the capacity of states to recognize past cooperation and defection.

1. *The shortness of the shadow of the future.* Three factors shortened the shadow of the future in 1914. First, many Europeans believed that a decisive war would soon settle the final control of Europe. This expectation shortened the shadow of the future by suggesting that the "game" would end in an early "round of play." Europeans expected war because they exaggerated one another's hostility, and because the other misconceptions outlined above—the cult of the offensive, bandwagon ideas, exaggerations of the economic value of empire, under-

[89] Kenneth A. Oye, in "Bargaining, Belief Systems, and Breakdown: International Political Economy 1929-1936," Ph.D. diss. (Harvard University, 1983), chap. 3, distinguishes between "blackmailing," "backscratching," and "bracketing," and discusses the greater credibility costs of concession to blackmail, and the greater likelihood that demands supported by blackmail will therefore be resisted.

[90] The Kaiser wrote of the Slavs during the July crisis: "How hollow the whole so-called Serbian power is proving itself to be; thus it is seen to be with all the Slav nations! Just tread hard on the heels of that rabble!" July 25, 1914, quoted in Geiss (fn. 10), 182. On the other side, the Russian general staff magazine in 1913 expressed contempt for the Austrian army's discipline and cohesion: "The Austrian army represents a serious force. ... But on the occasion of the first great defeat all this multi-national and artificially united mass ought to disintegrate." Quoted in Fuller (fn. 13), 21.

estimates of the cost of war, and hypernationalism—led many Europeans to recommend warlike policies. They expected a *decisive* war because the cult of the offensive suggested the possibility of a clear military decision, and because bandwagon theories indicated that the winner of even a small victory could parlay this success into hegemonic dominance by using conquered power assets to intimidate weaker states into submission.

Second, some Europeans foresaw that the control of Europe might be settled by peaceful shifts in the balance of power. This perception shortened the shadow of the future by persuading declining states that they had to win early rounds of competition to keep the game going. Expectations of a peaceful decision reflected the logic of the cult of the offensive and of bandwagon theories, since both suggested that relatively small shifts in military strength could prove decisive. These expectations caused the leaders of declining states to prefer victory in early rounds of competition over the prospect of cooperation in later rounds whenever power assets were at stake in early rounds. They were therefore drawn toward bellicose policies to freeze the balance of power—such as Germany's efforts to rupture the Entente by intimidation, and German and Austrian programs for preventive war. Although such policies sacrificed the possibility of future cooperation, this was a small sacrifice in the minds of leaders because the results of later rounds of competition would be determined by the results of earlier rounds. If the earlier rounds were lost, little else would matter.

Third, the relative secrecy of 1914 had the effect of aggregating decisions into a few, large transactions, which shortened the shadow of the future by magnifying the importance of each transaction relative to the next. Had both sides been fully aware of every political and military move by the other as it occurred, the Entente might have been able to deter the Central Powers from instigating the July crisis by immediately punishing each small political move that the Central Powers took, hour by hour, from the Sarajevo assassination onward. Each side might also have deterred the other's mobilization by threatening to keep perfect pace with it. Secrecy made this kind of deterrence impossible, however, because states were unaware of the acts that required deterring as they happened. As a result, the shadow of the future was shortened; statesmen felt that they could get away with so much before being punished that the relative importance of eventual retribution dwindled.

2. *Poor "recognition."* The conflict between Germany and the Entente developed partly because Germany misread retaliatory reaction by the Entente as unprovoked aggression. This in turn produced an "echo" or

"spiral"[91] effect that intensified the dispute. The distorted history taught in German schools rendered Germans immune to the idea that they could be perceived as threatening others, and the German version of recent diplomatic history played down the role of German provocation in creating the Entente. The Germans therefore saw defensive Entente reactions as malicious predations, which stiffened their resolve to respond forcefully. Holger Herwig summarized the German reaction to the Entente's hostility: "That this 'encirclement' had largely been self-imposed and that it could have been overcome easily by a peaceful foreign policy apparently never dawned on the statesmen in Berlin, absorbed as many of them were in social Darwinistic visions of the rise and fall of world empires."[92]

This "echo" continued until 1945. Between 1919 and 1945, the Germans maintained that Entente hostility during 1914-1919 was the unprovoked expression of British "encirclement" conspiracies, and concluded that this history demonstrated the boundless aggressiveness of Germany's neighbors.[93] These myths laid the logical basis for Nazi expansionism.

C.   THE NUMBER OF PLAYERS IN THE GAME:
     CONSEQUENCES OF MULTIPOLARITY

Political power in 1914 was dispersed among a relatively large number of European states—six great powers and several medium-size powers. The dispersion of power increased the costs of information and transaction, which in turn fostered blunders and miscalculations. It also made it harder to fashion discriminating sanctions that punished an aggressor without harming the aggressor's allies; as a consequence, retaliatory sanctions tended to spread rather than to dampen conflict.[94] While large numbers can damage cooperation independently, in this case these effects

[91] The classic essay on spirals, and on the opposite danger of deterrence failure, is Robert Jervis, *Perception and Misperception in International Politics* (Princeton: Princeton University Press, 1976), 58-113.
[92] Herwig, "Looking-Glass House: Germany in the Eras of Tirpitz and Moltke," unpub. (1980), 48. The British Ambassador to Berlin, Sir Frank Lascelles, noted of the imperial Germans: "They were the most sensitive people in the world, and at the same time it would never enter into their heads that they could by any possibility be offensive themselves, although in reality they often were ..." Geiss (fn. 11), 62-63. When the British papers spoke of the "German menace," the Kaiser angrily denied the charge, writing "We challenge nobody!" on the margin of one such article in 1905. "It is British vainness and overheated fancy that styles our [naval] building so" Steinberg (fn. 34), 22.
[93] On the efforts organized by successive Weimar governments to obscure German responsibility for the war, see Imanuel Geiss, "The Outbreak of the First World War and German War Aims," *Journal of Contemporary History* 1 (July 1966), 75-82. A longer treatment of this important subject is badly needed.
[94] On these concepts, see Kenneth Oye's introduction to this collection.

were produced in conjunction with the cult of the offensive, and with bandwagon thinking. In their absence, the malign effects of large numbers would have diminished or disappeared.

Blunders and miscalculations played an important role in causing the war. For instance, the Germans launched the July crisis in the mistaken expectation that Britain and Belgium would not resist their offensive, and that Italy, Sweden, Rumania, and Japan would fight on the side of the Central Powers. The British, partly because they were unaware that Russian mobilization meant war, failed to move forcefully to prevent it. The Russians began mobilizing in the false hope that Germany would acquiesce to their partial mobilization, and that their general mobilization could be concealed from Germany. Russian, German, and French officials also exaggerated one another's preliminary mobilization measures, which spurred all three to take further measures, fueling the spiral of mobilizations.[95]

In part these blunders reflected the confusion sown by the simultaneous action of eight states. The dispersion of power scattered each state's focus of attention. As a result, each was likely to misconstrue the actions, interests, and perceptions of the others. Large numbers increased the costs of information and raised the risk of error.

The blunders of the crisis also reflected the effects of the cult of the offensive, which made errors harder to avoid by fostering secrecy, and harder to reverse by magnifying their consequences. Germany miscalculated British and Belgian intentions while Britain was unaware that Russian mobilization meant war, partly because Germany pursued secret policies. By enlarging windows and preemptive incentives, the cult also enlarged the military estimates. As a result, each mistake provoked rapid, dramatic reactions that quickly made the mistake irreversible. Without the cult of the offensive, there would have been fewer blunders in 1914, and the statesmen could more easily have recovered and reversed those that occurred.

Together with bandwagon ideas, the cult of the offensive also encouraged the evolution of a tight network of offensive alliances that emboldened aggressors and spread local war. Alliances operated tightly and offensively because the security of the European powers was tightly meshed: each power felt that its own security rested precariously on that of its allies, and therefore felt compelled to rush to defend its allies— even when these allies had provoked their attackers. States also feared

---

[95] For documentation, see sources cited in Van Evera (fn. 4), 76-77, 99, 102-13; for sources on Russia's belief that Germany would acquiesce to Russia's partial mobilization, see Albertini (fn. 9), II, 550.

nearby mobilizations that were directed at others, or felt tempted to attack if these mobilizations briefly weakened an enemy's defenses by diverting opposing forces away from their frontiers. As a result, conflict spread as powers mobilized in defensive or offensive response to nearby mobilizations. Russian and German war plans had been designed to anticipate these processes, and thereby ensured that they actually operated. Russian plans would drag Germany into any Austro-Russian war, and German plans would force Belgium and France to fight in a Russo-German war, even if Russia was the provocateur. Bystanders were left with no option to avoid wars in which their allies were involved.

This situation emboldened states (especially Serbia and Russia) who knew they could count on the protection of their allies even if they provoked war. Thus, in a perverse way, provocative behavior was encouraged precisely because provocateurs could entangle all of Europe in any local wars they caused. The responsibility for this explosive situation lay partly with the large number of European powers: in a bipolar world, sanctions would have been focused on single target states, and aggressors would have had no allies behind whom they could hide. In this sense, the number of powers in Europe contributed to the problem.

In addition, the cult and bandwagon ideas were essential elements of the equation. They supplied the basic reason why the states of Europe believed their security to be tightly interdependent. Without these ideas, multipolarity could have operated to strengthen the peace in 1914: states could have exploited it to arrange defensive alliances, like those Bismarck had concluded in the 1880s. Aggressors would have been deterred because each would have been confronted by many enemies; status quo powers would have been safe in the knowledge that they had many allies. In fact, the alliances of 1914 had originally been designed as defensive alliances, and evolved into tighter and more offensive arrangements chiefly for reasons growing from the cult of the offensive.[96] Had this transformation been prevented, an important cause of the war would have been removed.

D.   WHY TIT-FOR-TAT FAILED IN 1914

A Tit-for-Tat strategy seeks to elicit cooperation from others by basing action on two principles: players must not defect first, nor play to "win" thereafter (i.e., they must be "nice"); and they must reciprocate defection. The European powers of 1914 did not consciously employ such strategies (or any other strategies) to elicit cooperation from one another, nor did they consider doing so. However, even if they had considered Tit-for-

[96] For details, see Van Evera (fn. 4), 96-101.

Tat strategies, they might well have rejected them, because such strategies become costly and ineffective in an environment like that of 1914. The reward for defecting first is large in such a world, and the penalty of defecting second is great, so the price of a "nice" strategy is high. Also, "nice" strategies are less likely to elicit cooperation; indeed, being "nice" may elicit even worse behavior from others. Punishing defections also may fail to evoke better conduct, or may even elicit worse behavior by provoking defectors to retaliate; therefore the net results of Tit-for-Tat are very poor.

Thus, although one cannot argue that Tit-for-Tat was tried in 1914 and failed, one can say that the 1914 environment would have discouraged its adoption and made its failure likely if it had been adopted. Five specific aspects of the 1914 situation rendered Tit-for-Tat strategies less than attractive and effective.

First, a "nice" policy seemed expensive because, due to the cult of the offensive and bandwagon and big-stick assumptions, small losses seemed hard to reverse. Both ideas made territory and other resources appear more additive, or cumulative. As a result, states found it harder to be the second to be "not nice." Instead, they pursued bellicose diplomatic styles, as illustrated in the various prewar crises and in July 1914. They also resisted making even small concessions, on the assumption that small losses would leave them too weak to prevent larger ones.[97] The logic of the cult, and of bandwagon/big-stick thinking, was simply incompatible with "nice" conduct.

Moreover, Germany might have behaved even worse had the Entente adopted a "nicer" policy. Like the Germany of 1938, the Germany of 1914 was likely to misconstrue final concessions to legitimate demands as craven surrender to intimidation. States often exaggerate their own role in forcing concessions from others.[98] This is especially true of aggressor states, and above all of militarized states such as Wilhelmine Germany, because their militaries are quick to claim credit for inter-

[97] Illustrating this mindset, one French observer warned during the July crisis that the demise of far-away Serbia would directly threaten French security, and that France had to fight immediately to prevent this:

To do away with Serbia means to double the strength which Austria can send against Russia: to double Austro-Hungarian resistance to the Russian Army means to enable Germany to send some more army corps against France. For every Serbian soldier killed by a bullet on the Morava one more Prussian soldier can be sent to the Moselle. . . . It is for us to grasp this truth and draw the consequences from it before disaster overtakes Serbia.

J. Herbette, July 29, 1914, in Albertini (fn. 9), II, 596.

[98] See Robert Jervis, "Hypotheses on Misperception," in *World Politics* 20 (April 1968), 454-79; reprinted in George H. Quester, *Power, Action, and Interaction* (Boston: Little, Brown, 1971), 104-32, at 129; Jervis (fn. 91), 343-48.

national successes by arguing that concessions were won by intimidation rather than by conciliation. With such states, "nice" strategies will merely encourage more demands.[99] The attitude prevalent in Germany in 1914 therefore rendered it relatively impervious to conciliatory inducements.

Second, a policy of fostering cooperation by reciprocating defection risked sparking a conflict spiral, because false history convinced both sides that the other had defected last and deserved punishment, while their own side was blameless. Thus, when the Entente responded firmly to German provocations, it touched off a hostile German response which was premised on the Germans' false view of recent history. Because recognition was poor, negative sanctions were as likely to foster retaliation as cooperation.

This illustrates that Tit-for-Tat strategies require that both sides believe essentially the same history; otherwise the players may be locked into an endless echo of retaliations as each side punishes the other's latest "unprovoked" transgression. Because states seldom believe the same history, however, the utility of Tit-for-Tat strategies is severely limited in international affairs. Strategies to promote international cooperation through reciprocity may therefore require parallel action to control the chauvinist mythmaking that often distorts a nation's view of its past.

Third, because Europeans widely assumed that the offense had the advantage, a Tit-for-Tat policy under the conditions of 1914 risked provoking a conflict spiral by threatening the security of states. Under conditions of perceived offense dominance, strategies of punishment grow more dangerous because acts of punishment may develop offensive implications by threatening the other's defensive capabilities. If so, the sanctioner runs the risk that, instead of eliciting the sanctionee's cooperation, the sanctions will provoke it to take forceful measures to defend itself. British leaders hesitated to organize a firm allied resistance to the Germans during the July crisis partly out of fear that the Germans would see this as an offensive threat;[100] and although the British were probably mistaken, their reaction illustrates a general problem that arises when the offense is strong. Negative sanctions must be carefully chosen and deftly applied to avoid threatening the other's defensive capabilities, but that is often impossible if states believe their security to be precarious.

Fourth, a policy of encouraging cooperation by practicing reciprocity

[99] Indeed, it is hard to recount the history of the period without concluding that the Entente did not "defect" first; so in this sense a "nice" strategy *can* be said to have been tried and to have failed.

[100] See Schmitt (fn. 18), II, 90.

collided with the German belief in bandwagon theories, which persistently led the Germans to underestimate Britain's willingness to retaliate if Germany misbehaved. Instead, this belief suggested that Britain would become "nice" if Germany remained nasty, thereby inoculating the Germans against the warning that reciprocal defection was meant to convey. As a result, the British needed to punish the Germans again and again to drive their message home—and ultimately even this was unsuccessful. Despite the firm foreign and naval policy the British had followed for a decade before 1914, and the many warnings that had emanated from London, the Germans still hoped that Britain could be browbeaten into neutrality. This obtuseness reflected the Germans' false theories of international affairs. They would have had to unlearn these theories before the lessons taught by negative sanctions could have sunk in.

Finally, because of the secrecy that concealed German plans, the British were unaware that Germany planned to move for continental hegemony. They therefore did not emphasize sufficiently that Britain would fight. As a result, Germany misbehaved without anticipating the full weight of the retaliation that would follow. Reciprocation failed to produce cooperation, not because it was not practiced, but because it was not expected. The lack of "transparency" in the system undercut the effectiveness of cooperation-through-reciprocity by depriving the British of the opportunity to emphasize that they would repay German misconduct in kind.

In sum, because the conditions required for the successful application of a Tit-for-Tat strategy were missing in 1914, Europe was infertile ground for Tit-for-Tat strategies. These conditions are often absent in international affairs; the syndromes of 1914 were merely pronounced varieties of common national maladies. It follows that we will fail to foster cooperation, and may create greater conflict, if we rely on Tit-for-Tat strategies without first establishing the conditions required for their success.

It does not follow that another strategy would have done any better in 1914. Tit-for-Tat was probably as good as any alternative, and the statesmen of 1914 might as well have tried it (assuming they were willing to pay the price of adopting "nice" strategies.) But *any* tactical strategy for eliciting cooperation is bound to fail in an environment like that of 1914. No strategy can induce cooperation in such a world. Statesmen who seek to promote cooperation in such a world should first try reforming payoff structures and the strategic setting before considering specific tactics.

III. Could World War I Have Been Prevented?

World War I was a war of illusions, caused by the misperceptions that afflicted contemporary European societies. In an immediate sense, the war grew from the perverse payoff structures and strategic setting of 1914, and from dangers of multipolarity that were magnified by these conditions. These immediate causes were a reflection of the false ideas that had overtaken Europe. A clear-sighted Europe would have suffered no perverse payoff structures, no perverse strategic setting, fewer pathologies of multipolarity—and probably no war. There would have been less international conflict, and the conditions that allow a peaceful resolution of conflict would have been abundantly present.

Accordingly, the prevention of the First World War would have required dispelling the misperceptions then prevalent in Europe. Steps to change actual political, military, or economic arrangements—to further strengthen the defense on the battlefield, or to post observer corps to prevent surprise, for instance—might have brought marginal improvement. But misperceptions were the taproot of the war; any realistic program for peace would have required their elimination.

Any program that corrected Europe's myopias probably would have preserved the peace, since Europe had little else to fight about. The principal European questions of the late 19th century—those arising from the unification of Germany and Italy—had been resolved by 1914, leaving only problems of Slavic and South Slavic nationalism, which were farther removed from the heart of Europe. The partition of Africa, a source of conflict since the 1870s, had been settled by the Agadir agreement of 1911. No vital economic quarrels remained unresolved. Germany in particular had little cause for complaint: her national demands had been granted by the European powers between 1864 and 1871, and Germany had the largest and fastest-growing economy[101] and the strongest army in Europe. Thus, Europe was relatively free of genuine conflicts of interest. If the myopias of individual states had somehow been corrected, the First World War could probably have been avoided.

The correction of these myopias should thus have been the first order of business for the European peace movement. Yet this was probably infeasible. European myths were purveyed by powerful and willful elites and institutions who wanted to further their vital domestic political, economic, and organizational interests. Combating these ideas would have failed unless the opposition had equally powerful institutions on

---

[101] See Paul M. Kennedy, "The First World War and the International Power System," *International Security* 9 (Summer 1984), 7-40, at 12-14, 18-19.

its side. In Germany, the most myth-ridden European power, the political order was too repressive to allow groups who would fight these myths to operate successfully, as the sad history of the Wilhelmine German peace movement attests.[102]

The idea of curing misperceptions like those of 1914 thus seems quite farfetched. National perceptual engineering on the scale required in 1914 has been conducted successfully, but never under such adverse conditions. To mention some successful efforts, mythmaking in the German schools was nearly eliminated by the allied occupation authorities after 1945, and nationalist mythmaking in the schools of other West European countries was greatly reduced after 1945 by international projects organized by UNESCO and the international schoolbook movement. European academic historical writing also became less nationalistic under the influence of a new generation of historians—exemplified by the Fischer school—who experienced firsthand the disasters produced by the mendacity of their predecessors.[103] However, these reforms were achieved in a benign political climate, in conjunction with a military occupation, following social changes that left Europe less severely stratified (thereby lessening the elite's motivation to make myths), and two world wars that provided object lessons in the risks of allowing mythmaking to run rampant. It seems unlikely that such efforts could have succeeded in pre-1914 Europe. Thus, while perceptions are usually more malleable than hard realities, the misconceptions of prewar Europe probably would have resisted correction by measures less violent than those that finally brought them under control.

These conclusions point toward a rather gloomy outlook. The case of 1914 suggests that international cooperation may require controlling national misperception, but that plausible strategies for doing this are hard to devise. Large-scale national perceptual engineering is a utopian notion that seems feasible only under special conditions. Nevertheless, the 1914 case warns that we must consider how national misperceptions can be corrected, since peace will be threatened if misperceptions like those of 1914 ever reappear on the same scale. Milder forms of these misperceptions persist today in both East and West, and we risk disaster if we fail to devise methods to keep them under control.

[102] See Chickering (fn. 42), throughout. This account suggests, however, that even a more powerful German peace movement might have made little difference, since the movement failed to dispute the specific factual and theoretical falsehoods that fueled German expansionism, instead misdirecting its energies toward arbitration schemes, disarmament proposals, and general public consciousness-raising.

[103] On the de-nationalization of European education after 1945, see E. H. Dance, *History the Betrayer* (London: Hutchinson, 1960), 126-50, and Kennedy (fn. 42), throughout; on the Fischer school, see Moses (fn. 70), throughout.

ARMS RACES AND COOPERATION

By GEORGE W. DOWNS, DAVID M. ROCKE,
and RANDOLPH M. SIVERSON*

I. INTRODUCTION

A GOVERNMENT interested in reducing the level of arms competition with a rival can attempt to realize this goal in a variety
of ways. It can choose to shift military expenditures from offensive to
defensive weapons in the hope that this will solve the "security dilemma"
by increasing its security without decreasing that of its opponent. It can
attempt to convince its rival of the futility of increased arms expenditures
by announcing that it will henceforth spend neither more nor less on
defense than the rival. Or it can propose that the two states initiate
formal arms talks. Each of these actions represents a different type of
strategy designed to promote cooperation. Shifting expenditures to primarily defensive weapons is one type of *unilateral* strategy that has been
discussed at length by Jervis.[1] Tying defense expenditures to those of
the rival state is an example of the *tacit bargaining* strategy of reciprocity
that plays a critical role in Schelling and in Axelrod's recent work on
the Prisoners' Dilemma.[2] Formal arms talks are a variety of the strategy
of *negotiation*.[3]

In this paper we explore the advantages and disadvantages of each
of these strategies for reducing the intensity of arms races that are
motivated by different patterns of preferences and complicated by different sources of uncertainty. The essay contains a substantial amount
of both formal and historical analysis. To rely on formal analysis alone
would tend to obscure the fact that arms races have taken place under
a far broader set of conditions than might be predicted on the basis of

* We wish to acknowledge the support of the College of Letters and Science, University
of California, Davis, the University of California's Institute on Global Conflict and Co-
operation, and the Institute of Governmental Affairs, University of California, Davis. Greg
Gleason provided research assistance on the Washington Naval Conference and the Hague
Conference. We also benefited from the helpful comments of Robert Axelrod, Robert Jervis,
Kenneth Oye, Glenn Snyder, Stephen Van Evera, and Frank Zagare.
[1] Robert Jervis, *Perception and Misperception in International Politics* (Princeton: Princeton
University Press, 1976); and, more notably, Jervis, "Cooperation under the Security Di-
lemma," *World Politics* 30 (January 1978), 167-214.
[2] Robert Axelrod, *The Evolution of Cooperation* (New York: Basic Books, 1984).
[3] Howard Raiffa, *The Art and Science of Negotiation* (Cambridge: Harvard University
Press, 1982).

a narrow game-theoretic representation, and that they can be affected by factors that are not conventionally dealt with in formal analysis. For example, when states employ "bargaining chip" strategies or attempt to convince a rival that they are stronger than they really are in order to gain policy leverage in other areas (as the Soviet Union did in the late 1950s), an arms race may develop or accelerate even though the structure of the payoffs suggests that cooperation should result. Moreover, we will see that it is possible to propose a strategy that can successfully promote cooperation in a world of perfect information and control, but fail miserably in the uncertain world in which states must interact.

An approach that attempts to evaluate alternative cooperative strategies solely by examining the historical record of the 19th and 20th centuries faces still greater problems. This is not, as one might assume, simply because there are relatively few instances in which arms races have been peacefully reversed. Although their number is not large enough to isolate the impact of an individual strategy in cases where several were pursued simultaneously, they are more numerous than many pessimists might imagine.[4] The chief difficulty lies instead in the disconcerting fact that the majority of arms races that have ended in cooperation have done so not because one side adopted a particular cooperative strategy, but because the basic character of the race was altered by events that were not directly connected with it.

Such events, which collectively might be called the "tilt of the board," spring largely from economic circumstances and changes in the larger political order outside the relations between the two states engaged in the arms race. From a historical point of view, the most important determinant of cooperation that can be classified under this heading is the activity of a third power. Consider the series of Anglo-French naval races that took place during the last half of the 19th century. The race of 1852-1853 was "peacefully" resolved when the two nations joined

---

[4] Both Samuel Huntington, in "Arms Races: Prerequisites and Results" *Public Policy* 8 (1958), 41-86, and Paul Kennedy, in *Strategy and Diplomacy* (Ayelsbury, England: Fontana, 1984), 163-78, offer examples of arms races that did not result in war. Huntington's list, which is the more comprehensive of the two, follows:

1. France vs. England	1840-1866
2. France vs. Germany	1874-1894
3. England vs. France and Russia	1884-1904
4. Argentina vs. Chile	1890-1902
5. England vs. Germany	1898-1912
6. England vs. United States	1916-1930
7. Japan vs. United States	1916-1922
8. United States vs. Soviet Union	1946-

Kennedy, who concentrates his attention upon only the major powers, recognizes all of the above except Argentina and Chile between 1890 and 1902; there are minor differences in some of the dates.

forces to fight the Russians in the Crimean War; that of 1859-1861 gradually dissipated as Napoleon III turned his attention and limited resources to coping with Mexico and the rising power of Prussia; and that of 1884-1904 ended in the face of increased German power and aggressiveness.[5] Although these races came to a halt without the rivals going to war (at least with each other), they hardly provide ideal cases for making inferences about the effectiveness of alternative strategies to induce cooperation. Fortunately, while the relatively minor role played by cooperative strategies in resolving past arms races limits our ability to evaluate their merits directly, that does not mean that historical analysis has nothing to contribute. As we shall see, it can substantially enrich the formal analysis of arms races by identifying variables that might otherwise be omitted, and by prompting speculation about which of the wide variety of "games" that can theoretically lead to an arms race are actually being played.

II. Arms Races, Perfect Information, and Cooperation

To begin to understand the merits of the three strategies and the important variations in arms races with which they may have to cope, it is useful to consider the least complicated abstraction of two utility-maximizing antagonists with perfect information about each other's preferences and behavior. Let us treat an arms race as a sequence of plays of a 2 x 2 game with the standard payoff matrix shown in Figure 1.[6] To understand the conditions on the payoffs necessary for an arms race to exist, consider the payoffs to one of the participants.[7] In this setting of full information, an arms race—defined in this context as continual mutual defection—cannot exist among rational opponents un-

[5] Richard Cobden, *The Political Writings of Richard Cobden* (London: William Ridgway, 1868); Kennedy (fn. 4); Arthur J. Marder, *The Anatomy of British Sea Power* (New York: Octagon Books, 1976).

[6] The key here is the preference structure; for our purposes, the other conditions for a 2 x 2 game do not necessarily have to hold. The sequential-play-of-the-game structure seems the most reasonable in spite of Wagner's argument that one should allow each player to act conditionally on knowledge of the other's play. See R. Harrison Wagner, "The Theory of Games and the Problem of International Cooperation," *American Political Science Review* 77 (June 1983), 330-46. This seems more like defining away the problem than solving it: if information moves quickly enough and control is fine enough so that one can respond to an opponent's move after one week, then one models this as a-game-a-week. The analysis in extensive form that is used by Wagner seems unnecessarily cumbersome.

[7] In order to reduce the number of cases that have to be discussed, the analysis here is carried on with respect to the payoffs of one of the participants rather than to those of the whole game. Once the analysis of the individual orderings has been made, the actual games can be constructed using combinations of preference patterns. Terms such as "Prisoners' Dilemma," which conventionally refer to symmetric games, are also used for the preference pattern of one of the participants.

FIGURE I

2 X 2 REPRESENTATION OF AN ARMS RACE

Country B

		Cooperate	Defect
Country A	Cooperate	C,C	C,D
	Defect	D,C	D,D

less DD > CD; otherwise the response to defection would be cooperation.[8] If this requirement is fulfilled for both participants, we say that the game is defection-stable in the sense that once either party defects, both will defect from that point on. A second requirement for an arms race between rational opponents is that CC > DC and CC > DD cannot both be true. If CC > DC, cooperation is preferred to unilateral defection, so there is no incentive to defect from mutual cooperation (a condition described as cooperation stability); if CC > DD, this stable outcome is preferred to mutual defection.[9]

The following nine orderings of the outcomes for each side fulfill the above conditions:[10]

1. DD > CC > CD > DC
2. DC > CC > DD > CD   (Prisoners' Dilemma)
3. DD > CC > DC > CD
4. DD > CD > CC > DC
5. DC > DD > CC > CD   (Deadlock)
6. DD > DC > CC > CD   (Deadlock-type)
7. DD > CD > DC > CC
8. DC > DD > CD > CC   (Deadlock-type)
9. DD > DC > CD > CC   (Deadlock-type)

[8] The game Chicken, which violates this condition, has been used by several authors for representing conflict situations. For an example, see Glen Snyder and Paul Diesing, *Conflict Among Nations: Bargaining, Decision-Making, and System Structure in International Crises* (Princeton: Princeton University Press, 1977). Chicken is highly unstable, however, and not a realistic model for an arms race as *continual* defection.

[9] We shall see later that some of these excluded games can lead to arms races when the assumption of perfect information is relaxed.

[10] The terminology for the various games is presented in Snyder and Diesing (fn. 8) and Jervis (fn. 1). Snyder and Diesing use a different selection of games since they are interested in international crises—events of short duration—rather than the more extended arena of arms races. Jervis focuses mostly on Stag Hunt, which is an important sub-case that we deal with in a subsequent section.

A. DEADLOCK

Four of these orderings are related to the game of Deadlock in that the two most preferred outcomes involve defection by the side whose preferences they reflect. Because Deadlock provides so little opportunity for the generation of a cooperative solution, and because such a single-minded preference for defection seems to make war inevitable, there has been a persistent tendency on the part of social scientists to imply that it is descriptive of no more than a handful of deviant cases (for instance, Hitler's Germany). Such an apocalyptic view of Deadlock may be naive for a number of reasons. Contrary to the theories of Richardson[11] and others, there is no compelling evidence that even substantial periods of continuing arms increases necessarily lead to war.[12] They may persist in an uncomfortable but generally peaceful, dynamic equilibrium or, more commonly, be brought to a peaceful conclusion by some exogenous shock. More important, Deadlock and Deadlock-type preferences may be characteristic of decision makers who share none of Hitler's impe-rialistic dreams. Consider, for example, a situation where internal con-stituencies press for military expenditures to increase the well-being of the arms industry. If this internal component carries sufficient weight in determining defense expenditures, the preferences of decision makers will be those of Deadlock: they will choose to defect regardless of the action of the rival state. In this case, their preferences are those of Deadlock—not because of an insatiable lust for war, but because they place a premium on a particular domestic constituency.

Nor is this the only situation in which Deadlock preferences may arise. If a government believes that its weapon systems are superior to those of its rival, or that the strategy that will guide their use is superior, it may prefer mutual defection to mutual cooperation. Whether it does or not depends (at least under our assumptions of rationality) on which option offers the greatest net benefit. There is some evidence to suggest that, before World War I, the Germans' belief in the superiority of their dreadnoughts and crews led to a perception that a matching shipbuilding effort on the part of the British was preferable to mutual cooperation. This belief was probably reinforced by another sort of utility calculation

---

[11] Lewis F. Richardson, *Arms and Insecurity* (Chicago: Quadrangle, 1960).

[12] Recent research by Michael Wallace draws a very close connection between arms races and war. See Wallace, "Arms Races and Escalation: Some New Evidence," *Journal of Conflict Resolution* 23 (March, 1979), 3-16, and "Armaments and Escalation" *International Studies Quarterly* 26 (March 1982), 37-56. Subsequent analysis casts very serious doubt on the relationship, however; see Henk W. Houweling and Jan G. Siccama, "The Arms Race—War Relationship: Why Serious Disputes Matter," *Arms Control* 2 (September 1981), 157-97.

that seems to have played a critical role in a number of arms races: that of relative strength. If state A has 10 tanks and state B has 50, the decision of A to acquire 5 tanks increases its total forces by 50 percent and increases its strength relative to B by 30 percent. Should B choose to match this increase, A still increases its relative strength by 27 percent. Thus mutual defection leaves A nearly as well off as unilateral defection, and possibly better off than mutual cooperation. The logic of this situation constituted the underpinnings of Tirpitz's German naval policy as it developed after 1899, and almost certainly played a role in defining the Deadlock-like preferences of the Germans in the 1930s and of the Soviets in the 1950s. Both began from a position that was so weak relative to their natural rivals that it could reasonably be expected to improve under mutual defection.

Finally, the presence of Deadlock or Deadlock-type preferences would help to explain the most striking findings associated with the evolution of cooperation in 19th- and 20th-century arms races: the relative scarcity of national strategies to end them, and the important role of exogenous events. What easier way to explain why nations so infrequently employed one of our three strategies to promote cooperation than to hypothesize that their preference was to arm regardless of what their rival did? What simpler way to explain why outside factors proved critical in ending an arms race than to suggest that the participants had no other incentive to do so? Although there are other explanations for both findings, their joint occurrence suggests the possibility that Deadlock is far more prevalent than is usually thought to be the case.

Let us now consider the ability of each of the three cooperative strategies to cope with a Deadlock-driven arms race. We will begin with the unilateral strategy, which increases the potential for cooperation without requiring any active participation or consensus on the part of the rival state. It does this by providing a state with the benefits of security that it would normally get from arms without provoking the rival to increase its armaments and therefore the intensity of the arms race.[13] A unilateral strategy possesses the virtue of leaving the initiating state better off (in the sense of gaining security) than it would be under a variety of other more formal cooperative arrangements, such as a bilateral freeze.

There are at least four types of unilateral strategies that can reduce the intensity of an arms race. The first (and the one that has received the most theoretical attention) involves a concentration on defensive as

[13] Jervis (fn. 1).

opposed to offensive weapons.[14] Recent proposals to increase the invulnerability of ICBMs to preemptive attack by hardening silos, employing mobile launch platforms, or developing a system of silo-defense ABMs instead of simply increasing the number and accuracy of ICBMs, have all been justified at least partly on the grounds that they will make the United States more secure without provoking a new round of arms escalation.[15] Curiously, historical examples of defensive weapons being acquired because of their ability to defuse an arms race seem to be quite rare. States have often chosen to build defensive rather than offensive weapons during an arms race, but they usually appear to have done so because they believe that such weapons offered the greatest amount of security for the money spent, and not because they thought that such weapons would lead to an end of the arms race. Thus, the British adopted a policy of building picket ships and fortifying the coast during their naval race with France in 1859-1861 without giving any particular thought to how the French would respond, or what impact it would have on their arms race.[16] These moves simply seemed to provide greater security than could be obtained through an exclusive reliance on ships of the line. The same absence of any unilateral strategy logic characterized Britain's defensive response to Germany's bomber build-up prior to World War II. The British chose to build fighters, radar, and anti-aircraft guns rather than bombers—not because they were afraid of provoking the Germans to still greater bomber production, but because they thought it was the optimal way to compete with them.[17]

A second type of unilateral strategy that can be used to break out of the security dilemma is the formation of defensive alliances. In the purest case, these function in precisely the same fashion as the acquisition of defensive weapons. The only difference is that, in this instance, defensive weapons are being "purchased" through the formation of an alliance instead of directly, thus permitting states to increase or maintain their level of security without engaging in the budgetary expenditures that weapons increases would entail. Just as in the case of a shift from offensive to defensive weapons, however, there are many instances of defensive alliances, but there have been few one could confidently assert to have been undertaken as part of a strategy to solve the security dilemma. When France and Russia entered into their alliance of 1894, they were well aware that their defensive capabilities were significantly

[14] *Ibid.*
[15] Freeman Dyson, *Weapons and Hope* (New York: Harper & Row, 1984).
[16] Cobden (fn. 5), 367.
[17] Ian Colvin, *The Chamberlain Cabinet* (New York: Taplinger, 1971).

enhanced; but they did not believe that their alliance would leave Great Britain (or Germany) undisturbed—which indeed it did not. The Byzantine pattern of defensive alliances that characterized Bismarckian Europe appears to have been more successful in preventing sustained arms races; but again, it is not clear that this was the primary intent of the actors.[18]

A third type of unilateral strategy involves the creation of buffer states. Ideally, this strategy provides both sides with greater security simultaneously. The creation of a neutral and independent Belgium in 1832 is a good example, although here the motivation had less to do with defusing an ongoing arms race than with avoiding one.[19]

A fourth type of unilateral strategy is based on the acquisition and surrender of intelligence information. The more accurate the information the United States possesses about Soviet weapons development, and the more quickly it is obtained, the more costly it is for the Soviets to try to escalate the arms race covertly. Providing the enemy with intelligence information voluntarily in order to convince it that its worst fears are unjustified is rare, but it has occurred. In 1853, the French Minister of Marine invited members of Parliament to visit French shipyards to allay British suspicions of a massive naval build-up.[20]

Because Deadlock creates no incentive to cooperate, it may appear that the various unilateral strategies are irrelevant to the problem of arms race de-escalation in such an environment. Although this is true in the sense that, under Deadlock, states do not choose to pursue a unilateral strategy in order to promote cooperation, they can nonetheless choose to do so from other motives with similar effect. Suppose, for example, that the motivation that lies behind a state's present preference for defection is a desire for greater security. If it believes that the net benefit in added security to be gained from an increased expenditure on defensive arms is greater than it would be if it cooperated and

[18] A.J.P. Taylor, *The Struggle for Mastery in Europe*, 1848-1914 (London: Oxford University Press, 1971).
[19] As British Foreign Minister Palmerston wrote after the London Conference:
France ought to feel the great advantages which this arrangment confers upon Her. By one stroke of the pen, the whole line of Belgick fortresses, so far as they constituted points of attack upon her territory, at once disappear; and this upon a frontier the nearest to her Capital, and the least protected by defenses of nature or of art. England voluntarily interdicts Herself . . . while the Northern powers of Europe, of their own accord, close the door through which they would naturally approach the French frontier in the event of hostilities leading them there. France ought therefore to see in this Protocol the most signal and unequivocal proofs of the pacific spirit which animates the other Powers of Europe . . .
Quoted in William Lingelbach, "Belgian Neutrality: Its Origin and Interpretation," *American Historical Review* 39 (October 1933), 60-61.
[20] Cobden (fn. 5), 259.

maintained the status quo, then it would adopt Deadlock-like preferences, but *behave* as if it had adopted a unilateral strategy. As we have
noted above, this is what seems to have been going on in the case of
British fortress and picket-ship construction. The behavior resembled
the implementation of a unilateral strategy, but the motive was Deadlock: the British preferred building forts and ships to mutual cooperation
with the French. It also seems to describe the logic of various members
of the Reagan administration with regard to the antiballistic missile.
That is, they appear inclined to proceed with an ABM system regardless
of whether the Soviets increase the number and sophistication of their
ICBMs, because they believe the United States would be better off with
such a system than it would be under a nuclear freeze. In cases like
these, the motivation is security rather than cooperation, but the outcome
is the same. The successful implementation of a perimeter defense system
in the case of the British, or an antiballistic missile system in the case
of the United States, reduces the marginal benefit of shipbuilding by
the French or the manufacture of ICBMs by the Soviets. If the French
and the Soviets were also motivated primarily by security considerations
rather than a desire to expand their ability to influence their rivals, these
actions should slow the respective arms races.[21]

Tacit bargaining differs from a unilateral strategy in that the actions
taken are made dependent on those of the other state; it differs from
conventional negotiation in that the role of verbal interaction is relatively
insignificant, and no attempt is made to create a formal agreement.
Perhaps the closest parallel is the reinforcement schedule used in behavior modification to reward and punish a subject in such a way that
he or she eventually "learns" a desired behavior. Of course, each state
here is simultaneously both "subject" and "experimenter." Tacit bargaining is not relevant to Deadlock-driven arms races, since neither state
has an incentive to cease defecting and to send a positive signal or, for
that matter, to pay attention to such a signal if it were sent.

---

[21] The question of whether it will in fact slow the arms race is a complex one. One could
argue that the other side will build fewer offensive weapons since the marginal benefit of
each is reduced; one could also argue that more will be built since more will be required
to obtain a given objective. Without further assumptions, either result is possible. Suppose
that one side established defenses so that each weapon of the other side is 10% less effective
than it was. This has two simultaneous effects. First, it raises by 10% the price of what
might be called a weapon effectiveness unit; that is, the amount of a weapon required to
accomplish a given objective. Second, it increases the number of weapons required per
weapon effectiveness unit by 10%. If the price elasticity of demand for weapon effectiveness
units is -1, then the 10% increase in price will result in a 10% decrease in the number of
weapon effectiveness units purchased. However, since 10% more weapons are needed for
each effectiveness unit, the number of weapons remains the same. If this elasticity is greater
than -1 (say -0.5), the number of weapons built will increase; whereas, if the elasticity
is less than -1 (say -1.5), the number of weapons built will decrease.

Negotiation, like tacit bargaining, may seem to hold little promise for reducing the intensity of a Deadlock-motivated arms race. Why negotiate if mutual defection is preferable to mutual cooperation? The answer lies in the fact that, while both states may prefer defection to cooperation within the confines of a particular game (i.e., the missile game, the dreadnought game, etc.), negotiation offers the possibility of linking that game to other issues (e.g., access to raw materials, recognition of territorial claims) in such a way that the net marginal benefit that each gains from cooperating within this larger game is greater than that of defection. Expressed more formally, the presence of additional issues transforms a basically zero-sum distributive game with no zone of agreement into a non-zero-sum integrative game in which both sides can benefit simultaneously.[22]

The trick is that, whatever these goods or policies are, they cannot have been freely exchanged prior to the negotiation. In that case, they would already have been exchanged for each other directly at an optimal level and there would be nothing to gain by introducing defense issues. The goods and policies must be linked to defense questions in such a way that an optimal level of exchange cannot take place in the absence of a negotiated arms agreement. In most arms races, they are not difficult to find. The U.S. and other states have frequently restricted the trade of raw materials, petroleum products, and various finished goods to countries with which they are engaged in an arms race. Any of these might plausibly be the basis for negotiating the end of a deadlocked arms race.

The role that sub-optimally exchanged goods and policies can play in ending a deadlocked arms race suggests that a national leader who has placed numerous economic and social restrictions on the state's interactions with a rival may be more able to negotiate the end of a deadlocked arms race than a leader who has imposed no such restrictions. This may help to explain why leaders with a reputation for great mutual hostility are often able to negotiate a settlement where their more moderate colleagues have failed. It is not simply because, as it is usually argued, they are both in a position to coopt their conservative followers as well as their more liberal opponents, but because they have so thoroughly linked other issues to the arms race that they have more to offer each other in return for cooperation.

B. PRISONERS' DILEMMA

Each of the cooperative strategies can be effective in coping with an arms race inspired by a Prisoners' Dilemma. Moreover, because mutual

[22] Raiffa (fn. 3), 131 ff.

cooperation in a Prisoners' Dilemma is more attractive than mutual defection, there will be an incentive to invoke these strategies. There are two problems with unilateral strategies in the context of the Prisoners' Dilemma with perfect information. One lies in the implicit assumption that the motivation of the rival is primarily that of security. If this assumption is correct, the rival state will not be motivated to respond to the initiating state's acquisition of defensive weapons, a defensive alliance, and so forth, because it will feel no more threatened than it did prior to such an action. If, on the other hand, the rival is motivated by a desire to exert influence over the other's policies, it will respond to a build-up of defensive weapons or a defensive alliance in roughly the same way (in terms of effort if not technology) as it would to a build-up of offensive weapons or the creation of an aggressive alliance.

The other problem with unilateral strategies is that a cost-effective alternative to the development of offensive weapons is assumed to exist. Frequently, however, this is simply unavailable, or decision makers do not think it is available. Before the development of the submarine there was no defensive alternative to the acquisition of capital ships, just as there has been no real alternative to the ICBM. Similarly—although one could argue that the problem was perceptual—on the eve of World War I national leaders saw no real alternative to responding to troop build-ups by other countries except with build-ups of their own.

The virtues of alternative tacit bargaining strategies in contexts of Prisoners' Dilemma have recently been explored in a most interesting way by Axelrod.[23] He found that a policy of reciprocity—or Tit-for-Tat—that begins with cooperation and thereafter prescribes a response that reflects the rival's behavior achieved the best results when competing with a host of other strategies in an iterative Prisoners' Dilemma computer simulation. This strategy is effective, not because it links the game to other issues, but because it forges a link between current behavior and future iterations of the same game. The "defect" strategy is clearly the one for both players engaging in a single-play Prisoners' Dilemma game, since it maximizes the individual benefit of each regardless of what the other chooses. That is often not the case, however, in a mutiple-play version of the same game where the number of plays is large and unknown. Here the advantages of a defection in any single game can be outweighed by the expectation that such a decision will cause the opponent to respond by defecting in subsequent plays. This can be costly because the gain to be obtained from a single defection may be quite modest when compared to the difference between mutual cooperation and mutual defection if the latter is multiplied by a large number that

[23] Axelrod (fn. 2).

represents the times the game is likely to be played in the future. Axelrod points out that this explains why firms only infrequently violate their contracts even in contexts where legal recourse is impractical. The gain from any single violation is small compared to the gain to be realized through subsequent dealings with each other.

The prospect of iteration plays a central role in arms decisions because there is always the possibility that any rate of arms increase or technological innovation will inspire a new race or intensify the existing one. Everything else being equal, the larger the number of expected iterations in a Prisoners' Dilemma arms game, the more likely it will be that the short-term benefits of an arms lead will be judged to be less than the long-term costs of a protracted arms race. A government interested in promoting cooperation can take advantage of this fact by convincing its rival that it will respond aggressively to any arms escalation by increasing its own armaments, and that it has the resources to do so indefinitely. That is very close to the official policy adopted by Britain at a number of junctures during the 19th century, perhaps most explicitly in the "two-power standard" by which the British government announced that it would maintain a navy that was at least as large as the combined forces of the next two most powerful fleets. The power of iteration to promote cooperation can also be seen in the tendency of arms agreements to focus on weapons that would make continued iterations especially costly (e.g., dreadnoughts rather than destroyers) and on new, unproven weapon systems that yield only modest short-run benefits for the "lead" state and promise vastly increased costs in the future (e.g., ABMs, space weapons).

An interesting but widely neglected aspect of increased intelligence capabilities is that they not only reduce the short-term advantages of arms increases and innovations by permitting one state the opportunity to catch up to the other before the difference in capabilities is strategically significant, but that they further increase iterativeness by providing an opportunity for many timely responses. As we shall see, this can be quite beneficial in the execution of tacit bargaining strategies.

Of course, in security matters it is not always possible for decision makers to convince themselves, much less an opponent, that the long-term benefits of cooperation outweigh the short-term benefits of defection. As Van Evera makes clear, the cult of the offensive created a situation prior to World War I in which each government believed that a slight advantage in forces or weaponry could quickly be translated into a military victory.[24] Under these circumstances, the long-run advantages of cooperation (which Axelrod terms "the shadow of the fu-

[24] Stephen Van Evera, "Why Cooperation Failed in 1914," pp. 80-117 of this collection.

ture") pale before the benefits of victory or the cost of defeat, and the threat of future non-cooperation becomes irrelevant. Obviously this is the same argument that is used to justify an absence of cooperation in the nuclear arms race. Not surprisingly, perhaps, there seem to have been few if any arms races in the last 200 years where the rhetoric of government officials on one or both sides has not been filled with warnings that everything will be lost if there is any delay in matching the arms growth of the rival. For example, in the 19th century the cost of a future arms race cast only a small shadow in Great Britain, when news of the first French ironclad raised the specter of imminent invasion across an "iron bridge" spanning the English Channel.[25]

As in the case of Deadlock, the key to the capacity of negotiation to cope with arms races inspired by Prisoners' Dilemma lies in its ability to transform the game (or at least reduce the relative benefits of defection) by creating linkages to other games and issues. Sometimes, when the advantage of unilateral defection over mutual cooperation (DC − CC) is small and the advantage of mutual cooperation over mutual defection (CC − DD) is large, this linkage may be modest and implicit. If state A violates the agreement, state B will go back to defecting (just as in the case with tacit bargaining) or refuse to negotiate on other issues where there is a mutual advantage that might be realized. At other times the linkage is made more formally. In either case, there must be a capability to withdraw the issue or game to which the linkage is made if a defection takes place; otherwise there is no incentive to continue cooperating.

While one is hard-pressed to find historical examples of arms races that have been partially de-escalated through the use of a unilateral strategy or tacit bargaining, there appear to be three instances in which negotiation has played an important role in settings in which the participants can plausibly be argued to have Prisoners' Dilemma preferences. These are the Washington Naval Treaty of 1922 and SALT I and II. The Washington Naval Treaty of 1922 put a limit on the battleship-building efforts of what were then the world's three great naval powers: Great Britain, the United States, and Japan. To assess the contribution of negotiation, we need to know how complicated the agreement was that produced the compromise of the capital-ship tonnage ratio of 5:5:3, and to what extent issues over and above that of battleship construction were necessary to bring it about. In answer to the first question, the agreement involved a number of Pacific security and trade issues un-

[25] Cobden (fn. 5).

related to battleship construction.[26] Great Britain and the United States received guarantees of an open-door policy regarding trade in China and the Pacific, and the return of Shantung province and key trans-portation systems to the Chinese. They also received guarantees that, with certain specified exceptions, Japan would not increase fortifications on the Pacific islands taken from Germany during World War I. The latter provisions were especially important to the U.S., which found itself controlling areas such as the Philippines and Guam that would have been virtually indefensible if the Pacific were dotted with Japanese naval bases. Both sets of guarantees were also important to the British since they could now avoid having to keep a large navy in the Pacific. In addition, the Washington Treaty provided the British with an excuse not to extend the possibly entangling 1902 Anglo-Japanese alliance that was about to expire. For its part, Japan received the *de jure* right to administer the possessions north of the equator that it had taken from Germany, and was able to head off the possibility of a mutual assistance pact in the Pacific between Great Britain and the United States.

It is plausible that no capital-ship treaty would have been signed in the absence of these other agreements. Great Britain could not have afforded to reduce its presence in the Pacific without settlement of the China question. The United States, while probably the power least wedded to battleships as the core of its navy, was in the process of building more such ships (see the 1916 Defense Bill and the 1919 Defense Appropriations Bill); it might have increased their number still further if it had been necessary to defend its Pacific possessions and free trade in the East. The Japanese, who had only recently reconfirmed their commitment to a policy of two squadrons of eight battleships each, would almost certainly have built more ships sooner if faced with an Anglo-American Defense Pact (a likely outcome in the absence of the Washington Treaty) and continued U.S. insistence that they abandon the possessions taken from Germany.[27] The comments of Secretary of State Stimson to Senator Borah in a letter 10 years later attest to the importance of the multidimensional character of the final settlement:

It must be remembered also that this treaty was one of several treaties and agreements entered into at the Washington Conference by the various

[26] Harold Sprout and Margaret Sprout, *Toward a New Order of Sea Power: American Naval Policy and the World Scene, 1918-1922*, rev. ed. (Princeton: Princeton University Press, 1943; reprinted by Greenwood Press, 1969); Robert A. Hoover, *Arms Control: Interwar Naval Limitation Agreements* (Denver: Monograph Series in World Affairs, University of Denver, Vol. 17, Book 3, 1980).

[27] Quincy Wright, *The Existing Legal Situation as It Relates to the Conflict in the Far East* (New York: Institute of Pacific Relations, 1939).

powers concerned, all of which were interrelated and interdependent. No one of the treaties can be disregarded without disturbing the general understanding and equilibrium which were intended to be accomplished and effected by the group of agreements arrived at their entirety. The Washington Conference was essentially a disarmament conference aimed at the possibility of peace in the world, not only through the cessation of competition in naval armament, but also by the solution of other disturbing problems which threatened the peace of the world, particularly in the Far East.[28]

Thus, in the case of the Washington Treaty, additional dimensions had to be added to the capital-ship problem for an agreement to emerge; the result was complicated enough to have required negotiation.

To a somewhat lesser extent, the SALT I agreement was characterized by similar complexities. It contained provisions that allowed each state significant differences in the levels and "mixes" of its strategic arsenal. Even the most basic trade-off that permitted the Soviet Union an advantage in the area of throw weight, and the U.S. a greater number of missiles, would have been difficult to attain through tacit bargaining. Salt II, with the infusion of cruise missiles, Soviet bombers, and the issue of forward bases in Western Europe, was even more complicated. Talbott, for example, recounts the trade in which the maximum level of 1200 MIRVed warheads preferred by the U.S. was accepted by the U.S.S.R. in exchange for an American acceptance of the Soviet preference for a limit of 2,250 strategic launchers.[29]

The importance of being able to link different weapon systems and different dimensions of the same system, and to introduce non-weapon dimensions such as territory and trade, is also demonstrated by the fate of disarmament talks in which the negotiating parties did not have these options at their disposal. In the first Hague conference of 1899, the agenda was constructed in a way that carefully separated weapons limitation talks from discussions of every other issue; the representatives were primarily military experts who had neither the authority nor the expertise to introduce political, economic, or territorial issues. While it would be foolish to argue that the conference would have been a success if this situation had been different, it is not unreasonable to say that the narrowness of the mandate under which the representatives operated helped to create a problem of structural control that made the achievement of any real progress nearly impossible.[30]

[28] *Ibid.*, 102.
[29] Strobe Talbott, *Endgame: The Inside Story of SALT II* (New York: Harper & Row, 1979).
[30] Calvin DeArmond Davis, *The United States and the First Hague Peace Conference* (Ithaca, NY: Cornell University Press, 1962).

III. Sources of Uncertainty:
Problems of Information and Control

The decision environments in which arms races actually take place pose a number of information and control problems which increase the range of games that can lead to arms races and affect the ability of any given strategy to produce cooperation. They are somewhat analogous to the market imperfections that play such an important role in public finance, in the sense that they both complicate the decision problem— in this case, obtaining cooperation in an arms race rather than maximizing marginal social benefit—and reduce the applicability of purely deductive analysis. Moreover, just as the importance of externalities, natural monopolies, or consumer ignorance is determined less by logic than through the observation of real markets, so the discovery of these complicating characteristics is grounded in the evolution of actual arms races. We will begin by enumerating several problems of information and control and considering how they can function to expand the range of games that can lead to arms races. Then we will show how they can cause the conduct of other games to vary from how they would be played under the assumption of perfect information.

A. STRATEGIC MISREPRESENTATION

Strategic misrepresentation takes place in a bargaining situation when, in order to obtain an advantage, one party pretends to have preferences that it does not. In the context of arms negotiation, the classic situation is one in which a state pretends to want a weapon system more than it actually does, in an attempt to extort concessions from its rival for halting its development. Unfortunately such bluffs are sometimes called, in which case the desire to maintain future credibility may require that the threat to build the system be carried out. *This means that under sufficiently unlucky circumstances almost any game can result in an arms race.* Schelling's classic example of the ABM provides one illustration; another may be found in connection with the MX missile. One can argue that a majority of Congress believes that the nonmobile MX is unnecessary or undesirable even without Soviet restraint. That is, a plausible pattern for congressional preferences in the absence of the missile's role as a bargaining chip to encourage Soviet concessions might be CC > CD > DC > DD, a situation that could never lead to an arms race under full rationality and perfect information in an isolated game. Yet, if the missile fails in its role as a bargaining chip, substantial numbers may nonetheless be built.

Another important arms race-related behavior that can be placed under the heading of strategic misrepresentation involves a pretense about capabilities rather than preferences. In the fall of 1957, the Soviet Union announced that it had orbited a satellite by means of an ICBM. In the months following this announcement, Khrushchev, through a combination of frequent public display of a limited number of missiles, clever rhetoric, and American ignorance, systematically misrepresented (and exaggerated) the actual ICBM capability of the Soviet Union, which was not close to that of the United States.[31] He subsequently attempted to exploit this "missile gap" to increase Soviet influence in various policy areas. Although he achieved only sporadic success, he did manage to alarm the American government about its supposed strategic weakness. The most significant evidence of this concern, of course, is to be found in the report of the Gaither Commission, which recommended large increases in defense expenditures as a response. President Eisenhower's attitude toward the balanced budget prevented him from fully embracing those recommendations, but he sharply accelerated existing ICBM programs (and the arms race)—an action that he would not have taken had the Soviets not misrepresented their capabilities.

B.   IMPERFECT INTELLIGENCE

Imperfect intelligence can inspire an arms race that would not take place in the presence of perfect information, and can permit one to continue when it is "unjustified." Cobden and Hirst both argued that the British consistently overestimated the rate of French ship production and the size of the French fleet in each of the Anglo-French naval races, and that they responded with building programs of their own that wildly escalated whatever race may actually have existed.[32] In fact, on at least one occasion there is evidence that the size of the French fleet was actually declining while the British were convinced that they were in an arms race.[33] Similarly, a minor arms race was on the verge of taking place between France and Germany in 1875 because German intelligence reported heavy French purchases of cavalry horses. It took considerable effort on the part of the French ambassador to reassure the German government that its information was simply wrong.[34]

More recently, the adoption of "worst-case analysis"—in which rivals build weapons in response to the largest increases that their opponent could implement—has exacerbated the rate of arms escalation. In their

[31] Arnold Horelick and Myron Rush, *Strategic Power and Soviet Foreign Policy* (Chicago: University of Chicago Press, 1966).
[32] Cobden (fn. 5); F. W. Hirst, *The Six Panics* (London: Methuen, 1913).
[33] Cobden (fn. 5), 240.
[34] G. P. Gooch, *Franco-German Relations*, 1817-1914 (London: Longmans, Green, 1923).

discussion of how the Pentagon under McNamara assessed "how much is enough," Enthoven and Smith note the inclusion of generous assumptions about Soviet capabilities; although they were recognized as unlikely, "because such threats were conceivable and within Soviet technical capability, they were explicitly and systematically considered in the force planning process."[35] An even more outspoken statement of the tendency to assume that enemy capabilities are greater than they appear to be was offered by General Curtis LeMay in justifying the Air Force's strategic posture. "We have to have sufficient military power to knock out all of the targets we know he has, or all the weapons we know he has, and I would like to have a little cushion to take care of some that we might not know he has."[36]

Imperfect intelligence expands the range of games that can lead to arms races by raising the possibility that one side will think the other side has defected even though this may not have occurred. If we retain the requirement that $DD > CD$ so that defection (or apparent defection) on the part of one side will cause the other side to defect as well, three additional games become potential sources of arms races.

10. $CC > DD > DC > CD$

11. $CC > DC > DD > CD$ (Stag Hunt)

12. $CC > DD > CD > DC$

These three games are not often analyzed; under full rationality and perfect information, each should inevitably lead to mutual co-operation because both parties will observe that this outcome is optimal for each of them individually and collectively. Moreover, all three games are cooperation-stable in the sense that there is no incentive for either party to defect from a cooperative solution.

The first and third bi-stable games (10 and 12) are not particularly useful because they require the unlikely circumstance that one party prefers mutual defection to defecting while the opponent cooperates. Stag Hunt, however, may frequently be an accurate model of actual arms races. It describes, for example, the classic situation in which a state acquires a weapon it would not have built on its own initiative because it believes that the rival is building it.[37]

[35] Alain Enthoven and Keith Smith, *How Much is Enough?* (New York: Harper & Row, 1971), 178.

[36] Quoted in William Kauffman, *The McNamara Strategy* (New York: Harper & Row, 1964), 284.

[37] Jervis (fn. 1).

C.   PROBLEMS OF INTERPRETATION

The ideologies of decision makers and the experiences they have in operating in the international system inevitably color the way they process information as well as their vision of what arms race game they are engaged in. Whenever there is uncertainty about the likely impact of an action or the significance of another state's behavior—which is almost all the time—these factors play a major role in determining how they will assess the situation. Ideologies function like a prior distribution in conditioning assessments of probability under uncertainty. The difficulty, of course, is that there is no guarantee that this experience or ideologically guided vision is accurate. In terms of its effect on the games that can generate arms races, the impact of experience and ideology is identical with that of poor information; all create the possibility that an arms race will emerge from a Stag Hunt.

Instances where experience has colored national decision makers' estimates of the game in which they were engaged, and increased their tendencies to intensify the arms race, are plentiful. U.S. attitudes toward arms control immediately after World War II were heavily conditioned by the ultimate failure of the Washington Treaty to prevent Japanese arms increases. Secretary Forrestal opposed proposals for sharing the secret of making the atomic bomb with the Soviet Union in large part because he felt the Soviets were Asiatic in their mentality and hence, like the Japanese, could not be trusted to live up to arms limitation treaties.[38] Secretary Byrnes's position was not appreciably different: "America scrapped battleships, Japan scrapped blueprints. America will not again make that mistake."[39]

Experience is one source of problems of interpretation, but it is not necessarily the most important one. Ideology is a close rival. The available evidence suggests, for example, that John Foster Dulles's ideology was such that he had difficulty recognizing cooperative behavior on the part of the Soviet Union. Thus, in 1956, when the Soviets announced a reduction of 1.2 million in the size of their armed forces, Dulles, when questioned by reporters, emphasized the lack of trustworthiness of Soviet leaders. Similarly, Dulles greeted apparently conciliatory gestures by Stalin's immediate successors as the "tricks of rotten apples."[40] Whether Dulles's interpretation of these specific Soviet acts is correct or not is

[38] Ernest R. May, "Lessons" of the Past: The Use and Misuse of History in American Foreign Policy (New York: Oxford University Press, 1973), 33.

[39] Ibid., 35.

[40] David Finlay, Ole Holsti, and Richard Fagen, Enemies in Politics (Chicago: Rand McNally, 1967), 60.

unimportant. The point is that Dulles's ideology made it difficult for the Soviets to communicate interest in initiating an end to any facet of the arms race if they so desired. In this context, an ideology that inspires the judgment that the rival has defected performs precisely the same function as imperfect intelligence that suggests that the rival is still "racing" when in fact it is not. We shall see that problems of interpretation can cause as much difficulty in sending a cooperative signal as they can in receiving one.

D. PROBLEMS OF CONTROL

Control problems contribute to the continuation of arms races whenever decision makers who intend to signal their willingness to cooperate (or even to defect in order to punish defection) cannot do so because other parts of the government are not responsive to their instructions or desires. In the midst of the Cuban missile crisis, President Kennedy became aware of the fact that his earlier orders to remove a number of obsolete and vulnerable (perhaps even provocative) Jupiter missiles in Turkey had not been followed. He again gave direct orders for their immediate removal, but such were the control problems that the initial result was nothing more than an examination of the options for defusing them.[41] What were the Soviets to make of all this? Were they dealing with a government willing to help them save face on the Cuban missile issue, or did the Americans intend to be provocative? For that matter, what were they to make of the Senate's failure many years later to ratify SALT II?

The control problem goes beyond the straightforward issue of whether or not direct orders are executed. As Halperin has pointed out, a well-timed leak to the press can significantly damage any policy that does not have wide support, and negotiations still in progress can frequently be destroyed by an untimely indiscretion.[42] Perhaps it is this realization that prompts national leaders to make use of personal envoys and summit meetings at critical stages in arms talks. Although the conventional explanation is that it is an adaptive response to overload in the regular channels of communication, it could also be due in some measure to a realization that the stakes are too high to risk a failure of control.

Uncertainty complicates the application of unilateral strategies in sev-

[41] Graham Allison, *The Essence of Decision* (Boston: Little, Brown, 1971), 142. An interesting line of inquiry challenges this account of the missiles in Turkey; see Barton Bernstein, "The Cuban Missile Crisis: Trading the Jupiters in Turkey?" *Political Science Quarterly* 95 (Spring 1980), 97-125.

[42] Morton Halperin, *Bureaucratic Politics and Foreign Policy* (Washington, DC: Brookings Institution, 1974).

eral ways. First, as we have already noted, if the rival is motivated more by ambitions to extend its power than by security concerns, then the unilateral steps the first state takes in order to feel more secure may only inspire still greater efforts on the part of the rival to exert its influence. The Maginot Line and the British fighter force both led the Germans to escalate their arms production and their tactical innovations. No doubt one of the reasons why the employment of unilateral strategies to promote cooperation is so rare is that governments are usually suspicious that their rival is motivated less by security than by the desire for greater policy leverage.

Second, the basic character of a particular weapon system or alliance is frequently a matter of interpretation. An example of this difference in interpretation can be found in the World Disarmament Conference held in Geneva in 1932. There it was proposed that offensive weapons be outlawed, while defensive weapons be allowed to remain in existence. Although they were able to agree that heavy tanks were clearly offensive weapons, the states that were represented at the conference disagreed about the character of *every* other weapon. The aircraft carrier, for example, was viewed to be offensive by the Japanese but defensive by the Americans.[43] Similar difficulties occurred in the different interpretations of frontier fortifications by the German and French governments in the 1930s. To the French, who by 1932 had invested a considerable amount in the Maginot Line, frontier fortifications were defensive. The German government, however, saw the region behind the Maginot Line as an area where troops could be concentrated for an attack on Germany. This view probably contributed to the construction of the fortresses on the Siegfried Line, which were placed directly opposite those of the Maginot Line.[44]

Although many alliances are intended to be defensive, they are not necessarily viewed as such by prospective opponents. The Anglo-French Entente of 1904 was created as a way of stabilizing Anglo-French relations in troublesome policy areas. Yet by 1905, the Germans saw the alliance as a design to threaten several of their interests, most notably their commercial interests in Morocco.[45]

The impact of the other complicating factors on the success of unilateral strategies is smaller than the impact of interpretation and often interacts with it. The quality of intelligence information can obviously

[43] George Quester, *Offense and Defense in the International System* (New York: Wiley, 1977).
[44] Anthony Kemp, *The Maginot Line: Myth and Reality* (London: Frederick Warne, 1981).
[45] Taylor (fn. 18), 404.

be important. The more open a government is about the character of its weaponry, the less likely it is that the worst-case scenario will dominate the other state's response. If a unilateral strategy is being pursued to mitigate an arms race, it is essential that the other side be convinced that any ABM system is useful only for silo defense, or that the work taking place at the missile silos is intended merely to harden them rather than to install multiple warheads.

Before exploring the impact of problems of information and control on tacit bargaining strategies, as represented by Tit-for-Tat, it is useful to distinguish the merits of reciprocity as an evolutionary strategy from its virtues as a strategy to end or reduce the intensity of a single arms race. As an evolutionary strategy, it is potentially applicable to the long-run development of everything from single-celled organisms to civilizations, and derives its strength from success or failure over many iterations. As a strategy to end a particular arms race, however, it depends on the expectations it creates about the probable consequences of arming or not arming to reduce the net benefit of defection or to transform the game from a Prisoners' Dilemma into something more benign. Not surprisingly, however, these expectations can be influenced by our set of complicating factors in such a way that the effectiveness of the Tit-for-Tat strategy is degraded. It should be noted that in Axelrod's experiments, Bayesian routines performed poorly;[46] nevertheless, expectations would still seem to be of great importance for tacit bargaining among states, for at least two reasons. First, a state faces another state with much more accurately established priors than if it faced a computer program of potentially arbitrary design. Second, a state has a much greater variety of information to condition on during the arms race than the computer program, which could only use the sequence of past defections and cooperations.

To appreciate the extent to which the effectiveness of Tit-for-Tat can be diminished by problems of information and control, it is helpful to construct a simple model. First, consider the problem of control. For reasons already discussed, when decision makers intend to perform a certain action X, such as taking missiles out of Turkey, there is only a certain probability (call it c) that X will be correctly implemented. Second, there is the problem of information flow. The action X that was initiated by the first party may or may not be accurately perceived by the second party. For example, the number of missiles put into or taken out of operation may be over- or under-estimated by the competing state.

[46] Axelrod (fn. 2), 192ff.

Third, the action X that may have been intended as cooperation (defection) may not be interpreted as such by the other state. This problem is especially acute when initiatives can potentially take place over a large number of weapon systems. If one side stops building ships but raises the rate of tank production, or slows its rate of constructing missile-carrying submarines but slightly increases cruise-missile production, will that be perceived as cooperation or defection? Can the initiating state be certain how such actions will be interpreted? Can the other state be certain how such actions were intended?

These problems may be hard to distinguish in practice. When information is poor, what one supposes the opponent to have done is heavily dependent on prior beliefs, conditioned by previous interactions. For this reason—and to keep the present discussion from becoming too complex—we will model problems of information and of interpretation together. If the opponent has done X, intended to be cooperation, let the probability that it will be perceived and interpreted as cooperation be q_1. If the opponent has done Y, intended to be defection, let the probability that it will be accurately perceived be q_2. In reality, control, information, and perception are not dichotomous; they occur in many shades along a continuum. Neither are defection and cooperation binary choices. Nonetheless, the simple model in which one pretends that all these factors are dichotomous is useful in that it eliminates many unnecessary complications.

It is interesting to see how complex the analysis may become in the presence of these factors. Suppose that state A decides to cooperate. If the action is correctly implemented (an event of probability c), cooperation is perceived with probability q_1. If it is incorrectly implemented (an event of probability $1 - c$), cooperation is perceived with probability $1 - q_2$. Thus, the probability of state B perceiving cooperation if A intended to cooperate is given by the upper right-hand value in Figure 2. Similar calculations lead to the other entries in Figure 2.

In the traditional, full-information, complete-control version of the model, the parameters c, q_1, and q_2 are all equal to one. If each party begins with cooperation, then with perfect information under Tit-for-Tat, the outcome is always CC. We may represent this as a vector of probabilities for the four states, CC, CD, DC, DD of (1.0, 0.0, 0.0, 0.0). Let us assume, however, that $q_1 = q_2 = 0.99$. With this only slightly more realistic assumption of a 1 percent chance of misperception (there is every indication that most arms races are plagued with a far higher figure), the long-run probabilities of the four outcomes are (0.25, 0.25, 0.25, 0.25). This means that the game stabilizes with at least one party

FIGURE 2

PROBABILITIES OF ACTUAL RESPONSES BEING PERCEIVED IN
VARIOUS WAYS ACCORDING TO ONE MODEL OF INFORMATION AND CONTROL

A's Intention	Chance that	
	B perceives Cooperation	B perceives Defection
Cooperate	$cq_1 + (1-c)(1-q_2)$	$c(1-q_1) + (1-c)q_2$
Defect	$c(1-q_2) + (1-c)q_1$	$cq_2 + (1-c)(1-q_1)$

defecting 75 percent of the time. Axelrod's results for a misperception variant of his tournament show it to be still superior to the other strategies entered, but those other strategies were designed under the assumption of perfect information.[47]

One reason for the sub-optimal outcome for Tit-for-Tat under conditions of imperfect information is that each side was too ready to defect after the apparent previous defection of the opponent. In this case, a little more patience would seem to be called for. A possible extension of this class of strategies is probabilistic Tit-for-Tat, in which the opponent's cooperation is followed by our cooperation with probability s and by our defection with probability $1 - s$, and in which the opponent's defection is followed by defection or cooperation with probabilities s and $1 - s$, respectively. When the opponent appears to have defected, we will defect with some probability less than 1, thus being somewhat more patient. To see how this works, let us assume that both countries have perfect control and that $q_1 = q_2 = 0.95$. Suppose that both countries decide to behave more forgivingly, treating a defection as a defection only part of the time: they behave as if q_2 were less than 0.95, say 0.5. In that case, the long-run probability vector is (0.83, 0.08, 0.08, 0.01), a much more satisfactory outcome. Even if only one country behaves forgivingly while the other pursues Tit-for-Tat, the outcome is (0.74, 0.10, 0.14, 0.02).

Axelrod has suggested that retaliation in Tit-for-Tat should be less than 1 in order to alleviate the consequences of a single defection, which under Tit-for-Tat with perfect information and control can lead to endless rounds of echoing or mutual defection.[48] It might be wisest to

[47] Ibid., 182ff.
[48] Ibid., 138 and 186ff.

combine this tactic with probabilistic Tit-for-Tat to produce a strategy that is, in effect, a probability distribution on the unit interval (where $0 =$ defection and $1 =$ cooperation) and values between 0 and 1 represent partial defection.

The same consequences of imperfect information hold true in an evolutionary sense. Suppose that conditions are such that $q_1 = q_2 = 0.95$. Under Tit-for-Tat (TFT), the state will cooperate on the first move and later do whatever the opponent is perceived to have done on the previous move. Modified Tit-for-Tat (MTFT) is similar except that it is more forgiving, behaving as if $q_2 = 0.5$. Using Axelrod's payoff matrix, the long-run payoff of TFT vs. TFT is 2.25, the payoff of TFT facing MTFT is 2.94, the payoff of MTFT vs. TFT is 2.74, and the payoff of MTFT vs. MTFT is 2.90. This means that a large population of TFT can be successfully invaded by MTFT so that TFT is not collectively stable under imperfect information. Of course, MTFT is not stable either; in equilibrium and in large populations, equal payoffs would be obtained if the population were 82.5 percent MTFT and 7.5 percent TFT. No doubt there is a strategy superior to either of these, but this remains a problem for future research.

The foregoing should not, of course, be taken as an indictment of tacit bargaining in general. Hirst credits a policy of reciprocity with having brought about the longest period of cooperation between the British and French during the 19th century.[49] In addition, Schelling has noted the emergence of several instances of arms restraint between the United States and the Soviet Union which were apparently achieved on the basis of tacit bargaining.[50] Nonetheless, it is important to recognize that tacit bargaining strategies can be very susceptible to problems of control, information, and interpretation. In a given context, the best solution may be to employ a Modified Tit-for-Tat, but an equally practical alternative may simply be to take elaborate measures to minimize control and information problems by bypassing normal channels, employing hotlines, and so forth. If these problems are effectively dealt with by either method, tacit bargaining strategies can prove invaluable in providing an opponent with incentives to cooperate in Prisoners' Dilemma or Stag Hunt.

The relationship between negotiation and problems of information and control is more indeterminate than was the case with the strategies

[49] Hirst (fn. 32), 39.

[50] Thomas Schelling, "Reciprocal Measures for Arms Stabilization," in Donald Brennan, ed., *Arms Control, Disarmaments, and National Security* (New York: George Braziller, 1961), 175. More recently, Russell Leng has shown the effectiveness of reciprocity-based tactics in Soviet-American relations. "Reagan and the Russians: Crisis Bargaining Beliefs and the Historical Record," *American Political Science Review* 78 (June 1984), 338-55.

of unilateral action and tacit bargaining. In part this is because one of the great strengths of negotiation lies in its ability to cope with the same information problems that can undermine the other strategies. The fact that the United States and the Soviet Union place a different value on throw-weight versus number of missiles, or that the Germans and the British placed a different value on numbers of battleships versus broadside weight can play havoc with a strategy of tacit bargaining, since neither side can fully understand what the other would view as reciprocity. Yet the difference in utilities that can be the source of so many problems of interpretation is precisely what negotiation can exploit in order to create an agreement.

The strategic misrepresentation that attends negotiation can occasionally create problems of information and interpretation that lead to still greater arms escalation. Before the onset of British mediation in the naval race of 1894-1902 between Argentina and Chile, the exaggerated claims and aggressiveness employed by both countries in their intermittent negotiations seemed to inspire ever greater hostility in the other party, and consequently increased arms competition.[51] Moreover, as we noted earlier, the use of bargaining-chip strategies, such as threatening to put in a weapons system that is really undesired in order to gain concessions from the other side, can lead to intensified arms competition that would never have taken place without negotiation.

The strategy of negotiation can also intensify an arms race by providing both sides with an incentive to bargain from as strong a position as possible. It is not difficult to deduce the arms-race implications of Richard Nixon's philosophy that no state should ever let its president go to the bargaining table as the leader of the second-strongest state in the world. Such states will prepare for peace talks by escalating the arms race, and probably feel compelled to maintain this pace if the talks collapse. Even more perversely, each will assume that the other will adopt this strategy—and this will increase the rate of arms acquisition still further. Note that this is different from the typical bargaining-chip strategy in that both states are arming rather than threatening to arm, and it is a problem that plagues neither unilateral action nor tacit bargaining.

IV. Conclusion

Both the "game" that underlies an arms race and the conditions under which it is conducted can dramatically affect the success of any strategy

[51] Robert Burr, *By Reason or Force: Chile and the Balancing of Power in South America, 1830-1905* (Berkeley: University of California Press, 1965).

designed to end it. If antagonists have Deadlock or Deadlock-type preferences, only negotiation can provide the means by which cooperation might be strategically achieved; even this possibility depends on the pre-existence of linkages between the arms race and the rules that govern interactions among the antagonists on other issues (for example, trade). Behaviors that resemble unilateral strategies may be employed and may reduce the intensity of the arms race, but they are not motivated by a desire for cooperation; they will only be adopted if they are optimal from the standpoint of security. Tacit bargaining strategies will not be employed at all. The possibility that Deadlock-driven arms races may be more common than is generally assumed helps to explain both why the use of cooperative strategies is relatively rare even in the set of arms races that have ended cooperatively, and why the cooperation that has occurred has often been prompted by an economic change and third-party intervention.

If an arms race can be described as a Prisoners' Dilemma (at least from the standpoint of preference orderings) conducted under conditions of perfect information, the outlook for cooperation and for the success of all three cooperative strategies is more sanguine—provided certain critical assumptions turn out to be correct. Assuming that both sides are driven by security needs rather than by a desire for policy influence—an assumption that may well be false—unilateral strategies may promote cooperation by reducing the benefit of an aggressive arms policy on the part of the rival, and the cost of subsequent cooperation for the state employing it. Assuming the benefits of future cooperation (the shadow of the future) to be great enough when compared to the potential costs of falling behind in the arms race—an assumption that states often seem reluctant to make—the tacit bargaining strategy of Tit-for-Tat can be an effective way of ending an arms race. Negotiation can succeed in a Prisoners' Dilemma environment by forging a link between the arms race and other games or issues. As long as the benefits of this linkage can be withdrawn to punish defections, there will be an incentive for continued cooperation.

When we drop the assumption of perfect information and admit the existence of problems of information and control that are often present in actual—as opposed to hypothetical—arms races, each of the strategies faces additional limitations. In the case of unilateral strategies, the biggest threat to success comes from problems of interpretation. What is viewed as defensive by a government interested in initiating the end of the security dilemma may not be so viewed by its rival. In the case of tacit bargaining, the problem of interpretation also looms largest, but those of information and control can be important too. Modest reductions in the probability that an action believed by the initiating state to be co-operative will be correctly executed, observed, and interpreted can lead to startlingly poor results for a tacit bargaining strategy that might succeed admirably under optimal conditions. In the case of negotiation, strategic misrepresentation can so muddle the character of interaction that what could have been a golden opportunity for cooperation is lost.

An understanding of the sources of uncertainty that frustrate the application of cooperative strategies also helps us to understand some of their special strengths. If the problems that are internal to their application can be overcome, they can help uncover critical facts about the nature of the arms race that is taking place, and defuse that com-ponent of it which derives from misperception rather than from fun-damental policy disagreement. Unilateral strategies can provide a par-ticularly safe avenue for trying to determine the motivations of an adversary and for identifying the game being played. If a defensive alliance or weapon system leads to far greater weapons activity than could reasonably stem from misperception alone, the game that the two states are playing is not Stag Hunt, and the rival state is motivated by policy influence goals as well as by security considerations. Simple tacit bargaining strategies conducted in a highly iterative setting with quick responses to small instances of cooperation and defection can provide a particularly good environment in which states can learn about each other's preferences and willingness to cooperate. Negotiation that is not itself plagued with misrepresentation can occasionally reveal information that, even in the absence of an agreement, leads both sides to believe that the intensity of an arms race can be safely reduced.

Finally, it might appear that the best way for a state interested in promoting cooperation to cope with the difficulties associated with each individual strategy is to pursue all of them simultaneously. Although certainly desirable from the standpoint of exploiting the ways in which they complement each other, this joint strategy suffers from the fact that they are often mutually exclusive. Negotiators may wish to maxi-mize their bargaining position and the credibility of their threats by increasing their weapons production and development prior to negoti-ations, but this precludes the give-and-take of a Tit-for-Tat bargaining strategy. When the weapons are offensive in character—as they often are in order to provide the rival with the maximum incentive to negotiate a halt to the race—unilateral strategies are difficult to implement. Tit-for-Tat is also somewhat inconsistent with unilateral strategies, since the "punishment" of an increase in offensive weapons on the part of the rival may necessitate a similar action in response. It is true, of course, that a unilateral strategy can be continued even as this punishment is being carried out, but the potential for misinterpretation will be dramatically increased by the heightened climate of tension that the act of punishment may produce. The existence of these incompatibilities makes it all the more important to understand their relative effectiveness under different circumstances.

TRADE WARS:
A Comparative Study of Anglo-Hanse, Franco-Italian, and Hawley-Smoot Conflicts

By JOHN CONYBEARE*

I. INTRODUCTION

IN trade wars, states are primarily concerned with economic objectives directly related to the traded-goods sector of the economy; the means used are restrictions on the flow of goods and services. This definition excludes phenomena such as wars of plunder, and embargoes to support military wars. Intervention in foreign trade became a major object of state policy in the early modern period, when the number of sovereign entities increased and trade expanded along inter-regional trade routes. With the possible exception of the 1930s, trade wars have received little *theoretical* attention. Political scientists and historians usually treat them as mere byproducts of larger political and military conflicts. Economists, more interested in questions of normative trade theory, tend to dismiss them as an irrational atavism.

Three trade wars are examined here with a view to suggesting factors that may promote or inhibit cooperation.[1] The Anglo-Hanse trade wars between the 14th and 17th centuries will be used to illustrate the problems of cooperation in situations of long, repeated conflicts, and to ask, in particular, why repetition did not lead to cooperation. A 10-year tariff war between France and Italy in the 1880s and 1890s will be explained in terms of the effects of structural asymmetry of payoffs on cooperation; to put it more simply, it will show that big powers can coerce small powers. Finally, the tariff wars centering on the U.S. Hawley-Smoot tariff of 1929 will exemplify some of the difficulties of achieving co-

* I acknowledge, with thanks, comments from Kenneth Oye and other contributors to this volume, as well as Jeff Frieden, Guilio Gallarotti, Charles Kindleberger, Todd Sandler, and David Yoffie.

[1] A study with a limited number of cases cannot purport to test theory, but it may aspire to the more modest objective of "history illuminated by theory." Since we are considering only cases in which trade wars actually occurred, illumination is restricted to the processes and outcomes of the wars, telling us little about why such wars occur. In order to answer the latter question, we would have to consider examples in which trade wars did not occur (e.g., the Anglo-German trade rivalry prior to World War I).

operation when a large number of countries are in the game. The relevance of these three dimensions (structure, iteration, and numbers) is briefly examined in Section II.

II. GAME-THEORETIC VARIABLES

A. STRUCTURE OF PAYOFFS

Variable-sum games[2] may be classified according to the players' preferences for outcomes. The three basic orderings of Prisoners' Dilemma (exemplified in the Anglo-Hanse case), Chicken, and Stag Hunt are explained in Kenneth Oye's introductory essay. Another possibility, also noted by Oye, is "Deadlock," in which actors have the preference DD > CC. Examples may be found in the U.S.-E.E.C. Chicken War of the 1960s, when the Common Market countries preferred to protect domestic chicken producers even in the face of U.S. retaliation against E.E.C. exports,[3] and in the 1983 case of U.S. restraints on imports of specialty steel, which resulted in retaliation by the E.E.C. Some of these preference orderings may be combined to produce hybrid games, of which those most relevant to the trade wars discussed here are Bully (where one player has a Deadlock preference ordering and the other has the ordering of Chicken) and Called Bluff (where an actor playing Chicken faces an actor playing Prisoners' Dilemma).[4] A trade war between a strong and a weak power (such as the Franco-Italian case below), or some of the bilateral conflicts during the Hawley-Smoot period (e.g., the United States versus Switzerland), may produce asymmetric payoffs approximating the Called Bluff or Bully games.

Cooperation in these games may be enhanced by reducing the gains from exploitation, increasing the costs of defection, and increasing the gains from cooperation.[5] In the Franco-Italian case, for example, France was able to increase the cost of defection to Italy. Reducing the cost of being exploited may increase cooperation if it transforms a game of Prisoners' Dilemma into Chicken (i.e., if the preference DD > CD is reversed). An increase in the probability of cooperation does not nec-

---

[2] There may also be zero-sum trade games, where the only type of cooperation we might observe would be the formation of "minimum winning coalitions," such as the current interest of the E.E.C. and Japan in excluding the developing countries from any share in the U.S. steel market.

[3] See Ross B. Talbot, *The Chicken War* (Ames: Iowa State University Press, 1978).

[4] The games of Deadlock, Called Bluff, and Bully are described in Glenn H. Snyder and Paul Diesing, *Conflict Among Nations* (Princeton: Princeton University Press, 1977), 41-48.

[5] See Robert Jervis, "Cooperation under the Security Dilemma," *World Politics* 30 (January 1978), 167-214.

essarily imply that the parties choose a higher degree of free trade. The probability that free trade will be chosen may involve conditions different from those just cited. Riezman argues that if the cost of being exploited is raised, the likelihood will increase that, if two countries cooperate to maximize joint income, the new equilibrium in a Prisoners' Dilemma tariff war will be free trade.[6]

The configuration of payoffs will be a function of at least four factors. First, the direct stakes in the issue are a function of such things as relative size, trade dependence, or stages of a business cycle. The pure theory of trade suggests that a large or sectorally hegemonic country should find its interest best served by raising trade taxes against weaker countries, thereby turning the terms of trade in its favor (i.e., raising its export prices and lowering its import prices).[7] The United States appears to have followed this strategy during much of the period described below as the Hawley-Smoot wars; so did England during its late-medieval monopoly on the supply of wool to Europe. Whether or not strong powers gain from restricting trade, they clearly have the ability to punish weaker countries by raising a weaker country's costs of defection while holding constant or even reducing their own costs at DD. The Franco-Italian case is an example. Finally, countries should perceive the gains from defection to be greater during periods of prolonged recession (e.g., the beginning of the Anglo-Hanse and Hawley-Smoot wars), or sectoral difficulties (e.g., the prolonged agricultural recession during which the Franco-Italian war occurred, or the current protection, by the developed countries, of industries in cyclical or secular decline, such as steel and textiles). The reason is that, if marginal utility for income rises as income falls (i.e., an extra dollar is worth more to you as your income falls), predatory trade policies will be more attractive during recessions.

A second factor consists of the dynamics of bargaining, including transaction costs, side payments, linkage to other issues, coalitions, and diplomatic skill. Transaction costs and the norms of violence figured

---

[6] Raymond Riezman, "Tariff Retaliation from a Strategic Viewpoint," *Southern Economic Journal* 48 (January 1978), 583-93. Specifying the payoffs in a two-dimensional utility space, Riezman's point is that the more acute the angle of the bargaining set bounded by CD-CC-DC, the greater chance that CC (representing free trade), rather than some other point on the line CD-CC-DC, will allow the countries to reach their maximum income (or highest joint indifference curve).

[7] The implications of this argument are explored in John Conybeare, "Public Goods, Prisoners' Dilemmas and the International Political Economy," *International Studies Quarterly* 28 (March 1984), 5-23. A quantitative example is provided by D. N. McCloskey, "Magnanimous Albion: Free Trade and British National Income," *Explorations in Economic History* 17 (July 1980), 303-20. McCloskey argues that Britain's national income was lowered by the transition to free trade in the 1840s.

prominently in the inability of the Anglo-Hanse relationship to maintain cooperative agreements. Linkage was involved in the trade war between France and Italy; it concerned the latter's renewal of its membership in the Triple Alliance in 1887.

Third, variables in domestic structure, particularly the relationship of the state to "rent-seeking" interest groups, may be both a determinant of and a constraint on state goals in a trade war.[8] International cooperation is usually reduced by such activities, as in the Anglo-Hanse and Hawley-Smoot cases, in which groups sought their private interests by urging uncooperative policies on the state.

Finally, there are cognitive factors. Just as a difference in religious background is a good predictor of divorce in the United States,[9] a state's stakes in cooperation will be affected by such factors as ideology, misperception, risk, and time preference. Weak powers, for example, may miscalculate their ability to influence a strong power, as in the cases of Italy raising tariffs against France in the 1880s and of Switzerland retaliating against the Hawley-Smoot tariff.

B.   ITERATION

In his introductory essay, Kenneth Oye notes that iteration, the "shadow of the future," may aid cooperation. Trade games are invariably iterated; a state can always respond to the other state's previous move (for example, by imposing a retaliatory tariff), thereby prolonging a trade conflict for as long as it sees advantages in doing so. Why then would we expect to see uncooperative outcomes in trade games? The interesting aspect of the Anglo-Hanse war is the question of why iteration over a long time did not help to sustain any lasting cooperation.

Iteration is a highly fragile means of effecting cooperation. Time may reduce cooperation as actors develop patterns of interaction that foster the escalation of conflict. The perceived payoffs of the game may also change over time, obscuring the iterativeness of the game. Institutional structures may reduce the iterativeness of games. The rules of the postwar General Agreement on Trade and Tariffs (GATT) on the arbitration of trade disputes (as in the case of the Chicken War) help to insulate a particular dispute from affecting future relationships in other trade areas, mainly by constraining the scope and magnitude of permissible

---

[8] Rent-seeking refers to groups that shift income to themselves by, for example, imposing tariffs on competing foreign goods; see David Colander, ed., *Neoclassical Political Economy* (Cambridge, MA: Ballinger, 1984).

[9] Gary S. Becker, Elisabeth M. Landes, and Robert T. Michael, "An Economic Analysis of Marital Instability," *Journal of Political Economy* 85 (December 1977), 1141-87.

retaliation. Paradoxically, this may reduce the incentive to cooperate in the dispute at hand.

The ability to direct retaliation properly so as to punish the actual perpetrators of uncooperative acts is critical to the success of contingent strategies in iterated games. This problem is usually present in trade wars. For example, when the American steel industry persuaded the U.S. government to restrict specialty steel imports in 1983, and the E.E.C. retaliated against other American exports, the steel industry could hardly be expected to moderate its protectionist demands. This problem may be avoided if the federal government can aggregate the total effect on the U.S. economy of steel import restraints and the attendant repercussions. In the Anglo-Hanse case, however, the chronic weakness of central government made it hard for retaliation to occur in a manner that would change the behavior of uncooperative, rent-seeking actors on either side. Thus, we have another set of factors affecting cooperation: large numbers and public goods.

C. NUMBERS OF ACTORS

Games in which it is difficult to retaliate against another player contain one element of a "public good" (namely, nonexcludability, where actors can take advantage of the cooperativeness of others while they themselves defect). Such games may become more uncooperative as the number of players increases, since each player's decision to defect and "free-ride" on the cooperativeness of others will have a decreasing effect on the total amount of cooperation occurring in the system.[10] Public-good games with large numbers of actors may degenerate into a Prisoners' Dilemma, in which each player's best strategy is to defect. This problem cannot be corrected by repeated plays, since iteration is only conducive to co-operation insofar as players can retaliate against defectors, which is not possible in the presence of publicness. The solution is either to construct institutionalized rules or "regimes" to constrain free-riding, or to remove the publicness from the game. GATT is an attempt at the former, and the Hawley-Smoot conflicts illustrate the latter strategy.

The principal means by which publicness enters modern, interstate trade policy is by way of the "most-favored-nation" (MFN) clause in treaties, specifying that a state cannot grant a concession (e.g., tariff reduction) to one state that it is not prepared to grant to all states with

---

[10] There is now a huge theoretical literature on the conditions under which large numbers will reduce public-good cooperation; for a recent critical analysis, see Richard Cornes and Todd Sandler, "Easy Riders, Joint Production and Public Goods," *Economic Journal* 94 (September 1984), 580-99.

which it has MFN treaties. MFN clauses caused some problems during the 19th century (such as in the Franco-Italian case), but were not a major obstacle to cooperation: there were relatively few players in the system (i.e., it was a small-number, public-good problem with little free-riding), and trade treaties were of short duration and generally re-negotiated all at once, which made it easier to prevent or remove any unrequited benefits conferred on other states. Most-favored-nation clauses created severe public-good problems in the 1920s, when there were more states in the system; the major trading state, the United States, itself attempted to free-ride by refusing to negotiate tariff re-ductions while claiming the benefits (through the MFN clause) of other countries' negotiations. The Hawley-Smoot case shows the techniques that may be brought to bear on free-riding in international trade: quotas, regional pacts, short treaties, "escape clauses," and negotiation with principal suppliers only.

III. ANGLO-HANSE TRADE WARS, 1300-1700: A CASE OF ITERATED NON-COOPERATION

A. HISTORY

Competitive toll-levying hindered medieval trade. A 13th-century English observer of the toll system on the Rhine clearly perceived the sub-optimal joint tax effect, describing it as the "raving madness of the Teutons."[11] One factor encouraging the development of international trade in the later medieval period was the rise of a consortium of northern European trading towns known as the Hanseatic League. The merchants and political leaders of these cities saw that there could be an advantage in collusion and monopolization of trade routes so as to maximize joint profits. The Hanse consisted of 200 cities, lead by Visby, Lübeck, Co-logne, and Danzig. Moving wool and cloth east, and raw materials (such as metals, furs, grain, and tar) west, the Hanse dominated northern trade through the economic and (rarely) military power of its members, ob-taining unreciprocated trading rights in critical ports such as London, Antwerp, Bergen, and Novgorod.

Foreign merchants were allowed to trade in Mercia (the English midlands) by a treaty between Offa II and Charlemagne in 796. German

---

[11] Quoted by M. M. Postan, "The Trade of Medieval Europe: The North," in Postan, *Medieval Trade and Finance* (Cambridge: Cambridge University Press, 1973), 108. See also Postan's "The Economic and Political Relations of England and the Hanse from 1400 to 1475," *ibid.*; Phillipe Dollinger, *The German Hanse* (Stanford, CA: Stanford University Press, 1973); and E. G. Nash, *The Hansa* (London: Bodley Head, 1924).

traders were in England at the time of Ethelred (978-1016), and were given special privileges by all the early Plantagenets. The Hanse established itself in the Steelyard (a small area on the Thames docks) by means of a royal charter (Carta Mercatoria) given by Edward I in 1303, and then spread to other English ports such as Lynn, Ipswich, and Boston. England had less extensive rights in Hanse towns. Xenophobia and the material interests of merchants who suffered discrimination in Hanse cities or competition in the English market demanded restrictions on the Hanse—mainly higher import duties and export taxes. Trade taxes became a major source of the Crown's revenue, especially under Edward III after the outbreak of the Hundred Years War in 1338.[12]

The conflict broke out when English merchants petitioned the King to redress their inequitable treatment in Hanse towns. Formal demands were made in 1377, followed by suspension of the Hanse's privileges until it granted equivalent rights in 1380. The agreements were not firm enough to prevent mutual restrictions on trade (including English piracy), leading to reprisals and counter-reprisals. Divisions within the Hanse led to a new treaty in 1388, reestablishing trade, limited rights of extraterritoriality, and restraint on trade taxes. The Hanse abrogated the treaty in 1398 and excluded English merchants, allegedly as a result of persisting piracy. Again, divisions within the Hanse as well as in England, together with the weakening effect of the Teutonic Wars on the Prussian Hanse towns, led to a new treaty in 1408. Both the first and second trade wars resulted in the Hanse's recognition of English trading rights in the Baltic, though these were still not equal to the Hanse's privileges in England.

The third trade war began in 1410, when Prussia revoked some English privileges in retaliation for English delays in fulfilling the financial terms of the previous treaty. England retaliated (again including piracy), Prussia counter-retaliated, and the conflict escalated until a truce was reached (1426-1430). England kept up the pressure for full trading rights in the Baltic, while English merchants in Prussia were forced to put up a bond which was to be forfeited if taxes were raised on the Hanse in England. As in the past, interests on both sides perceived the costs of defection. The English war in France was going badly, leading to a withdrawal from Paris in 1436. Loss of the alliance with Burgundy (1435) hampered the English cloth trade in the Low Countries, making

[12] See George Unwin, ed., *Finance and Trade Under Edward III* (Manchester: Manchester University Press, 1918); Jean Froissart, *Chronicles* (1369-1390; reprint trans. and ed. by Geoffrey Brereton, New York: Penguin, 1968). England had a near-monopoly on the supply of wool to Europe, and behaved like a rational hegemon, taxing wool exports heavily from 1275.

the Baltic trade more important. Parliament resisted war-financing measures, thereby increasing the need to rely on the trade taxes provided by the Hanse. The Hanse was also divided: Western Hanse towns were unwilling to lose their lucrative entrepôt trade with England because of Prussia's desire to exclude the English from the Baltic trade, and a group led by Lübeck threatened to conclude a separate peace. A treaty giving England full trading rights in the Baltic was concluded in 1437, but was not ratified by Prussia.

England initiated the fourth war in the course of the domestic disunity which culminated in the War of the Roses (1455-1485). A royal ordinance of 1442 had eased restrictions on privateering, leading to an attack on the Hanse trading fleet in 1449, followed by naval clashes. A truce in 1456 broke down quickly. A fifth war began in 1458, when English privateers under the Earl of Warwick plundered a large Hanse fleet on the pretext that it had refused to salute the English flag. England got the better of the ensuing naval wars, though merchants were unhappy about the loss of trade, particularly after the seizure of Hanse goods in London in 1468. Finally, the Hanse took advantage of the War of the Roses by financing and equipping Edward IV, who defeated the Lancastrians at Barnet (1471). Edward then concluded the Treaty of Utrecht (1474) which allowed the Hanse extensive privileges in England while English traders obtained virtually no rights in the Baltic. The Hanse's share of trade with England reached its highest levels around 1480, while the English trade in the Baltic dwindled.

The final conflict was played out over the next two centuries, as a comparative advantage in cloth, supported by an expanding shipbuilding industry, enabled England to dominate the nearby European markets and ultimately to break the Hanse's monopoly in the Baltic.[13] Hanse towns were induced to withdraw from or to exclude the League; Cologne and Hamburg concluded treaties with England in the 1560s. Regulated companies, such as the Merchant Adventurers in the west and the Eastland Company (chartered in 1579) in the Baltic, facilitated the English penetration of these markets. Edward VI abolished the Hanse's special privileges in 1552 and Queen Elizabeth closed the Steelyard in 1598. Though allowed to re-enter by James I, the Hanse never recovered. Its commercial monopoly was broken; and, squeezed by more powerful states (Denmark, Sweden, Prussia, Russia, Poland) during the Thirty

[13] This last period is covered by Henryk Zins, *England and the Baltic* (Totowa, NJ: Rowman & Littlefield, 1972); R.W.K. Hinton, *The Eastland Trade and the Commonweal in the Seventeenth Century* (Cambridge: Cambridge University Press, 1959); and J. K. Fedorowicz, *England's Baltic Trade in the Early Seventeenth Century* (New York: Cambridge University Press, 1980).

Years War (1618-1648), the League held its last diet in 1669. In any case, the focus of European trade was shifting away from the Baltic and toward the Atlantic.

The 17th century marked a period of aggressive English commercial expansion. Mercantilist writers of the time thought England should raise tariffs (on the grounds that English exports were "necessities" but imports were "toys"), and that this could be done while England claimed the benefit of most-favored-nation treaties with its trading partners.[14] This strategy not only demonstrates an understanding of modern trade theory (namely, that strong powers can increase their national income by raising tariffs; see fn. 7), but also bears a remarkable resemblance to that of another rising hegemon: the United States in the 1920s. Keynes once noted that the mercantilists "attained to fragments of practical wisdom which the unrealistic abstractions of Ricardo first forgot and then obliterated."

As the Hanse declined, English policy focused first on Holland and then on France. The Cockayne project banned the export of unfinished cloth, causing the Dutch to ban the import of finished English cloth, and in turn leading James I to ban the export of raw wool, until both sides gave up in 1617. England then resorted to the Navigation Acts (effectively a tax on imports and exports by foreigners) and finally to naval warfare (1652-1674). A much longer tariff war with France then ensued, beginning with Colbert's tariff on woolens in 1664. England retaliated by briefly banning French imports and then imposing prohibitive tariffs which were not alleviated until Pitt's commercial treaty of 1786.[15]

B. ANALYSIS

The Anglo-Hanse situation was a Prisoners' Dilemma in which both sides sought to further the interests of their own merchants and producers (and, on the English side, to tax trade for revenue) at the expense of the other side (outcomes DC and CD), and ended up with mutually undesired trade restraints (DD).[16] On many occasions the actors suc-

---

[14] See Jacob Viner, "English Theories of Foreign Trade Before Adam Smith," in Viner, *Studies in the Theory of International Trade* (1937; reprinted, Clifton, NJ: A. M. Kelley, 1975), 63.

[15] See George Edmundson, *Anglo-Dutch Rivalry During the First Half of the Seventeenth Century* (Oxford: Clarendon Press, 1911); W. O. Henderson, "The Anglo-French Commercial Treaty of 1786," *Economic History Review* 10 (August 1957), 104-12; Ralph Davis, *The Rise of the Atlantic Economies* (Ithaca, NY: Cornell University Press, 1973).

[16] The costs of restraints were more severe than at present because transport costs and taxes constituted a high proportion of the total price. Increases in taxes had a severe effect on trade flows, compounded by the loss of economies of scale in transport costs when taxes were raised, and thus further reducing trade.

ceeded in negotiating themselves back to relatively free trade (CC), but cooperation could never be sustained. The most interesting analytic question is why several hundred years of iterated conflict could produce no lasting cooperation. There are three categories of answers to this question: transaction costs, rent-seeking, and economic recession.

First, transaction costs (i.e., identifying the actors involved, bargaining with them, and monitoring the agreement) were very high. Time lags in negotiation were long. Putting together a negotiating party and sending it to the other side took several years and was physically dangerous for the negotiators—not only because of the long journey and exposure to violence, but also because, upon returning home, they might find that domestic coalitions had changed.

Second, changing domestic rent-seeking coalitions complicated negotiations. In England, there were divisions between merchant interests, consumers wanting cheaper supplies, and the Crown's need to tax foreigners for revenue. The first group was well represented in Parliament, which had by 1350 wrested control of trade taxes from the Crown and promoted the monopolization of trade by cartels such as the Company of the Staple, which controlled wool exports. The merchants were, however, divided between those who competed with the Hanse for the Baltic carrying trade (and had the mixed interest of the Prisoners' Dilemma); those who supplied products in direct competition with the Hanse, and had no interest in negotiation (preferring a Deadlock situation); and those who had no interest in the Baltic, but needed the Hanse's trade routes through the Low Countries into central or southern Europe, and hence preferred unilateral cooperation (i.e., the preferences of Stag Hunt). Consumer interests were represented by the nobility within the King's Council; the weight of interests fluctuated according to the relative strengths of baronial parties, relations with Parliament, and popular xenophobia against the Hanse. Some members of the King's Council (the Earl of Warwick being one example) were not above financing pirate attacks on Hanse ships when their private gains outweighed their interests as consumers of Hanse imports. English nationalism fitted in well with certain baronial and merchant interests. Finally, the Crown's interest in tax revenue opposed the interest of those who wished to cut the Hanse's trade to a minimum.[17]

---

[17] As in the case of OPEC today, the probable low elasticity of demand (i.e., response of demand to changes in price) for English cloth and wool meant that a tax on cloth or wool exported by the Hanse could raise revenue without greatly reducing the quantity of trade, everything else being equal (but cf. fn. 16). Cloth duties were less than 10%, but by 1470, wool taxes rose to the equivalent of 25% for denizens and 48% for aliens; trade taxes provided 30-50% of the Crown's revenue. See E. M. Carus-Wilson and Olive Coleman, *England's Export Trade, 1275-1547* (Oxford: Oxford University Press, 1963), 22-25, 194.

Similar divisions appeared in the Hanse. Western towns, such as Hamburg and Cologne, favored cooperation because their main function was to channel English cloth and wool into central and southern Europe. Towns that competed for the Baltic shipping trade (Lübeck) or produced competing cloth products (Danzig) were less cooperative and had little interest in compromise. Exacerbating these divisions were struggles between various Hanse towns for control over the League, and the tendency of individual towns to conclude separate trade agreements with rivals of the League. With several dozen major members and a total membership of over 200 cities, the Hanse had a severe internal Prisoners' Dilemma problem insofar as many members could do better by breaking the League's monopolistic restrictions. Though Hanse diets voted by majority rule, individual members could avoid compliance by absenting themselves from meetings. The major weapon against dissent was expulsion, which worked less and less well as the League lost its monopolistic control over trade routes and was unable to offer sufficient incentives to nondefectors. Because of the number and diversity of its cities, the League could maintain its existence only by insisting on strict adherence to its monopolistic goals; it was increasingly unable to enforce these as its hegemony over northern European trade declined.

Another rent-seeking factor operated directly on the shadow of the future, increasing actors' discounting to the point where, for many, there was no shadow at all. The use of violence as a Tit-for-Tat strategy of retaliation occurred in a manner conducive to escalation rather than to restraint because it effectively removed the shadow of the future for defectors. On the English side, privateers (often owned by members of the King's Council) could attack Hanse ships, safe in the knowledge that the aggrieved Hanse cities would retaliate by seizing the goods of English merchants in those cities rather than by seeking out the interests of the privateers. Similarly, Hanse merchants could press for the exclusion of English merchants from their towns in the knowledge that retaliation would not hurt them, but other groups of Hanse interests. In general, the system of reprisals promoted escalation by shifting the retaliatory or future costs of current defection to others. In the case of seizures of goods, plaintiffs could obtain from their home authorities a "letter of reprisal" entitling them to seize assets of equal value from *any* citizen of the country of the offender. This introduces a large-number public "bad," since defectors cannot be excluded (via reprisals) from enjoying the fruits of their defection in the future.[18]

---

[18] This example reinforces a point made in Section II, that large-number public-good problems may not evolve into cooperation because there is no mechanism for punishing

Third, even if we ignore domestic rent-seeking and consider the problem to be that of a bilateral Prisoners' Dilemma, the potential for cooperation was reduced by the effects of economic recession (see Section II). The wars began during the calamitous 14th century. Sustained economic depression, worsened by the plague and the Hundred Years War (1337-1453), enhanced the gains from defection even if these gains were short-lived due to retaliation. The final stage of the conflict occurred during a major English recession, which lasted from 1590 to 1640 and was aggravated by the Thirty Years War. These recessions raised the current marginal value of predatory income transfers. They may also have increased the rate at which the benefits of future cooperation would be discounted; more simply put, desperation reduces the shadow of the future.

England's subsequent trade wars with Holland and France had some of the same qualities. The conflicts with the Dutch started off over the same kinds of issues that had inflamed Anglo-Hanse relations, but quickly developed asymmetries as England used its naval supremacy to finish off the trade war and Holland as a world power. The war with France was more symmetrical, and also bears some resemblance to the Anglo-Hanse wars, particularly in the pattern of division of domestic interests. On at least one occasion—the Treaty of Utrecht (1713)—domestic interests on both sides prevented trade from being reopened.[19] The development of cooperation was hindered by two additional factors not as evident in the Anglo-Hanse case. The prevailing doctrines of mercantilism promoted a view of trade as a zero-sum game in which there was no gain to cooperation. Perhaps even more important was the linkage of the Anglo-French trade dispute to larger, chronic military conflicts—the Wars of the League of Augsburg (1689-1697), Spanish Succession (1702-1713), Austrian Succession (1740-1748), the Seven Years War (1756-1763), and the American War of Independence (1776-1783).[20]

IV. The Franco-Italian Tariff War of 1887-1898: Cooperation with Asymmetric Payoffs

The 19th century is often wrongly described as the century of free trade. Freer trade among the developed countries did not preclude

---

defection. On the problem of violence as a public "bad," see Philip Neher, "The Pure Theory of Muggery," *American Economic Review* 63 (June 1978), 437-45.

[19] Viner (fn. 14), 117.

[20] See Derek McKay and H. M. Scott, *The Rise of the Great Powers: 1648-1815* (London: Longman, 1983).

policies that hindered the primary exports and industrial development plans of the then less developed areas of Europe. The major trade treaties of the mid-century were instances of "but a brief moment when the self-interest of the developed nations temporarily suggested mutual tariff reductions at the expense of others."[21] The Franco-Italian and two other tariff wars of the period—between France and Switzerland and between Germany and Russia—might well be subtitled "the visible boot." They illustrate the problems that arise for a weak power that provokes a tariff war with a strong power without realizing the extent to which the strong power can inflict massive punishment and force the weaker one to make important concessions to bring the game back to a semblance of mutual cooperation.[22]

A. HISTORY

Italian tariffs on French goods had been constrained by agreements arrived at in 1859, 1863, and 1881. The Italians, desirous of stimulating their manufacturing industry and providing themselves with bargaining chips for access to other markets for their agricultural exports, imposed a new tariff in June 1887 which levied an average import duty of 60 percent.[23] They renounced existing treaties and renegotiated those with Austria-Hungary, Switzerland, and Spain. The treaty with Germany was continued in order not to anger a powerful trade partner. In the case of France, the Italians miscalculated; France refused to negotiate a new treaty. The basis for this error was a belief that disruption of Italian agricultural exports to France would hurt the latter far more than themselves (Russia later made the same mistake in bargaining with Germany). In September 1887, Italy reinforced what it clearly thought was a strong bargaining position by adding the demand that France reduce its tariffs on the major Italian exports of silk, wine, oil, and cattle, threatening an even higher tariff on French goods if this demand was not met.

Without an agreement, French goods became automatically subject

[21] Alan Milward, "Tariffs as Constitutions," in Susan Strange and Roger Tooze, eds., *The International Politics of Surplus Capacity* (London: Allen & Unwin, 1981), 62.

[22] Though size and strength are highly correlated, vulnerability to the disruption of trade, rather than smallness *per se*, is the source of bargaining weakness. In these cases, vulnerability is a result of both a high level of agricultural production relative to GNP and a high degree of commodity and geographic concentration of trade; these factors are combined with, and partly reflected in, low total and per capita income.

[23] For background, see Frank J. Coppa, "The Italian Tariff and the Conflict Between Agriculture and Industry: The Commercial Policy of Liberal Italy, 1866-1922," *Journal of Economic History* 30 (December 1970), 742-69. The main source for the tariff wars described below is Great Britain, Parliament, *Parliamentary Papers* (Commons), "Reports on Tariff Wars Between Certain European States," Cmnd. 1938 (Commercial No. 1, February 1904).

to the high rates of the new Italian tariff.[24] In February 1888, Italy broke off negotiations after the French parliament had voted a punitive doubling of tariffs against Italy if it refused to take the old 1881 treaty as a basis for negotiations and to make additional concessions to France (which had already raised duties on some Italian agricultural exports). The British Embassy in Paris reported, "National pride prevented Italy from entertaining these proposals. France was unwilling to modify them, and the language used toward Italy in the French Chamber precluded further negotiations."[25] France applied the punitive duties to Italy on February 27, 1888; Italy's reprisal followed on March 1.

In July of the same year, Italy offered France a 50 percent reduction on the rates in the 1887 tariff. The French refused, insisting on the old rates in the 1881 treaty, which, even with a 50 percent reduction, were lower than the 1887 rates. Italy gradually gave ground, and by December 1889 agreed to abrogate the penalty tariff against France. France did not remove its penalty tariffs against Italy until 1892, when the new Meline tariff came into effect, and even then kept Italy on the maximum rates of this dual tariff. It was not until 1898 that France gave Italy minimum tariff status, except on wine and silk, which had been 58 percent of Italian exports to France in 1887. In return, Italy gave France minimum tariff status, and also reduced tariffs on some 60 goods of special interest to France.

An important factor throughout the dispute was that Franco-Italian political relations were inflamed by colonial rivalries and problems of the intra-European balance of power.[26] In 1881, France had established a protectorate over Tunis despite the large Italian settlement in that former part of the Roman Empire. More important was the Italian renewal of the Triple Alliance in 1887, the revised treaty including assurances of German support against France in North Africa. In July 1888, Italy persuaded Britain and Germany to warn France not to attack the Italian fleet at La Spezia.

During the early period of the conflict, France generally sought to use economic punishment, including not only tariffs but exclusion from French capital markets, as a way of forcing Italy away from the Triple Alliance. As this only appeared to worsen relations with Italy (the Triple Alliance was again renewed in 1891), France abandoned the linkage of

[24] Many tariff systems at this time had dual rates: on each commodity there was a low MFN rate for countries that granted similar concessions and a higher general rate for countries that did not.

[25] Great Britain (fn. 23), 15.

[26] On the diplomatic background to the tariff war, see Walter B. Harvey, *Tariffs and International Relations in Europe, 1860-1914* (Chicago: University of Chicago Libraries, 1938).

economic sanctions to alliance diplomacy, though it did require Italy to give up its claims to Tunis (agreed in 1896), and did not relinquish the economic objectives of the tariff war. The end of the tariff war coincided with a period of general Italian weakness, both domestic (the bread riots of 1898) and foreign (military defeat by the Ethiopians in 1896).

The magnitude of the costs to Italy may be gauged by noting that between 1887 and 1897 Italian exports to France fell by 57 percent (an annual loss of FF176 million in revenues), while French exports to Italy fell by 21 percent (an annual loss of FF41 million). Italian exports to France were 40 percent of total exports in 1887, while French exports to Italy were less than 6 percent of total exports. With a national income half that of France, there is little doubt that Italy suffered more heavily. Between 1880 and 1900, Italy's relative per capita income declined from 74 percent to 64 percent of that of France.[27]

Two other tariff wars which occurred during this period were almost identical to the above case.[28] From 1892 to 1895, the French were involved in a tariff war with the Swiss, which stemmed from Switzerland's refusal to accept the new rates in the 1892 Meline tariff, even though it had been offered the minimum rate. The Swiss applied new, higher tariff rates to France, which retaliated by putting Switzerland on the highest rates in the Meline tariff. The war ended when the Swiss accepted an offer that left them with less than they had been offered in 1892.

At the same time, Russia and Germany were engaged in a tariff war that originated in Russia's attempts to raise its tariffs on manufactures for development purposes and simultaneously lower Germany's agricultural tariffs. Believing their grain supplies to be indispensable to Germany, the Russians attempted to force the issue by raising tariffs on German manufactures to the maximum provided by their latest (1891) tariff rates. Germany retaliated with a 50 percent penalty tariff, and Russia counter-retaliated with a similar penalty. The war, which lasted from August 1893 to March 1894, ended when Russia accepted Germany's original response to its demands: Russia was granted the minimum agricultural tariff that it had desired, but had to reduce tariffs on some 120 German manufactures in addition to giving most-favored-nation status to Germany.

[27] In 1970 U.S. dollars, Italy's per capita income in 1890 was $466, and its GNP was $15 billion; France's per capita and GNP were $668 and $26 billion. Data from N.F.R. Crafts, "Gross National Product in Europe 1870-1910: Some New Estimates," *Explorations in Economic History* 20 (October 1983), 387-401.

[28] See Great Britain (fn. 23); and U.S. Department of Commerce, Bureau of Foreign and Domestic Commerce, *Tariff Relations Between Germany and Russia (1890-1914)*, by L. Domeratzky, Tariff Series No. 38 (Washington, DC: GPO, 1918).

B.   ANALYSIS

The games played here had primary goals of promoting the balance of trade by increasing exports and reducing imports. Countries that were less developed (Italy, Russia) also desired to expand their "infant" manufacturing sectors. The original structure of payoffs in these games appears to have been Prisoners' Dilemma. Unilateral exploitation (DC) was clearly the first preference of all parties, and CC was preferred to DD since the trade war hurt both sides. The preference DD > CD, the critical factor distinguishing Prisoners' Dilemma from Chicken, is less clear; however, since retaliation could recoup at least some of the costs of being exploited, the Prisoners' Dilemma preference of DD over being exploited is the most plausible inference.

In all three cases, the weaker country initiated defection by denouncing trade treaties and unilaterally raising tariffs against the more powerful one. The strong power then moved quickly to increase the costs of mutual defection for the small power, mainly by punitive tariff surcharges. Though the stronger country's "fighting" tariff would be roughly equal in *ad valorem* terms to the surcharges imposed by the weaker one, the latter was hurt relatively more due to its smaller size and the greater proportion of its trade that was concentrated on the stronger trading partner.

The strong powers made it clear that they could increase the costs of defection for the weak ones—possibly making the game Chicken for the latter, while themselves treating it as Prisoners' Dilemma. This would have created the game referred to in Section II as Called Bluff. In any case, the costs of mutual defection were sufficiently high to the weak powers for them eventually to make major concessions in order to return the game to a higher level of cooperation—but one that was more favorable to the strong power than when the conflict began (i.e., an outcome leaving the weak power better off than at DD, but worse off than if it had left the game at CC in the first place).

In the course of the conflict, the strong states may even have come to see advantages in punishing the weak states (i.e., DD > CC), resulting in the asymmetric game of Bully. France's belief that the economic punishment of mutual tariffs might pull Italy away from the Triple Alliance may have been strong enough to cause a preference reversal to DD > CC. Germany, just before its tariff war, began to diversify its sources of agricultural imports away from Russia by concluding trade treaties with alternative suppliers, which may have caused a similar reversal of preference.

These games are fairly well explained by the rational strategic consequences of differences in power, and there is little need to resort to a lower level of analysis. Though rent-seeking interests were obviously affected by the strategies employed, they do not seem to have been markedly at variance with the goals sought by the economic diplomacy of decision makers; the intensity of preferences may have differed across actors, however. Hence our game analysis need not deviate much beyond the rational incentives revealed by the structure of the game itself. The one question is why the weaker powers provoked or even initiated defection in the first place.

The weaker powers seem to have either misperceived the nature of the game (Italy, Russia) or attempted to free-ride on the stronger power's tolerance of minor exploitation (Switzerland). In each case, the less developed country wanted to increase its manufacturing tariffs while inducing the other to lower its agricultural barriers. Italy and Russia both believed that France and Germany could not do without their agricultural products, and their statesmen may have thought they were playing a game of Chicken that could be won with a provocative demonstration of resolve, such as denouncing a trade treaty and unilaterally raising tariffs against the stronger power.

The weaker powers may also have underestimated the ability or desire of the stronger ones to link tariff conflicts to military alliances. French alarm over the Triple Alliance added to the incentives for punishing Italy that already existed in the tariff game. Raising Italy's costs in a tariff war was thought to help the French campaign to force Italy out of the Triple Alliance, though it hindered the resolution of the trade conflict by requiring conspicuous compliance with an act of compellence. The trade war did not end until France abandoned this demand. Linkage also played a role in the Russo-German tariff war, though in this case it was less explicit and was initiated by the weaker power. In December 1893, at the height of the tariff war, Russia signed a military convention with France. Though it is impossible to say how much this benefited Russia in the negotiations to end the tariff war, the Kaiser himself was reported to have said that he would not risk war for the sake of "a hundred crazy Junkers" who stood to gain from tariffs on Russian agriculture.[29]

Finally, the long agricultural recession in Europe, lasting from the late 1870s to the mid-1890s, was more painful for the less developed countries. They derived a major part of their national income from agriculture, and their stronger trading partners purchased most of their agricultural exports. The recession led both France and Germany to try

[29] Cited in Harvey (fn. 26), 84.

to export their domestic agricultural problems by "beggaring" their suppliers with high agricultural tariffs. The precariousness of the weaker countries in this situation might have led them to believe that they would be better off having a tariff conflict while they still had large market shares in France or Germany, giving them a degree of bargaining leverage that might not always be present; Germany, as we have noted, was actively reducing its reliance on Russian agriculture, thus producing a *negative* shadow of the future for the weak country. A similar situation might be faced by a state that attacks another state, not because it has great confidence in victory, but because it believes that in the future it will be more vulnerable.[30]

That such asymmetric games should gravitate toward the DC outcome for the more powerful country is hardly surprising, and may be observed in contemporary trade conflicts. The current U.S. policy of reducing steel imports to 18.5 percent of the American market will require that steel from developing countries be substantially shut out. The costs to the exporters will be very high, since they have few substitute markets and their capacity for retaliation against the United States is minimal. Hence they are playing a game of Chicken in which the costs of mutual defection are very high for the developing countries but not for the U.S., which can play a Prisoners' Dilemma strategy of not cooperating regardless of the actions of the developing countries.

V. The Hawley-Smoot Trade Wars: Cooperation with Large Numbers in a Public-Good Game

A. HISTORY

The Hawley-Smoot tariff wars illustrate how the introduction of a public-good element into international trade (namely, the most-favored-nation or nondiscrimination norm) may, when combined with large numbers of actors, produce chronic defection even when the game is iterated. They also demonstrate how hegemonic predation (via high tariffs) may be countered by collective retaliation. In this case, it was primarily the United States that attempted, successfully during the 1920s, to free-ride on the rest of the world by demanding that other countries accord it MFN status without any reciprocal tariff concessions. The predictable result was that American tariffs remained high while the U.S. benefited from tariff reductions by the rest of the world. This

---

[30] See Stephen Van Evera, "Why Cooperation Failed in 1914," in this collection, on "windows" of vulnerability as a cause of World War I.

situation was possible in part because of the publicness of MFN systems and in part because of the economic power of the United States. The solution adopted by the other members of the system was to reduce the degree of publicness with exclusionary devices (such as country quotas), thus turning the problem of large numbers into a set of bilateral interactions where retaliation—the shadow of the future—could foster cooperation.

The problem of most-favored-nation clauses had existed prior to World War I, but was greatly exacerbated by developments stemming from the war—such as new, war-created industries, new countries, and reparations. Most important was the fact that many more countries were involved in tariff negotiations, producing the large-number public-good problem. International tariff conferences, such as the World Economic Conference of 1927, were able to slow the escalation of the problem. However, in the wake of the rise of U.S. tariffs in 1929—known as Hawley-Smoot—the Geneva Conference of 1930 concluded that multilateral solutions should be abandoned in favor of bilateral negotiations.

The United States had had few successful experiences with tariff bargaining before the 1934 Reciprocal Trade Agreements Amendment (RTAA). Several tariff acts of the 1890s gave the Executive the authority to offer reciproal concessions, but these agreements (the Argol and Kasson treaties) were rejected by Congress. Prior to the 1890s, U.S. tariff acts had provided only for retaliation. A 1934 report by the Tariff Commission noted that from 1840 to 1923 the U.S. had concluded only three reciprocity treaties (with Canada, Newfoundland, and Hawaii), and these more for political than for economic purposes. The 1922 Fordney-McCumber tariff initiated an approach to bargaining that exemplified the power of a rising hegemon: the U.S. declared that its tariffs were "autonomous" (set to equalize costs of production and therefore not negotiable); at the same time, the United States also wished to negotiate most-favored-nation treaties with other countries so as to benefit from their tariff negotiations, and was prepared to apply penalty duties of up to 50 percent to any country that refused. By 1934, only 29 unconditional MFN treaties had been concluded, mostly with small or weaker countries.[31] Following the 1929 passage of the Hawley-Smoot tariff, 61 other countries raised trade barriers; some formed regional blocs, and many insisted on the strict bilateral balancing of trade. The

[31] United States, Tariff Commission, *Tariff Bargaining Under Most Favored Nation Treaties* (Washington, DC: GPO, 1934). The difficulties of negotiating MFN treaties while an autonomous tariff was in effect were not lost on contemporary observers; see Percy W. Bidwell, "Tariff Reform: The Case for Bargaining," *American Economic Review* 23 (March 1933), 137-51.

RTAA authorized the President to reduce tariffs by up to 50 percent in bilateral negotiations, and 21 such agreements were made by 1940.

Though the Hawley-Smoot tariff represented the peak of the tariff war, other countries contributed to the breakdown of the most-favored-nation system.[32] France, for example, had attempted to abandon MFN clauses in 1919, but concluded a number of intra-European MFN treaties in 1927. Under threat of retaliation, France gave the same benefits to the United States even though no MFN treaty existed between them. Thereafter, France circumvented the MFN clause by means of country quotas and cartel arrangements with Germany, Holland, Belgium, and Czechoslovakia. In the wake of Hawley-Smoot, France retaliated by reducing U.S. quotas while still giving MFN tariff treatment to the United States; it also renegotiated many of its other treaties with a view to making MFN "conditional" (i.e., benefits were extended to third parties only in return for reciprocal concessions). As a result, there were some tariff wars with other states (e.g., with Brazil in 1931). In general, France sought to construct an economically unified Europe on the basis of quotas and cartels—the same objective that it now has in the E.E.C., though it is currently called "organized free trade."

The consequence of Hawley-Smoot was that Britain, Germany, and France began to make regional and barter arrangements with smaller client states. The U.S. tariff helped to precipitate the formation of a full Empire-preference system. Some Commonwealth countries had already retaliated against the United States; Britain, having failed to convince other European countries of the case for tariff reductions, gave in to pressure from Australia and Canada for Empire preference, hoping it could be tied into some scheme for European unity. Introducing the Import Duties Act of 1932 to the Commons, Chancellor of the Exchequer Neville Chamberlain stated, "We also mean to use it for negotiations with foreign countries which have not hitherto paid very much attention to our suggestions, and, at the same time, we think it prudent to arm ourselves with an instrument which shall be at least as effective as those which may be used to discriminate against us in foreign markets."[33] The British tariff of 10 percent did not provoke retaliation because other countries were relieved that it was not higher, and because Britain concluded 15 bilateral agreements with interested (non-Empire) countries.

Smaller countries dealt with Hawley-Smoot in a more circumspect

[32] Tariff conflicts before and after Hawley-Smoot are described in Joseph M. Jones, *Tariff Retaliation* (Philadelphia: University of Pennsylvania Press, 1934).
[33] Quoted from Hansard, *ibid.*, 234.

manner. Italy raised tariffs and conducted a domestic campaign against the purchase of American cars and radios. Spain's tariff of 1930 raised duties on major imports from the United States. Switzerland, fearful of retaliation if it denied MFN status to the U.S., retaliated with public boycotts of American products, raised tariffs generally, and instituted country quotas on imports. Austria did the same, and negotiated disguised preferential trading groups with neighboring countries. Other small countries formed discriminatory regional arrangements (e.g., the Benelux countries in 1932).

B. ANALYSIS

These tariff wars occurred primarily over balance-of-trade goals, though the ultimate objective was to improve domestic employment at the expense of other countries. Most participants ended up at a mutually uncooperative outcome with lower employment. The Depression enhanced the benefits of predatory employment and income transfers, raising the gains from a strategy of unilateral defection in a trade game. The key to understanding the Hawley-Smoot wars is, however, the role of the MFN clause in creating a large-number public-good problem, which for most actors suggested a Prisoners' Dilemma payoff structure.

Some of the smaller countries tried to play a Stag Hunt game, retaliating only after having failed to persuade larger powers to restrain tariff increases. Switzerland, for example, lobbied heavily in the United States to prevent Hawley-Smoot tariff increases on major Swiss exports such as watches, and retaliated only after these efforts had failed. The reasons for this more cooperative strategy are that the costs of mutual defection and the gains from mutual cooperation are higher for small countries, since relatively more of the gains from trade go to the small countries in the first place; furthermore, small countries could only hurt themselves by applying a unilateral or a retaliatory tariff to a much larger trade partner (i.e., $CC > DC$ and $CD > DD$).[34] A sizable portion of their national income was produced in the traded-goods sectors of their economies, and their exports had a high level of both commodity and geographic concentration with respect to their larger trading part-

[34] This is a standard result from the pure theory of trade, deriving from the argument that trade will occur at prices set by the domestic prices in the larger country, due to the size of its market; hence the smaller country will have higher export and lower import prices, implying more favorable terms of trade and greater overall gains from trade. By the same logic, a large country will improve its terms of trade and welfare by imposing a tariff on a smaller country's exports. The smaller country can only lower its welfare by applying a tariff to the larger country, because it cannot change the terms of trade but only reduce the volume of trade, thereby hurting itself and possibly the larger country.

ners,[35] which meant that there was less publicness due to their greater vulnerability to retaliation, even within the constraints of an MFN system. Hence these small countries faced a payoff structure that combined Chicken and Stag Hunt (i.e., stating the small power's policy first: $CC > DC > CD > DD$), in which they hoped to get large-power cooperation by threatening and (for credibility?) carrying out retaliatory defection, even though this hurt the smaller power more than the larger one. A U.S. tariff should have lowered the price of Swiss watches, raising U.S. welfare (and employment in the American watch industry); Switzerland retaliated with a tariff that could not lower the price of American cars, but reduced trade, and probably made both parties worse off (see fn. 34). Yet defection in an iterated game of Chicken may make dynamic sense if it induces the stronger party to cooperate.

The period from the mid-1930s to World War II was marked by the evolution of a moderate degree of cooperation, most of which was due to the use of techniques that constrained the public-good problem inherent in MFN clauses.[36] The most widely used device was to make MFN "conditional" or to superimpose geographic quotas, exchange controls, or explicitly discriminatory regional arrangements on it. Some treaties also contained damage-limiting devices such as short renewal periods and what have now come to be known as "escape clauses," providing for the withdrawal of concessions under vaguely specified contingencies.

More subtle tactics involved formal adherence to MFN principles but limited the geographic scope of negotiations. One of these was to avoid multilateral negotiations in which all parties would agree to general, across-the-board tariff cuts (the benefits of which would be unevenly distributed across states) in favor of purely bilateral negotiations in which uncompensated benefits could be more closely monitored. The strategy adopted by the United States in implementing the RTAA after 1934 was to negotiate only with principal suppliers, giving tariff reductions on merchandise imported primarily from one other country, in exchange for which that country reduced tariffs on merchandise imported mainly from the U.S. Even more devious was the tactic of restricting tariff reductions to raw materials, which actually *raised* a country's effective rate of protection.[37]

[35] See Albert O. Hirschman, *National Power and the Structure of Foreign Trade* (Los Angeles: University of California Press, 1980), 98-116.

[36] On the techniques for internalizing MFN publicness, see Richard C. Snyder, *The Most Favored Nation Clause* (New York: King's Crown Press, 1948); Snyder also classified 510 trade treaties on this criterion in "Commercial Policy as Reflected in Treaties from 1932 to 1939," *American Economic Review* 30 (September 1940), 787-802.

[37] The effective rate of protection is the nominal tariff weighted downward by the penalty

The 1930s provide us with another example of the predatory opportunities available to large powers. As noted above, a hegemonic power can use its monopolistic presence in the market to extract "rents" or income redistributions from the rest of the world by imposing optimal trade restrictions. Most-favored-nation norms make optimal predation slightly more difficult since the hegemon cannot impose optimal tariffs on each commodity from each country and must be content with a single tariff on each commodity. Furthermore, a predatory strategy may be difficult if smaller powers retaliate in unison, as they did immediately after the passage of the Hawley-Smoot tariff. The adoption by the U.S. of the principal-supplier method of negotiation ameliorated both of these problems. It inhibited any coordinated opposition by offering benefits of value only to each individual country with which the United States was prepared to negotiate, approximating the tactic of divide-and-conquer. By limiting negotiations to commodities exported primarily from one country, it also circumvented the problem of optimizing a tariff structure under the MFN condition of disallowing geographic discrimination.

Despite the common belief that the RTAA represented a dramatic change in U.S. trade policy, the evidence is more consistent with the thesis of hegemonic predation. By 1940, average nominal tariffs in the U.S. had declined to 36 percent—far below the 54 percent of 1933, but not much less than the 39 percent of 1928. The RTAA gave away little. Tariff reductions were allowed only when import-competing industries would not suffer "unduly burdening" costs. Most of the agreements were concluded with small or weak countries supplying raw materials to the United States. Of the total 899 "concessions" granted by the U.S. between 1934 and 1939, only 258 were on manufactures. Between 1934 and 1947, average nominal tariffs fell by 43 percent on foodstuffs, 31 percent on crude materials, 21 percent on semi-manufactures, and 19 percent on finished manufactures.[38] As the tariff on inputs fell more than the tariff on outputs, the effective rate of protection (see fn. 37) on manufactures was reduced by very little during the 1930s—certainly by less than 19 percent. The trade policies of the 1930s represented a change in the tactics rather than in the overall strategy of the United States. It is likely that the high tariff raised the national income, as it did for

---

value of inputs that are imported and pay a tariff. Hence, a country that lowers its tariffs on inputs such as raw materials, leaving output tariffs constant, will raise the effective level of protection for the output good.

[38] United States, Tariff Commission, *Operation of the Trade Agreements Program, July 1934-April 1948, Part III, Trade Agreements Concessions Granted by the U.S.* (Washington, DC: GPO, 1948), 66.

Britain as a result of its 1932 tariff.[39] In the absence of coordinated retaliation by the rest of the world, large powers can create games with asymmetric payoffs that give them relatively greater gains from defection.

VI. CONCLUSION

The preference structure of the static Prisoners' Dilemma is less conducive to cooperation than that of Chicken or Stag Hunt. Economic recessions exaggerate the Prisoners' Dilemma problem by raising the actors' marginal gains from predatory income transfers. Unfortunately, this game appears to be common in trade conflicts, except where there is asymmetry of size among the actors. Asymmetries, however, may not immediately inspire cooperation on the part of small or weak countries, because they may miscalculate (e.g., overestimate the larger power's incentive to cooperate), perceive the conflict as inevitable (and more desirable sooner than later), or perhaps feel the need to maintain credibility by defecting, even at some cost to themselves. Asymmetry may foster cooperation once the weaker power has been punished enough to prefer compromise to further resistance. A strong country may see little need to cooperate with a weaker one, partly because its market power may make high tariffs attractive even in the face of retaliation.

Issue linkage should, in the absence of high transaction costs, facilitate cooperation by enabling preferences to be more accurately expressed. Confusion or miscalculation of the intensity of preferences is one such transaction cost. Linking the Triple Alliance to its trade war with Italy did not bring that conflict to a close because France tried to make its cooperation in the trade war conditional upon Italy's pulling away from the Triple Alliance. The linkage had the unintended effect of pushing Italy closer to Germany, delaying the end of the trade war. On the other hand, Russia's military flirtation with France probably encouraged Germany to cooperate by presenting the latter with potential costs that were more important than total victory in the trade war. In some cases, linkage simply may not be credible, as in the threatened linkage of U.S. troop levels in NATO to the removal of E.E.C. tariffs on U.S. chickens in the early 1960s. Finally, linkage may not be accompanied by any real

[39] Several studies argue that by 1938 Britain's national income was about 2.3% higher than it would have been in the absence of the tariff; see Forrest Capie, *Depression and Protectionism: Britain Between the Wars* (London: Allen & Unwin, 1983), 106; see also McCloskey (fn. 7). One study of U.S. tariff policy suggests that U.S. welfare is raised slightly by a tariff; see Giorgio Basevi, "The Restrictive Effect of the U.S. Tariff and Its Welfare Value," *American Economic Review* 58 (September 1968), 840-49.

bargaining offers; France and England used their tariff war in the 18th century to add to the military damage they were inflicting on each other, but rarely attempted to bargain over the link.

All trade conflicts are iterated, but some are more iterated than others, and the shadow of the future affords states the opportunity for sequential bargaining that may lead to cooperation. Yet such cooperation may easily be disrupted by domestic rent-seeking actors who have no stake in cooperation, by transaction costs and particular norms of retaliation, and by the existence of publicness. The publicness of MFN rules, combined with large numbers, removes the shadow completely unless exclusionary devices or a coercive regime are available.

The GATT experience illustrates how some of the problems mentioned in this paper may be ameliorated by institutional incentives to cooperate. Most important is that GATT raises the payoff for cooperation and the costs of defection by way of the norms of "reciprocity" (rewarding concessions by other countries with concessions of equal value) and "retaliation" (sanctions—including revocation of most-favored-nation status—against free-riders). In the 1960s, this enabled the public-good benefits of MFN to be retained and enhanced by the shift from bilateral to multilateral negotiations.[40] GATT is also a forum for discussion, which not only emphasizes the iterativeness of the game, but also provides a circumscribed arena that helps prevent contagious trade disputes from spilling over into other issue areas or even into trade issues other than the one in question—though it may also reduce the shadow of the future (see Section II). GATT may also mitigate the problem of asymmetry with its generalized norms of equality among members and the promotion of its ideology ("Free trade is good for you"). Clearly, if GATT is to continue to play this role, states must refrain from taking issues out of the GATT regime and into bargaining environments where asymmetry, linkage, and domestic rent-seeking may reduce cooperation.

The main problems here are the nontariff barriers negotiated outside of GATT. Since states cannot be forced to bring such issues within the purview of GATT, the best tactic might be to present GATT as a forum that would facilitate bargaining over nontariff barriers rather than attempt to ban them. The first objective would be to construct a code of measurement so that these barriers could be cardinally comparable (e.g., as equivalents of an *ad valorem* tariff). States could then be given a

[40] Moving from bilateral to multilateral negotiations increases the amount of public-good spillover (see Section V), particularly favoring small countries when in the form of across-the-board tariff reductions. However, multilateral talks may also increase transaction costs; the Kennedy Round of multilateral negotiations from 1963 to 1967 took considerably longer than the previous Dillon Round of bilateral negotiations in 1960-1961.

number of marketable "points" (based on value of trade diversion or welfare losses) that permit a predefined amount of protection. These points could then be traded in the same way that firms in the United States can buy or sell pollution permits.[41] This method of lowering transaction costs will not ensure cooperative trades, but it might encourage states to keep their negotiations within the rules of GATT without sacrificing the short-term flexibility required for political reasons. It is unlikely that GATT can do anything to alter the underlying structure of payoffs beyond smoothing the path for negotiations. Increasing the punitive powers of GATT to raise the costs of defection is more likely to drive states out of the regime completely. Nor can GATT do much more to increase the benefits of joint cooperation, since the gains from trade are exogenously determined by, among other things, factor endowments, technology, product cycles, and demand patterns.

[41] See T. H. Tietenberg, *Emissions Trading* (Washington, DC: Resources for the Future, 1985).

THE STERLING-DOLLAR-FRANC TRIANGLE:
Monetary Diplomacy 1929-1937

By KENNETH A. OYE*

I. INTRODUCTION

THE interwar years encompass a full spectrum of international monetary cooperation and conflict. Between 1925 and 1931, Great Britain, France, and the United States formed and maintained a gold exchange standard. The monetary powers established parities between each key currency and gold, increased international liquidity by using both gold and key currencies as reserve assets, and defended parities through coordinated intervention on exchange markets and through domestic deflation. Between 1931 and 1936, monetary relations were marked by serial devaluation and compartmentalization. The devaluations of sterling in 1931 and the dollar in 1933 were paralleled by movement toward bilateralism and the emergence of competing economic blocs. Between 1936 and 1939, Britain, France, and the United States jointly managed the devaluation of the franc and the depreciation of sterling. Although exchange rates were not stabilized under the Tripartite Stabilization Agreement, the central monetary powers avoided renewal of wholesale commercial and monetary conflict.[1]

Why, and how, did Great Britain, the United States, and France cooperate in some periods and not in others? To explain the pattern of oscillation between monetary cooperation and conflict, this essay focuses on transitions between the periods. The first section, "From Cooperation to Conflict: 1929-1933," treats the final year of the gold exchange standard and the subsequent cycle of currency devaluation and economic compartmentalization. The next section, "From Conflict to Cooperation:

* I am grateful for comments by or consultations with Jeff Frieden, Claudia Goldin, Joanne Gowa, Stephen Krasner, David Lake, Timothy McKeown, Arthur Stein, Mark Trachtenberg, Martin Wolfe, and the other contributors to this volume.

[1] See Figure 1: Exchange Rates, 1920-1939, for the value of sterling and the franc relative to the dollar. Between 1920 and 1925, the dollar was tied to gold, while sterling and the franc floated. Uncertainty over the ultimate disposition of the controversies over war debts and reparations, a shortage of international liquidity, national differences in postwar inflation, and the burdens of postwar reconstruction delayed what all parties viewed as the inevitable restoration of a gold standard.

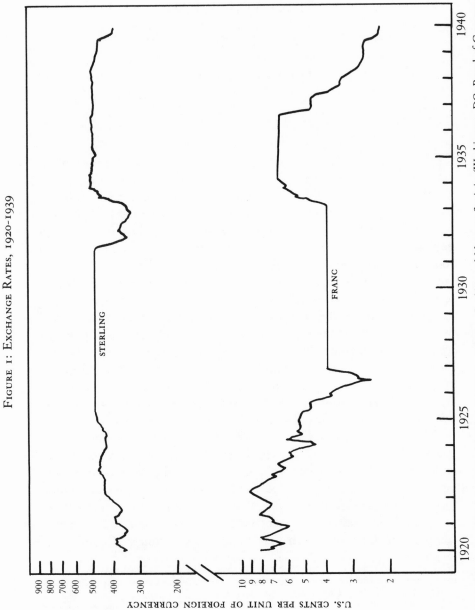

FIGURE 1: EXCHANGE RATES, 1920-1939

STERLING

FRANC

U.S. CENTS PER UNIT OF FOREIGN CURRENCY

Source: U.S. Board of Governors of the Federal Reserve System, *Banking and Monetary Statistics* (Washington, DC: Board of Governors

1934-1937," treats the devaluation of the franc and the beginnings of Tripartite Stabilization. To account for differences between these transitional periods, each study examines, in turn, intrinsic characteristics of international monetary politics, contextual determinants of national interests, and strategic responses of the central monetary powers.

As a first cut, this essay explains the transience of monetary cooperation and conflict in terms of the inherent characteristics of gold exchange and floating monetary systems. Paradoxically, the fruits of cooperation under the gold exchange standard in the years 1925-1931 impeded monetary cooperation during the early 1930s. Increasing misalignment of exchange rates eroded confidence in parities, and growth in official foreign currency reserves increased possible one-time losses from devaluation: misalignment reduced interest in stabilization, and the growth of official holdings of currencies shortened the shadow of the future. Conversely, the detritus of monetary conflict during the early 1930s facilitated monetary cooperation in the years 1936-1939. The realignment of exchange rates through cycles of devaluation improved the prospects for stabilization, while reductions in official foreign currency reserves lengthened the shadow of the future. Each of the studies begins by examining monetary policy options, tradeoffs across options, and associated problems of coordination under the two systems.

As a second cut at the question, the studies examine environmental determinants of British, French, and American interests in monetary policy alternatives. Although monetary options, tradeoffs, and problems of coordination are perennial, interest in options, the terms of tradeoffs, and the prospects for successful coordination are highly context-specific. During the interwar years, macroeconomic conditions, politico-military developments, and changes in economic beliefs had pervasive effects on monetary diplomacy. Swings between prosperity and depression, between peace and threat of war, and between monetary orthodoxy and inflationist heresy altered perceptions of interest in international monetary arrangements. These exogenous developments—factors largely beyond the realm of monetary diplomacy *per se*—partially determined whether the central monetary powers shared common interests that could be realized through monetary cooperation.[2] Payoff structure, the

[2] Proponents of the theory of hegemonic stability maintain that a fundamental exogenous factor, the international distribution of power, explains economic cooperation and conflict. They contrast the turbulence of the interwar years with the tranquility of British and American hegemonic orders, and argue that concentration of power is a necessary, though not sufficient, condition for openness. Revisionists have challenged the conventional interpretations of the late 19th and late 20th centuries. As this essay suggests, interwar economic cooperation was more extensive than is commonly realized. In any event, modest changes in power distribution during the brief interwar period cannot account for the oscillations

shadow of the future, and number of players serve as intervening concepts that relate these environmental changes to the strategic setting that confronted the central monetary powers.

As a third cut at the problem, the two studies examine the strategic responses of the central monetary powers. The actions of the governments of Great Britain, the United States, and France followed from and shaped the circumstances that they confronted. Payoff structure, the shadow of the future, and number of players were susceptible to willful as well as to unintentional manipulation. The central monetary powers consciously restructured the situations they confronted, with varying degrees of success. To create mutual interests, they joined issues; in 1931 and 1932, for example, Great Britain linked monetary, commercial, and financial issues to draw the Scandinavian countries and Argentina into the sterling bloc. To lengthen the shadow of the future, they reduced single-play games and enhanced iterated attributes of situations. For instance, the "24 Hour Gold Standard" provision of the Tripartite Stabilization Agreement was designed to minimize one-time gains and losses from devaluation. To reduce the number of players, they sought to privatize the benefits of cooperation. In the wake of the manifest failure of cooperation between the central monetary powers in the period 1931-1933, for example, Great Britain and France sought cooperation on a lesser scale. Their turn toward bilateralism, currency blocs, and empire permitted the realization of limited mutual economic interests between a different set of actors. Through strategies of composition across issues and strategies of decomposition across time and actors, the central monetary powers improved their ability to make credible commitments under monetary anarchy.

II. FROM COOPERATION TO CONFLICT: 1929-1933

During the 1920s, the central monetary powers created and maintained a gold exchange standard. First, they fixed the value of the central

---

between conflict and cooperation at that time. On hegemonic stability, see Stephen D. Krasner, "State Power and the Structure of International Trade," *World Politics* 28 (April 1976), 317-47; Charles P. Kindleberger, *The World in Depression: 1929-1939* (Berkeley: University of California Press, 1973); and Robert Gilpin, *U.S. Power and the Multinational Corporation* (New York: Basic Books, 1975), 258-59. For contrasting views, see Timothy McKeown, "Hegemonic Stability Theory and 19th-Century Tariff Levels in Europe," *International Organization* 37 (Winter 1983), 73-91; Kenneth A. Oye, "Belief Systems, Bargaining, and Breakdown: International Political Economy 1929-1936," Ph.D. diss. (Harvard University, 1983); David Calleo, "The Historiography of the Interwar Period: Reconsiderations," in Benjamin Rowland, ed., *Balance of Power or Hegemony: The Interwar Monetary System* (New York: New York University Press, 1976). For a conditional refutation of the

currencies in terms of gold. In a time of prosperity, these conservative governments acted on the orthodox belief that the defense of parities, through intervention on exchange markets if possible and through domestic deflation if necessary, was essential to the preservation of business confidence, the pursuit of financial preeminence, and the promotion of economic growth. Second, the central monetary powers departed from pure orthodoxy by treating foreign currencies as well as gold as reserve assets. At the Genoa Conference in 1922, the British proposed "gold economy" measures to mitigate deflationary pressure associated with a return to the gold standard. Key currencies were to be backed by gold, while other currencies were to be backed by reserves composed of both key currencies and gold. The British proposal was actualized over the course of the 1920s, as the share of currencies as a component of official reserves grew steadily. By 1928, foreign exchange comprised 45 percent of the official reserves of all continental European states, with foreign currency amounting to 51 percent of France's official reserves.[3] American and British official reserves consisted entirely of gold, while British payments deficits provided most of the new international liquidity. By permitting states to rely more heavily on intervention, rather than deflation, to alleviate pressure on parities, this second aspect of the gold exchange reinforced the orthodox view on complementarity between exchange-rate stability and domestic prosperity.

Prior to the onset of the Depression, the preservation of gold parities and domestic prosperity were viewed as complementary, not competing, objectives. Not only did the governments of Britain, France, and the United States prefer mutual adherence to the rules of the gold-exchange standard to a breakdown of that system, but they also preferred to adhere to the gold standard irrespective of the actions of others. In the absence of incentives to defect, Harmony prevailed, and nominal international monetary cooperation was extensive.

The Depression ended prosperity, brought down governments, and shattered monetary orthodoxy. The manifest inability of conservative governments to bring about recovery through monetary orthodoxy dis-

---

theory of hegemonic stability, see Robert Keohane, *After Hegemony* (Princeton: Princeton University Press, 1984).

[3] Calculated from "The Adequacy of Monetary Reserves," *IMF Staff Papers* 3 (1953-1954), Table 1, p. 201. Under a *pure* gold standard, reserves of all states consist entirely of gold; exchange disequilibria trigger gold shipments that reduce the national money supply and restore equilibrium to foreign exchange markets. Peter Lindert notes that leading currencies were an important component of official reserve assets under the often idealized "pure" gold standard. See his *Key Currencies and Gold: 1900-1913*, Princeton Studies in International Finance, No. 24 (Princeton: Princeton University, International Finance Section, 1969).

credited the governments as well as the orthodoxy. Monetary politics in the early 1930s were conditioned by recognition of a short-term tradeoff between domestic recovery and exchange-rate stabilization, and governments of the left confronting high levels of unemployment preferred devaluation to deflation. The devaluations of Britain in 1931, the United States in 1933, and France in 1936 permitted resort to reflationary domestic monetary policies, irrespective of the actions of other nations, and conferred a temporary commercial advantage as long as other nations did not devalue. In each instance, no mutual interest existed in preservation of old parities. The monetary harmony of the late 1920s was replaced by the monetary Deadlocks of the early 1930s. Conflict, defined in terms of departure from parities with gold, was inevitable. Even after accepting the inevitability of devaluation in terms of gold, two issues remained unresolved.

First, each successive devaluation imposed substantial costs on other countries and eventually triggered offsetting devaluations. The full cycle of devaluations was the equivalent of a fairly uniform devaluation of all currencies in terms of gold.[4] Why were reciprocity, and the prospect of iteration, of limited import during the early 1930s? Why were the central monetary powers unable to generate effective countervailing inducements and threats against states that depreciated their currencies, and unable to engage in joint reflation?

Second, conflict among the central monetary powers engendered cooperation between central and peripheral states. The period 1931-1936 is marked by the formation of monetary blocs. Why did the focus of monetary diplomacy shift from center-center relations to center-periphery relations during the early 1930s? How and why were the central monetary powers able to cooperate with secondary powers in forming economic blocs?

A. CYCLICAL DEVALUATION

An inherent feature of the gold-exchange standard rendered that system vulnerable to the shock of depression, and impeded monetary cooperation after the system fell. In practice, payments deficits of key currency countries were the primary source of growth in international liquidity; over the short term, the creation of liquidity reduced the costs associated with maintaining stable exchange rates. Intervention to alter foreign-exchange market conditions is distinctly less disruptive domestically than deflation. However, over the long term, payments deficits

---

[4] As Figure 1 indicates, exchange rates across currencies in late 1936 were not substantially different from exchange rates in early 1931.

may well promote exchange-rate instability by giving rise to virtually insoluble N-person single-play games. Under all systems in which payments deficits are an important source of liquidity—gold-exchange and *de facto* dollar standards—substantial international cooperation is required to check a congenital tendency toward oscillation between monetary crunch and monetary crisis.[5] In 1959, Robert Triffin argued that the Bretton Woods system was inherently unstable. He noted that if the United States corrected its persistent payments deficits, the world would confront a liquidity crunch; but if the United States continued to run deficits, the world would confront a crisis of confidence in the dollar.[6] Triffin's dilemma is central to all monetary systems that rely on payments deficits as a source of liquidity.

The stability of these systems rests on cooperation among holders of reserve currencies, and between holders of reserve currencies and reserve currency states. First, governmental and nongovernmental actors in many countries must continue to accept and hold the reserve currency even as doubts may surface about its future value. Under gold-exchange standards, holders of the reserve currency could not convert currency into gold without heightening pressure on pars between the reserve currency and gold. Under the *de facto* dollar standard, holders of dollars cannot convert dollars into other assets without reducing the value of the dollar. If a currency is under pressure, dumping it to avoid exchange losses is individually rational. Failure to convert, if others do so, may produce substantial one-time losses. But mass conversion—into gold or other assets—is certain to bring about a depreciation of the reserve

[5] This situation is also characteristic of other international monetary systems. Under the Bretton Woods system, the United States was expected to maintain full convertibility between the dollar and gold, and the monetary authorities of other states were encouraged to accept the dollar as a portion of their international reserves. American payments deficits provided international liquidity. Under the current *de facto* dollar standard, the international money supply is determined largely by the balance of payments of the United States. Dollars put into international circulation by American payments deficits are held and used by national monetary authorities and private banks, corporations, and individuals engaged in trade and finance. International liquidity may also be derived from other sources. Under a pure gold standard, where national currencies are backed by 100% gold cover, the international money supply would be determined strictly by the availability of newly mined gold. Under a pure Special Drawing Rights (S.D.R.) or European Currency Unit (E.C.U.) standard, international or regional money supply would be determined strictly by the collective decisions of members of the International Monetary Fund (I.M.F.) or European Monetary System (E.M.S.). These alternative approaches to the creation of liquidity remain ideal types. Neither will be treated in this essay.

[6] See Triffin, *Gold and the Dollar Crisis* (New Haven: Yale University Press, 1961), 3-14. For an argument that the recognition of mutual interdependence on the part of key participants in the international monetary system, coupled with a desire to preserve the system, may impart a much greater degree of endurance to the system than Triffin suggests, see Lawrence H. Officer and Thomas D. Willett, "Reserve-Asset Preferences and the Confidence Problem in the Crisis Zone," Quarterly Journal of Economics 83 (November 1969), 688-95.

currency. Holders of a reserve currency confront an N-person single-play game. Unless they are insured against exchange risk, defection is likely.

Second, the currency holders' dilemma gives rise to a further problem of cooperation. The holders' interest in retaining balances of a reserve currency is contingent on the actions of the reserve-currency nation as well as the decisions of other holders. Unless the reserve-currency nation is willing to stem depreciation of its currency, *and* holders are willing to act on the assumption that the reserve currency nation will subordinate domestic economic goals in order to stem depreciation, the value of the reserve currency will oscillate sharply. Holders have a strong incentive to defect first, for reserve losses may be minimized by preemptive conversion into gold. Issuers also have a strong incentive to defect early, in order to prevent conversion of outstanding currency balances into gold. The shadow of the future is short in the holder-issuer game.

These congenital flaws in the gold-exchange standard—a long-term tension between cooperation on liquidity creation and cooperation on exchange-rate stabilization—lie at the core of the monetary problems of the 1930s. The exogenous shock of the Depression and associated governmental and ideological changes explain departures from gold parities, and the single-play nature of the games between holder-holder and holder-issuer nations impeded joint management of devaluation.

In September 1931, Great Britain decisively violated the rules of the gold-exchange standard that it had helped to create during the 1920s. By suspending convertibility and permitting sterling to depreciate relative to gold-backed currencies, the U.K. reversed the direction of an international monetary policy that had been committed to maintaining an overvalued pound. During the 1920s, the Bank of England found that manipulation of the bank rate served to defend the pound against short-term pressure without shipping gold or experiencing domestic deflation. In his testimony before the Macmillan Committee in March 1930, Governor Montague Norman of the Bank of England declared that market operations were generally not necessary to effect a change in bank rates. Short-term capital inflows were responsive to changes in the bank rate, and usually proved sufficient to strengthen the pound. Lord Norman saw domestic economic performance, export performance, and financial position as complementary interests best served over the long term by maintenance of parity. John Maynard Keynes, in his questioning of Lord Norman, presented a radically different view of the tradeoffs across these economic objectives. Keynes believed that market operations and consequent credit tightening were necessary to effect an increase in the bank rate. Therefore, parity could only be preserved at the cost of export performance and domestic economic growth. Norman and Keynes thus held diametrically opposed views on the effects of efforts to preserve the sterling/gold par on British commercial and domestic economic prospects.[7]

During the summer of 1931, the Austrian financial crisis and the ensuing sterling crisis resolved the debate over the existence of the tradeoff between international monetary stabilization and domestic economic performance, while domestic deflation tilted the terms of the tradeoff. The traditional expedient of adjusting the bank rate without engaging in market operations proved insufficient to stem conversions of sterling into gold. The overvaluation of sterling had produced chronic payments deficits, and accumulating sterling balances abroad had intensified the single-play characteristics of the holder-holder game. Austrian and German financial defaults and the freezing of British long-term credits in Central Europe triggered the (at least *post hoc*) predictable mass conversion of sterling into gold. Although foreign central banks offered to support sterling with credits and intervention, international efforts at stabilization could not preserve the sterling/gold parity without substantial adjustment in British domestic economic policy. British fiscal austerity was a requisite of continued access to foreign funds, while monetary contraction was necessary to effect changes in the bank rate.

How was the holder-issuer game played out? After the Bank of England had exhausted initial intervention credits from the United States and France, the British asked the New York Federal Reserve Bank to raise additional funds to increase British resources. Because the New York Federal Reserve Bank was prohibited by statute from lending directly to a foreign government, George Harrison, the Reserve Bank's governor, asked Morgan Guaranty to raise funds from commercial banks. Harrison informed the British that "an American contribution would be forthcoming only if an adequate program of economy obtained the approval of Parliament." This linkage between American financial and British fiscal policy rested on the belief that, unless the British budget were brought into balance and the British economy were put through a deflationary wringer, the British would be forced to request additional resources to defend sterling, and would ultimately not be able to make good on their international financial and monetary commitments. Fur-

[7] On the Norman-Keynes exchange, see R. S. Sayers, *The Bank of England 1891-1944*, Vols. I, II, and Appendixes (Cambridge: Cambridge University Press, 1976), 172-87. For the definitive economic analysis of the effects of British international monetary policy during this period, see Alec Cairncross and Barry Eichengreen, *Sterling in Decline* (Cambridge: Cambridge University Press, 1984).

ther, American authorities feared that Britain, as a reserve-currency nation, would attempt to stem further gold losses and avoid the resulting monetary contractions through a preemptive suspension of convertibility.

In the midst of the Depression, British Prime Minister Ramsey MacDonald could not sell fiscal austerity—severe cuts in unemployment relief, reductions in government salaries, and a tax increase—to all the members of his Labour government. In August of 1931, MacDonald resigned and formed a National Coalition government from elements of the Labour, Conservative and Liberal Parties. The new National Coalition government adopted an austerity budget, and French and American banks offered fresh credits. The fresh credits were quickly exhausted, the prospect of even more severe austerity measures threatened further erosion of the MacDonald coalition, and the United States and France were unwilling to provide further loans. In late September, Great Britain abandoned the gold standard.[8]

Ultimately, the exhaustion of reserves and the domestic economic costs of further belt tightening—fiscal, financial, and monetary—more than offset the dubious benefits of maintaining parity. British economic performance had lagged even before the global Depression. During the international boom of the late 1920s, British unemployment never fell below one million, and British industrial activity did not keep pace with the other advanced industrial countries.[9] During 1930 and 1931, British domestic economic activity declined from this already low baseline. The penalties associated with adopting a restrictive domestic monetary policy and an austerity budget under conditions of rising unemployment and declining industrial activity were unacceptable. Because the only path to sustaining gold pars involved trekking through deflationary swamps, mutual cooperation in defense of these parities became less attractive than mutual defection.

British devaluation imposed substantial costs on other governments, however, and triggered offsetting devaluations. As noted above, the full cycle amounted to a joint devaluation in terms of gold, with little change in exchange rates across the three central currencies. Preventive political exchange was impeded by intrinsic features of the gold-exchange standard. The central monetary powers could not influence each other by threatening or offering to alter exchange rates because any indication

---

[8] The best accounts of this episode are found in Sayers (fn. 7), II, 397-99, and in Stephen V. O. Clarke, *Central Bank Cooperation 1924-1931* (New York: Federal Reserve Bank of New York, 1967), 182-219.

[9] The British economic malaise was caused, in part, by the overvaluation of sterling. On structural causes of sluggish British economic performance, see Charles Loch Mowat, *Britain Between the Wars: 1918-1940* (Chicago: University of Chicago Press, 1955), chaps. 5-7.

that a change in parities was possible would have triggered a run on their currencies. Both private and public holders of sterling confronted a dilemma of collective action, and their willingness to refrain from converting sterling to gold was contingent on confidence that parities would not be changed. This attribute of the gold-exchange standard discouraged resort to reciprocity and to linkages between monetary and other international economic issues. Only after the gold-exchange standard had disintegrated, and holdings of foreign currencies had dropped substantially, were monetary reciprocity and monetary issue-linkages practicable.

Reconstructive political exchange was impeded by the public nature of monetary externalities. Britain's decision to suspend convertibility of the pound imposed serious costs on all nations that remained on the gold standard. The United States, France, Germany, and other nations found that the costs of sustaining parities to gold were increased by the depreciation of sterling. Each of the nations on the gold standard was forced to adjust to the British decision, but the gold-bloc members did not move effectively, either individually or collectively, to forestall the British move or to induce the British to check the slide of sterling. Each expressed its preference for Britain's return to convertibility, with varying degrees of emotional intensity. But none expended political resources to effect a change in general British monetary policy. The dearth of political coercion and political exchange directed at influencing British monetary policy requires explanation. The public nature of international externalities associated with the suspension of convertibility and the subsequent depreciation of sterling account for the absence of action aimed at bringing about a revision of British policy. All the nations on the gold standard would have benefited if Britain had established a new parity and intervened to check the depreciation of sterling. None could have been excluded from the benefits. And none were willing to commit private political resources to provide a public good.

Nations that remained on the gold standard suffered from increasing pressures on their currencies. Following the depreciation of sterling, short-term capital outflows pushed the dollar to the gold selling point. The Hoover administration, however, was adamantly committed to maintaining the dollar-gold parity. President Hoover subscribed to monetary orthodoxy. He believed that international monetary stability was the key to restoring world trade, building business confidence, promoting dishoarding, stimulating investment, and ultimately ending deflation. His views on the importance of maintaining parities were shared by the French. American and French views diverged, however, on the relative merits of the gold and gold-exchange standards. Even prior to the British float, the Bank of France was committed in principle to liquidation of its substantial foreign-exchange holdings. Following British suspension of convertibility, the Netherlands, Germany, and Switzerland converted reserves of dollars, and France developed systematic plans to dispose of sterling and to convert dollars into gold. This Franco-American divergence of views on the relative merits of the gold and gold-exchange standards was of more than theoretical interest. A wholesale liquidation of $600 million in Bank of France balances could have turned the run on the dollar in late 1931 into a full-scale crisis. Under such circumstances, the cost to the United States of maintaining parity through gold sales, intervention, and discount-rate changes would have been high.

The French offered to refrain from liquidating their dollar balances if the United States refrained from pursuing any policy that would endanger the gold standard, modified its Hoover moratorium on war debts and reparations, and raised American interest rates to make employment of French funds in New York more profitable. The New York Federal Reserve formally rejected this explicit linkage, but met some of the French terms nonetheless. In October 1931, the New York Fed raised its discount rate from 1½ percent to 3½ percent.[10] The French refrained from converting further dollar balances during the run on the dollar.[11] It should be noted that the compensation received by the French—the rise in the New York discount rate—not only benefited the French, but also contributed directly to stemming the run on the dollar. France and the United States realized a mutual preference for sustaining gold parities in the face of a conflict of preferences over the timing of liquidation of French holdings of dollars. In this instance, policy coordination was facilitated by the private nature of externalities associated with wholesale conversion of the Bank of France's dollar balances. The French resumed their gold withdrawals when the dollar crisis ended in December 1931, and completed their conversion program in June 1932.

The *de jure* depreciation of sterling and the *de facto* depreciation of

[10] To place these rates in real perspective, remember that domestic prices were falling rapidly during this period. The GNP implicit price deflator for 1929 is 30% higher than the deflator for 1933. See *Economic Report of the President 1982* (Washington, DC: GPO, 1982), Table B-3. Real interest rates did not approach these levels again until 1981.

[11] Policy coordination clearly served the preferences of both the French and American governments. I do not argue, however, that preferences and real interests coincided. The two-point increase in the New York discount rate in 1931 unquestionably intensified the Depression. This account of Franco-American monetary diplomacy in 1931 is drawn largely from William Adams Brown, *The International Gold Standard Reinterpreted* (New York: National Bureau of Economic Research, 1940), 1179-82, and Kindleberger (fn. 2), 168.

the mark and other currencies through exchange controls placed steady pressure on the dollar. The U.S. departure from gold in 1933 is best understood in terms of the conjunction of this effective appreciation of the dollar and changes in domestic economic circumstances and economic beliefs. With its large gold reserves, the United States could have adhered to the rules of the gold standard by shipping gold to defend parity. It was not pushed off gold by uncontrollable swings in short-term capital movements. It stepped off gold to permit domestic economic recovery.

Differences between the economic beliefs of Presidents Hoover and Roosevelt had consequential effects on international monetary relations. As noted earlier, Hoover had been willing to tighten the domestic money supply to maintain dollar parity because he believed that international monetary stability was a requisite of domestic recovery. In his view, international monetary stabilization and domestic recovery were complementary objectives. Roosevelt believed that raising domestic prices was a precondition of domestic recovery. He saw two paths to the proximate goal of reflation. The core programs of the First New Deal—the A.A.A. and N.R.A.—sought to restrain production, raise prices, and ultimately increase profits and employment. Roosevelt also subscribed to the view that a general rise in prices could be effected either through the conventional means of manipulating the discount rate or through the unconventional means of purchasing newly mined gold at a premium price. The old gold/dollar parity simply could not be reconciled with raising prices by either of these means. Because of these views, Roosevelt confronted a substantial tension between international monetary stabilization and domestic economic recovery.[12]

In March and April of 1933, Roosevelt banned gold exports except under Treasury license and halted all operations in support of the dollar. As Figure 1 indicates, both sterling and the franc appreciated sharply relative to the dollar. Although the action was widely denounced, countervailing political pressure was limited and Roosevelt was unresponsive.

During preparatory discussions for the World Economic Conference of 1933, Britain indicated that depreciation of the dollar had increased British difficulties in meeting war-debt payments, and suggested that monetary stabilization and intergovernmental debts should be discussed together at the London Conference. The Roosevelt administration ob-

[12] On domestic problems associated with raising prices through production restraints, see Ellis W. Hawley, *The New Deal and the Problem of Monopoly: A Study in Economic Ambivalence* (Princeton: Princeton University Press, 1966). For a defense of price raising through gold purchasing, see George F. Warren and Frank A. Pearson, *Gold and Prices* (New York: John Wiley & Sons, 1935).

jected; it would not participate in the conference if intergovernmental debts were placed on the agenda. The French reiterated their commitment to the international gold standard, and pointed out that depreciation of the dollar might force them to tighten their system of trade quotas in order to maintain parity between the Poincaré franc and gold. The U.S. delegation noted that it might be prepared to discuss monetary stabilization, and encouraged the French to dismantle their system of quotas. At the Conference, Roosevelt considered a joint French and British proposal for temporary currency stabilization, and instructed the American delegation to seek agreement on ever higher dollar/sterling rates. When one of the American offers was accepted, Roosevelt simply withdrew the offer.

Why did the United States reject the joint proposal? The concessions offered were simply not commensurate with the concession sought, a currency stabilization that Roosevelt believed would vitiate domestic reflation. In fact, rumors of the impending stabilization agreement had triggered a sharp decline in stock and commodity prices. This may have reinforced Roosevelt's views on the desirability of further dollar depreciation. Throughout the summer and fall of 1933, Roosevelt purchased newly mined gold at a high price and forced the dollar down relative to sterling and the franc.[13]

B.   BILATERALISM AND COMPARTMENTALIZATION

Relations among the central monetary powers during the early 1930s were marked by cyclical devaluation, financial closure, and endemic commercial protection. Great Britain, France, and the United States could not agree on exchange-rate alignments, reserve-asset composition, intergovernmental and private financial issues, or commercial access. How did other nations respond to this forbidding international economic environment? Paradoxically, world economic disintegration fostered economic reintegration on a bilateral and bloc basis. By bargaining with a narrower range of actors on a broader range of issues, governments were able to make credible commitments under international anarchy.

First, trilateral and global discussions were supplanted by bilateral and bloc-level bargaining. Great Britain drew Argentina, Sweden, Norway, and Denmark into the sterling bloc through a series of bilateral negotiations. Germany drew the nations of Eastern Europe into the

[13] See Herbert Feis, *1933: Characters in Crisis* (Boston: Little, Brown, 1966), 178-258, for a sensitive account of these episodes. See also Stephen V. O. Clarke, *The Reconstruction of the International Monetary System: The Attempts of 1922 and 1933*, Princeton Studies in International Finance, No. 33 (Princeton: Princeton University, International Finance Section, 1973), 19-39.

mark system through bilateral clearing arrangements. Economic discrimination privatized the international externalities associated with national policy choices, and thereby facilitated bilateral and bloc-level bargaining. Exchange controls, financial discrimination, quotas, and multiple-list tariffs permitted governments to channel costs and benefits toward particular negotiating partners. The discriminations of the early 1930s were economically inefficient. By introducing myriad factor-price distortions, these policies unquestionably reduced the magnitude of economic gains from cooperation. By permitting states to engage in political exchange, however, discriminatory policies facilitated the realization of limited mutual interests, albeit on a less than global scale.[14]

Second, the boundaries between issues broke down. Governments engaged in political exchange, trading off concessions on one issue for gains on another. Consider the Anglo-Argentine negotiations: Great Britain offered preferential access to British capital and to British domestic markets while Argentina agreed to hold reserves of sterling, peg the peso to sterling, favor British creditors, and grant preferential access to Argentine markets. Although nations often did not share common interests on any single monetary, commercial, or financial issue, they shared interests in packages of issues taken as a whole. Further, by linking the intrinsically single-play issue of reserve-asset composition to iterated commercial and financial issues, governments improved the prospects for cooperation by lengthening the shadow of the future.

The interwar economic blocs are commonly viewed as products of coercion; in fact, coercion did play a substantial role in forming the cores of the blocs. The sterling and franc blocs began as traditional empires; the British-Indian and French-Algerian relationships were based on the imperial denial of sovereignty through military occupation. The dollar bloc was built around a traditional zone of American military and political penetration, and Germany had often intervened in East-Central Europe; relationships between the United States and the republics of the Caribbean basin and between Nazi Germany and the Danubian states were less-than-ideal examples of cooperation in the realization of mutual interests. During the early 1930s, however, economic blocs expanded well beyond the traditional boundaries of imperial

---

[14] For conventional analyses of economic inefficiency of interwar bilateralism and discrimination, see League of Nations, *International Currency Experience: Lessons of the Interwar Period* (Geneva: League of Nations, 1944), 162-89, and Howard S. Ellis, *Exchange Control in Central Europe* (Cambridge: Harvard University Press, 1941). For analysis of the mutual economic benefits of German and East European exchange controls, see Frank Child, *The Theory and Practice of Exchange Control in Germany: A Study of Monopolistic Exploitation in International Markets* (The Hague: Martinus Nijhoff, 1958).

rule and military-political intervention. The decision of Argentina and the Scandinavian countries to join the sterling bloc in 1931 cannot be explained in terms of military coercion or denial of sovereignty. Even the scope of German bilateral clearing arrangements in the early 1930s greatly exceeded the reach of nascent German military power and political penetration. By the end of 1933, Germany had negotiated clearing arrangements with almost all continental European states. The expansion of the sterling bloc and the German bilateral clearing system was based largely on consent.

The British example provides a clear, though somewhat perverse, illustration of cooperation under anarchy. Even as it permitted sterling to fall, Great Britain sought to form a sterling bloc. The displacement of sterling by the dollar or the franc would further undermine the financial preeminence of the City of London. Britain hoped that other countries would hold sterling balances as reserves and peg their currencies to sterling. Sir Richard Hopkins of the British Treasury wrote:

> One of the leading objectives that we ought to have in mind as soon as we can keep sterling steady at a reasonable level, is to make it easy for as many as possible of the unsteady currencies to base themselves on sterling so that we may become the leaders of a sterling bloc which, pending our restabilisation on gold, would have the best opportunities of mutual trade and would give sterling a new force in the world.[15]

Unfortunately, holders of sterling would confront very private single-play exchange risks, and Great Britain could not insure holders of sterling against these private risks while pursuing a nondiscriminatory monetary policy. The British were unwilling to privatize the effects of sterling depreciation through adoption of a multiple exchange-rate system or exchange controls. Indeed, the British explicitly rejected *de facto* devaluation through exchange controls in favor of *de jure* depreciation because controls would have further undermined the financial preeminence of the City.[16] To transcend this contradiction, Great Britain used discriminatory commercial and financial policies to encourage other governments to move onto a sterling standard.[17]

[15] U.K. Treasury Papers, Memorandum, Richard Hopkins to Neville Chamberlain, December 8, 1931. Cited in Ian M. Drummond, *The Floating Pound and the Sterling Area* (Cambridge: Cambridge University Press, 1981), 10.

[16] The British also rejected a somewhat narrowly self-serving French suggestion that the Bank of England convert Bank of France sterling reserves into gold at the old parity, to the detriment of other central banks.

[17] Britain displayed some ambivalence on the desirability of appearing to urge other countries to join the sterling bloc. To disavow responsibility for the security and convertibility of foreign sterling reserves, British officials sought to appear "studiously aloof" on the issue. See Drummond, (fn. 15), 9. In fact, Britain used commercial and financial leverage to encourage others to join the sterling bloc.

In the months after suspension of sterling/gold convertibility, Britain shifted from nondiscriminatory commercial and financial policies to Imperial commercial and financial preferences. The Abnormal Importations Act of 1931 and the Ottawa Agreements of 1932 established a two-tiered tariff and a system of quotas that encouraged trade among Britain and the Territories, Colonies, and Dominions, and discriminated against exports from foreign countries.[18]

The collapse of the multilateral clearing system in 1931 gave rise to a compartmentalized system of international finance. When lenders ceased lending and borrowers defaulted, the pyramid of credit collapsed. Reliance on preferential lending and repayment may have helped to rebuild international credit. Following the financial crisis of 1931, the British government discouraged all new international lending and prohibited new lending outside the Empire.[19] Imperial commercial and financial preferences provided Britain with considerable leverage vis-à-vis non-Empire nations. The extent of the British commitment to the Empire was unclear, and Britain's trading partners feared that the Dominions might succeed in capturing even stronger preferences in the future. Further, potential borrowers could not tap into British credit. This fear of additional trade diversion and desire for financial access provided the impetus for Norway, Sweden, Denmark, and Argentina to enter into bilateral discussions with Britain.

British relations with the Scandinavian countries may be characterized as implicit long-term reciprocity. Tacit linkages between monetary, financial, and commercial issues were pervasive, but the issues were rarely linked explicitly in any single agreement. Anglo-Danish negotiations were typical. In December 1931, the central bank of Denmark applied "urgently" for credit from the Bank of England and indicated that credits would be used "to maintain the sterling basis" of the currency. The credits were granted. In April 1933, Britain and Denmark concluded a reciprocal trade agreement. Denmark was granted 62 percent of the British quota for non-Empire bacon, and an egg and butter quota just below 1932 levels. In return, Denmark eliminated, reduced, or froze duties on a wide range of British goods, and agreed to purchase 80 percent of its total coal imports from Britain. Immediately after the

[18] For provisions of the Abnormal Importations Act and the Ottawa Agreements, see Margaret S. Gordon, *Barriers to World Trade: A Study of Recent Commercial Policy* (New York: Macmillan, 1941); Joseph M. Jones, *Tariff Retaliation: Repercussions of the Hawley-Smoot Bill* (Philadelphia: University of Pennsylvania Press, 1934); and League of Nations, *World Economic Survey 1930-31* (Geneva: League of Nations, 1931), and *World Economic Survey 1931-32* (Geneva: League of Nations, 1932).

[19] See J. Henry Richardson, *British Foreign Economic Policy* (New York: Macmillan, 1936), 69-75, and Brown (fn. 11), II, 1135.

trade treaty was concluded, Britain admitted Denmark to the list of preferred borrowers in London. In early 1934, Denmark eased exchange controls and pegged the krone to sterling. In July 1934, the British government formalized its policy of permitting sterling loans to nations in the sterling bloc.[20] In tone, substance, and timing, the Anglo-Swedish and Anglo-Norwegian negotiations resemble the Danish case.

In May and September of 1933, Britain and Argentina negotiated reciprocal agreements that explicitly joined financial, commercial, and monetary issues. The agreements were as noteworthy for their detail as for their scope. The British agreed to impose no quantitative restrictions or new duties on an array of Argentine goods, to accept as much Argentine chilled beef as they had imported in 1931-1932, to add no restrictions on frozen meat, and to provide a sterling loan. Argentina agreed to reduce duties on a number of goods provided largely by Britain, to continue to admit coal on a duty-free basis, to service British loans on a preferential basis, to permit British companies to convert blocked peso accounts into sterling, and to abandon the French franc and peg the peso to sterling. By linking iterated commercial issues to single-play monetary and financial issues, Argentina and Britain lengthened the shadow of the future.[21] Although neither British gunboats nor international courts could have effectively enforced the terms of the agreements, both parties had a stake in continuing cooperation. The Anglo-Argentine agreements were worth making because they were worth keeping.[22]

The bilateralism and currency blocs of the early 1930s permitted governments to realize limited mutual interests on a less than global basis. During a period when global monetary stabilization, financial restoration, and commercial openness appeared impossible to attain, the adoption of strategies to privatize the costs and benefits associated with economic policies and to negotiate on a bilateral basis permitted the realization of mutual interests between pairs of nations. However, bilateral and bloc-level cooperation effectively diverted costs to third parties. Danish butter and Argentine beef entered the British market at the expense of American dairy farmers and ranchers. Argentine loans

[20] This account is drawn from Drummond (fn. 15), 8 and 10; Brown (fn. 11), II, 1135 and 1167; and Richardson (fn. 19), 69-75.

[21] Argentina was to make available sterling remittances equal to exchange derived from Argentine sales in Britain after retaining a "reasonable sum" to service other foreign obligations.

[22] The terms of the agreements are drawn from Richardson (fn. 19), 106-08; Brown (fn. 11), II, 1167-68; and Roger Gravil, *The Anglo-Argentine Connection: 1900-1939* (Boulder, CO: Westview, 1985), 179-212.

from London were serviced at the expense of Argentine loans from New York. And while the peso-sterling and krone-sterling rates stabilized, the peso-franc and krone-franc rates dropped.

III. From Conflict to Cooperation: 1934-1937

By the end of 1933, adjustments to the depreciation of the dollar appeared to be complete. International exchange rates and domestic prices were steady. In early 1934, President Roosevelt established a lasting "temporary" parity at the rate of $35 per ounce that had been produced by the float, and in the middle of that year, Great Britain pegged sterling to the dollar at the rate of $4.95, also produced by the float.[23] Still, the devalued but fully convertible dollar and the floating but pegged pound exerted continual pressure against gold-bloc nations. Pressure on the franc increased sharply following the American devaluation. The three-month future price for francs on franc-sterling markets fell from a .1 percent premium over spot prices in the summer of 1933 to a 33 percent discount by the summer of 1936.[24] The French supported the overvalued franc through rigorously deflationary domestic fiscal and monetary policies, by expanding their system of quotas on imports, and by drawing down their gold reserves.

The willingness of the French to continue to support the franc/gold par through deflation (despite domestic stagnation) can only be understood in terms of the widespread French belief in monetary orthodoxy. In Great Britain, the commitment to the 1925 sterling/gold par was an article of faith within financial circles and an article of controversy within commercial circles. In the United States, the Republican Party's belief in the complementarity between domestic recovery and support of the dollar/gold par was not embedded in the general culture. Indeed, disputes over the merits of gold, silver, and greenback monetary standards had been common since the economic contractions of the late 1800s. In France, the putative virtues of the orthodox gold standard were accepted by peasants, artisans, the middle class, manufacturers, and financiers. Even the Popular Front campaigned in 1936 on a slogan of "neither deflation nor devaluation," and Leon Blum declared that he would not

---

[23] The United States sought to privatize benefits associated with restoration of full convertibility between the dollar and gold. Countries on the gold standard were free to convert dollars into gold, while members of the sterling bloc were denied conversion rights. However, because the British were free to trade in the gold-backed Poincaré franc, the United States could not effectively privatize its international monetary policy.

[24] Paul Einzig, *The Theory of Foreign Exchange* (London: Macmillan, 1937), insert following p. 286.

lead a "coup d'état monétaire."[25] France moved off gold only after the tension between domestic reflation and preservation of the franc/gold par became extraordinarily acute. Blum's Popular Front government rejected fiscal austerity in late spring of 1936, and accelerating gold shipments drew down French reserves. Domestic tolerance of deflation and official reserves of gold neared exhaustion during the summer of 1936.

The devaluation of the franc in fall of 1936 was the last in the series of uncoordinated devaluations that began in 1931. Like Britain and the U.S., France could not simultaneously support an overvalued currency and reflate a stagnant domestic economy; it chose domestic reflation and exchange-rate depreciation. As in the earlier cases, exchange-rate realignment did not bring about exchange-rate stability. Figure 1 shows that the two-stage depreciation of the franc and the depreciation of the pound and franc relative to the dollar were as steep as the sterling devaluation of 1931 and the dollar devaluation of 1933. *In contrast with these earlier cases, however, the devaluation of the franc did not trigger offsetting devaluations, intensified commercial conflict, or imposition of exchange controls.* Despite profound exchange-rate instability, monetary and commercial conflict did not arise. What factors permitted the emergence of extensive monetary consultation and limited monetary coordination in the late 1930s?

Consider factors affecting payoff structure. During the two years before the devaluation of the franc, American and British officials gradually recognized that the French defense of an overvalued franc had adverse effects on commercial interests. In a 1935 memorandum to Secretary of State Cordell Hull, State Department economic advisor Herbert Feis wrote:

> From a long range standpoint, a prolonged effort by the gold bloc countries to maintain present gold parities might be at least as damaging to us as a sudden collapse of their currencies, because such an effort would involve increasingly severe restrictions on trade and a chronic gold drain to the United States. In this connection, it is significant that while the dollar value of our exports to all countries increased 32 percent from 1932 to 1934, our exports to the five principal European countries which have maintained their pre-depression gold parities—France, Germany, Italy, Holland, and Belgium—rose less than 3 percent.

Feis went on to argue that a 25-35 percent devaluation of the franc would permit French payments to balance without additional commer-

---

[25] Martin Wolfe, *The French Franc Between the Wars, 1919-1939* (New York: Columbia University Press, 1951), 144.

cial restrictions, and would provide a reasonable basis for stabilization negotiations. In summer of 1936, Chancellor of the Exchequer Neville Chamberlain stipulated that British support for a fair rate of exchange hinged on freedom from the quotas and other trade restrictions that were used by the French to defend the franc. With the devaluation of the franc in 1936, none of the three key international currencies were clearly over- or undervalued. All three governments hoped that limited coordination of international monetary policies would permit reconciliation of export expansion, exchange rate stabilization, and domestic reflation.[26]

This emerging economic mutuality of interest in stabilization was reinforced by developments in security affairs. In 1936, governing elites in Britain, France, and the United States were suspicious of Germany's rearmament programs and disturbed by Hitler's occupation of the Rhineland. An economically and militarily strong France could serve as a barrier to a rapidly militarizing Germany. All three monetary powers perceived further deterioration in the French economic position as undesirable, and saw devaluation of the franc as a necessary condition for French economic recovery. However, because of the widespread French belief in the sanctity of gold, devaluation itself could well have undercut the fragile Blum coalition and further polarized French politics. By sanctioning and legitimating devaluation, Britain and the United States could soften the domestic French political repercussions of devaluation. The possible threat from Germany tempered British and especially American pursuit of narrow national advantage. In explaining the Tripartite Agreement to his staff, Treasury Secretary Morgenthau exclaimed: "This is a threat to Italy and Germany. . . . This is a notice to the boys—Achtung!"[27] British and American officials both had an interest in France's economic performance and political stability, an interest best served by their acceptance of the franc's devaluation.[28]

Taken together, these changes in international monetary and security affairs transformed payoff structure. All three countries saw a moderate depreciation of the franc as preferable to maintaining the old gold par.

[26] On Feis, see National Archives, Record Group 59, 800.5151/88½, "Economic Stabilization," 4th Draft, pp. 7-8. On Chamberlain, see Sayres (fn. 7), II, 478-79. For general discussions of the consequences of exchange-rate misalignment, see Walter A. Morton, *British Finance 1930-1940* (Madison: University of Wisconsin Press, 1943); League of Nations (fn. 14).

[27] Morgenthau Diaries, September 18, 1936, Book 32, p. 10, cited in Scott Eric Ratner, "The Politics of Quiet Diplomacy: Henry Morgenthau Jr. and the Efforts of the American Jewish Establishment to Aid the Jewish Victims of Nazism" B.A. thesis (Princeton University, 1984), 121.

[28] On French efforts to reinforce perceptions of the connection between security and economic issues, see Sayers (fn. 7), 476-77, and Wolfe (fn. 25), 145-46.

Realignment was viewed as necessary to creating a system of stabilized exchange rates, stemming volatile short-term capital movements from France to Britain and the United States, and checking tendencies toward political instability in France. The British and the American governments had a substantial interest in promoting systemic monetary and financial stability and in containing movement toward the radical right or left on the continent. However, Britain and the United States feared depreciation of the franc below levels that would balance French exports and imports. Both governments remained concerned over how a deep decline in the value of the franc might damage their export-oriented and import-competing sectors. In short, their preferences regarding the value of the franc were not monotonic; both preferred a *little* franc depreciation to no depreciation or deep depreciation. From the French perspective, more depreciation was better. A mutual preference for moderate devaluation coexisted with a French preference for sharp devaluation.

The mere existence of a mutual interest does not guarantee realization of a common good. Changes in payoff structure were paralleled by changes in the iterativeness of monetary relations. During the turbulence of the preceding five years, states had prudently drawn down the foreign-exchange component of official reserves; that of official French reserves dropped from 51 percent in 1928 to 3 percent in 1936. The elimination of holdings of foreign exchange altered the structure of the situation by reducing one-time gains from unilateral defection and one-time losses from unrequited cooperation. Although commercial advantage could have been derived from unilateral devaluation, commercial benefits could be largely negated through future retaliation. Because export levels are slow to respond to exchange-rate changes, the benefits of unilateral defection and the costs of unrequited cooperation at any one time were limited. Although devaluation could affect medium-term commercial prospects, and threats to devalue could affect short-term capital flows, exchange-rate changes no longer jeopardized the value of official monetary reserves.

How did Britain, France, and the United States realize mutual interests under monetary anarchy? In fall of 1936, the central monetary powers issued the three parallel declarations that are known as the Tripartite Stabilization Agreement. The declarations were ambiguously defined and carefully hedged. Under the Tripartite Agreement, Britain, France, and the United States promised to refrain from seeking "unreasonable competitive advantage" through manipulation of exchange rates—without specifying what exchange rates might be deemed unreasonable. The three treasuries promised to consult on the buying and selling prices of gold targeted by their exchange equalization funds—without pooling resources, committing lines of credit to the defense of other nations' currencies, or establishing mechanisms for enforcement. Finally, this innocuous agreement was subject to termination on 24 hours' notice.[29]

The form of the Tripartite Agreement limited potential losses in the event of defection. The treasuries of Britain, France, and the United States were well aware that exchange risks had heightened monetary conflict in the past, and consciously sought to maintain a favorable setting for cooperation. Under the Tripartite Agreement, the parties committed themselves to settle outstanding balances in gold on a daily basis to ensure that gains from unilateral devaluation would be limited. That provision was both a response to unsatisfactory recent experience and part of a strategy to reduce single-play aspects of the central monetary game.

To what extent did Britain, France, and the United States cooperate under the loophole-ridden Tripartite system? The initial slide from 80 to 130 francs per pound was accepted by all; harmony prevailed because all preferred a moderate depreciation of the franc to no depreciation. Indeed, the Blum government sought and received explicit support for the devaluation of the franc from both Britain and the United States.

The real test of cooperation began after the initial devaluation. The ambiguities of the Tripartite Agreement and the instability of exchange rates added weight to the significance of international monetary stabilization during the late 1930s. French business, fearful of Blum's Popular Front, continued to move capital to London and New York even after devaluation. Pressure on the franc from capital flight was compounded by French domestic inflation. By mid-1937, rising internal prices more than offset the effects of the initial franc devaluation. The British, the Americans, and the French had underpredicted continuing pressures on the franc. Throughout most of 1936 and 1937, the three-month franc-sterling forward rate ran at a substantial discount under the spot rate.[30]

---

[29] To the Deputy Governor of the Bank of France, the agreement was "ni accord, ni entente, uniquement co-operation journalière." To an official British operator, it was "flimsy and ineffective." Quoted in Sayers (fn. 7), II, 480 and 482. For a superb account of how agreement was reached, see Stephen V. O. Clarke, *Exchange-Rate Stabilization in the Mid-1930s: Negotiating the Tripartite Agreement*, Princeton Studies in International Finance, No. 41 (Princeton: Princeton University, International Finance Section, 1977). For trenchant commentary on the weaknesses of the Tripartite Stabilization Agreement, see Ian M. Drummond, *London, Washington, and the Management of the Franc, 1936-39*, Princeton Studies in International Finance, No. 45 (Princeton: International Finance Section, 1979).

[30] Einzig (fn. 24), 480; Wolfe (fn. 25), 138-71.

Modest interventions through each country's exchange equalization accounts were not up to the task of supporting the franc.

How did the central monetary powers respond to this situation? Despite French efforts to support the franc by selling gold, capital flight pushed the franc below levels that would balance French exports and imports. The British treasury offered to assist in floating a loan on private London markets if France would swallow conservative medicine by tightening fiscal policy and attenuating Popular Front reforms. The French adopted some of the British suggestions and used funds raised in London to support the franc. The British pegged sterling to the franc, and utilized their exchange-equalization fund to resist changes in the sterling-franc rate.

The United States Treasury continued to utilize its exchange-equalization fund to maintain parity between the dollar and gold, and thereby provided indirect support for the franc. American support for France stopped short of extending credit: France was in default on war debts, and the Johnson Act prohibited loans to governments in default on official obligations to the United States. Treasury Secretary Morgenthau horrified the British by advising the French to impose capital controls and offering to track down fugitive private French assets in the United States. Morgenthau's indignation at French capital flight may well have been intensified by empathy for French "New Dealers," for Blum had explicitly based elements of the Popular Front program on the New Deal. The French rejected Morgenthau's advice as impracticable, and continued to draw down their gold reserves to slow the decline of the franc.[31]

In January 1937, the French Stabilization Fund announced that it had exhausted its entire gold allotment in defense of franc-gold parity. Although the Fund's resources were partially replenished through a loan by the Bank of France, pressure on the franc intensified. In February, the Blum government announced a pause in social and economic reforms, cancellation of some public works expenditures, and other measures to check capital flight by restoring the confidence of the business community. Although these actions succeeded in stemming pressure on the franc for a few months, renewed capital flight in June 1937 exhausted the resources of the French Stabilization Fund. During the ensuing financial crisis, the Blum government fell.[32] The deep depreciation of the franc in 1936 and 1937 elicited consternation but no reprisals from Britain and the United States. France supported the franc by selling

[31] Because New Deal capital controls were never tested by strong capital outflows, the American experience was of limited relevance to France.

[32] This account is drawn from Drummond (fn. 29), and Wolfe (fn. 25).

gold and altering domestic policies. Britain and the United States did not regard ineffectual French efforts to support the franc as an attempt to obtain unreasonable commercial advantage, and both offered limited support to France.

Why did cooperation continue under the Tripartite system even though each of the states was free to defect? The U.S. commitment to the $35-per-ounce parity was explicitly revocable, Britain refused to establish any official parity between sterling and gold or other currencies, and France was free to engineer a large or a small drop in the value of the franc. Yet the United States maintained par, Britain pegged sterling to the franc, and France engineered a modest devaluation of the franc and then sought to defend a new par. Payoff structure and the shadow of the future explain both the emergence and the robustness of co-operation. A very large devaluation of the franc might have stemmed capital flight from France and worked to the advantage of French exporters, but France feared retaliation by Britain and the United States. The expectation of retaliation in the future reduced France's incentive to defect in the present. Raising the dollar price of gold might have raised domestic American price levels and worked to the advantage of American exporters, but the United States feared retaliation by Britain and did not want to weaken the economy of France. Engineering a drop in the value of sterling might have stimulated the British economy and worked to the advantage of British exporters, but Britain was wary of weakening France and fearful of retaliation by the United States. The realignment of exchange rates over the previous five years and the emerging German security threat created a mutual interest that could be realized through cooperation. The disorder of the previous five years caused these three governments to limit their vulnerability to one-shot devaluations. These nations had demonstrated their willingness and ability to pursue strategies of monetary reciprocity. Finally, the consultative mechanisms established under the Tripartite system furnished a means of continually revising and updating definitions of cooperation in light of changing circumstances, and provided early warning of defection. Although the Tripartite system did not achieve monetary stability, cooperation among the central monetary powers prevented the decline of the franc from triggering another round of monetary and commercial conflict.

IV. Conclusion

Conventional wisdom holds that, during the interwar period, nation-states could not transcend dilemmas of collective action. In that view, they succumbed to the short-term temptations of beggar-thy-neighbor policies, and were unable to realize long-term mutual interests; by striving to improve their welfare at the expense of others through tariffs, currency depreciation, and foreign-exchange controls, governments invited inevitable retaliation. Thus, each was left in a worse position from having pursued its own gain. This common image of the failure of cooperation under anarchy during the interwar period legitimates British hegemonic leadership before World War I as well as American hegemonic leadership after World War II. Finally, this view of the 1930s suggests that the erosion of American hegemony in the 1980s may lead toward economic closure.[33]

The disintegration and reintegration of international monetary relations may be better understood by analyzing the changing structure of games rather than by focusing on how the games were played. During the first transitional period (1929-1933), there were no dilemmas of collective action for the central monetary powers to transcend. The conjunction of intrinsically flawed monetary and financial systems, deteriorating macroeconomic conditions, and changing economic ideologies produced monetary Deadlocks. The swing from prosperity to depression and from monetary orthodoxy to reflationist heresy altered British and American perceptions of their interest in international monetary arrangements. Although the states that remained on the gold standard opposed the devaluations of sterling and the dollar, neither devaluation should be viewed as a failure of international cooperation.

While the central monetary powers did not share perceived common interests during this period, they did cooperate with others. The turn toward bilateralism and bloc diplomacy accommodated divergent tastes for monetary expansion and reflation between the blocs while affording some measure of exchange-rate stability within blocs. In the Anglo-Danish and Anglo-Argentine cases, economically inefficient discriminatory policies permitted bilateral political exchange. Further, by joining iterated commercial issues to single-play financial and monetary issues, these states were able to raise their mutual interests while lengthening the shadow of the future.

In 1936, the British, American, and French governments saw a mutual interest in devaluation and stabilization of the franc, and realized that mutual interest. Inadvertent exchange-rate adjustments of the previous period, reductions in holdings of foreign exchange, the emerging German security threat, and improving macroeconomic circumstances in the United States and Great Britain converted monetary Deadlock into

[33] See especially Kindleberger (fn. 11), 26-28.

an iterated three-nation dilemma of collective action. In short, when the central monetary powers perceived common interests that could be realized through cooperation, cooperation in fact materialized.

Differences in macroeconomic circumstances and economic ideology undercut analogies between the 1930s and the 1980s. However, the difficult problem of transcending contemporary dilemmas of collective action may be rendered somewhat more tractable by the continuing hold of this inappropriate analogy. One of the most consequential differences between the periods is the existence of the analogy between them. The specter of international economic disintegration brought about by the mindless and short-sighted pursuit of narrow national interests provides a powerful spur to cooperation. The fable of the 1930s may be spurious; the moral is not.

BANKERS' DILEMMAS:
Private Cooperation in Rescheduling Sovereign Debts

By CHARLES LIPSON*

I. INTRODUCTION

DURING the 1970s, the less developed countries started borrowing substantial sums from commercial banks in the Eurocurrency markets. Although this borrowing began well before the Arab oil embargo, its pace accelerated markedly in mid-decade, after oil prices had quadrupled and export earnings collapsed. Economic growth inevitably slowed worldwide, but heavy borrowing still allowed creditworthy LDCs to pursue significantly higher growth paths than those of Europe and North America.[1] The associated deficits were financed, in large part, by commercial credit.[2]

Much of this credit was extended to state-owned enterprises, which grew steadily while foreign direct investment lagged. In effect, one form of foreign capital was substituted for another.[3] Since the new funds could be used quite flexibly, this substitution of loans for direct investment gave state managers substantially more control over domestic economic

* I wish to thank Jeff Frieden, Christopher Holoman, Mark Hornung, Robert Keohane, C. K. Ko, Peter Lange, and Duncan Snidal for their helpful comments. Discussions with Kenneth Oye, and the seminar sessions he led, were valuable at every stage. My research and interviews were supported by a fellowship grant from the German Marshall Fund of the United States.

[1] From the late 1960s until 1983, the less developed countries consistently grew faster than the industrial countries. The biggest contrast was in 1975, when O.E.C.D. economies actually contracted slightly while less developed countries grew by approximately 4%. Between 1973 and 1979, Gross Domestic Product (GDP) in LDCs rose by 5.2% annually, and even faster (5.6%) among so-called middle-income oil importers. Advanced countries, by contrast, adjusted much more rapidly to the new factor prices and grew by only 2.8% annually. World Bank, *World Development Report 1984* (New York: Oxford University Press, for the World Bank, 1984), 11-12, Table 2.1, Figure 2.1.

[2] Benjamin J. Cohen, "Balance of Payments Financing: Evolution of a Regime," in Stephen D. Krasner, ed., *International Regimes* (Ithaca, NY: Cornell University Press, 1983), 315-36; Cohen, in collaboration with Fabio Basagni, *Banks and the Balance of Payments* (Montclair, NJ: Allanheld, Osmun, 1981).

[3] Jeff Frieden, "Third World Indebted Industrialization: International Finance and State Capitalism in Mexico, Brazil, Algeria, and South Korea," *International Organization* 35 (Summer 1981), 407-31.

activity and more control, at least initially, over the articulation between the national and the world economy.

There was, as we know, a terrible reckoning. It came in the early 1980s after a second oil crisis, another deep recession, and soaring real interest rates. Since Eurocredits had been extended on floating rates, interest obligations rose rapidly, both absolutely and relative to export earnings.[4] The terms of repayment were, of course, fixed contractually and were unrelated to national economic performance. They became increasingly onerous as interest rates rose and export earnings fell.

Still, when international credit was initially provided, it seemed to offer state planners more autonomy and wider choices than direct investment. State managers could choose the sectoral distribution of funds, and could emphasize capital-intensive infrastructure projects. They were no longer dependent upon the investment choices of multinational firms. Nor did the foreign loans carry the implications of external control and dependence so often associated with direct foreign investment.[5] Or so it seemed at the time.

But in a moment of crisis, when fixed repayment schedules are beyond reach, international loans offer only hard choices and little discretion. The debtor typically needs some breathing space: postponement of principal payments falling due over the next few years, and perhaps an infusion of new funds to keep interest payments current. In return, creditors want some assurance that, if they do renegotiate, they will be repaid promptly. They want some evidence that the debtor country can earn more foreign exchange and that it intends to meet its new repayment schedule. They have demanded, and received, agreement from debtors to undertake severe austerity programs.

In practice this means that the troubled debtor must approach the International Monetary Fund (I.M.F.) for conditional balance-of-payments support. To secure this support, a member country must reach agreement with the Fund on its future economic policies and performance targets.[6] Actually, as far as both debtors and creditors are concerned,

[4] In 1977, the developing countries paid nearly $40 billion in interest and principal. By 1984, that figure had quadrupled. Interest payments by the 25 largest borrowers rose from 10% of export earnings to 25%. Another 11% of export earnings went to repay principal, so that by 1984 debt-service represented well over one-third of total export earnings. The rise in this debt-service ratio was most marked between 1980 and 1982. *IMF Survey*, January 7, 1985, p. 3 (table); International Monetary Fund, *World Economic Outlook* (September 1984), revised projections by I.M.F. staff, Tables 35-36.

[5] On these critical attitudes toward direct foreign investment, see Thomas J. Biersteker, *Distortion or Development? Contending Perspectives on the Multinational Corporation* (Cambridge: MIT Press, 1981), chap. 1.

[6] Negotiations between Argentina and its major creditors demonstrated that the banks

the I.M.F.'s own credits are far less important than its approval of the proposed austerity measures. Without such approval and the continuing oversight that goes with it, the creditors (both public and private) simply will not reschedule sovereign debts.[7]

This critical status has given the I.M.F. some leverage in dealing with banks as well as with debtors. By refusing to sign a stabilization package, the Fund could effectively sabotage any agreement between the creditors and the debtor, and thus jeopardize the creditors' interests. It has used this threat, as we shall see, to provide residual coordination for banks—reinforcing the banks' own efforts to renegotiate their loans and to provide new credits to the impoverished debtor.

As the stakes in rescheduling have risen—with the biggest borrowers on the brink of default—the whole process has become more contentious. It is clear that loans to Third World borrowers entail losses; no one would value them at par. What has been unclear is who will bear these losses. That is what the fighting is really about—between creditors and debtors, between creditors and their monetary authorities, and among the creditors.

The debtors, most notably Argentina, have resisted the I.M.F.'s recommendations to reduce domestic demand and increase net exports. They have done so because I.M.F. programs are politically painful, usually requiring currency devaluation, deep budget cuts, limitations on new domestic credit, and suppression of real wage growth. The debtors have pushed instead for concessions on their outstanding obligations: below-market interest rates, longer grace periods for repayment, and postponement of several years' principal payments rather than merely one or two.

Creditors have refused to make significant concessions on interest rates, since that would not only lower bank earnings but would also acknowledge that a portion of the debt was uncollectible. They have made concessions, however, on other issues. Now that the first wave of "crisis reschedulings" is over and economic austerity programs are in place, creditors are willing to restructure debts over longer terms. They are less insistent on penalty rates and renegotiation fees, and more attentive to the problems of resuming economic growth. The smaller

---

require fully approved stabilization programs, not simply statements about "significant agreement with the I.M.F." or substantial progress in negotiations. *Wall Street Journal*, August 16, 1984, p. 27, and August 17, 1984, p. 16.

[7] Obviously, this informal requirement can apply only to member countries of the I.M.F. Since most states of Eastern Europe are not members, the creditors' oversight of economic programs there is inevitably weaker and less institutionalized. Commercial lenders have understandably sought to widen I.M.F. membership to include these states.

creditors have accepted the new terms proposed by larger banks—as they apply to outstanding debts. What they have not always accepted so easily is the obligation to provide new funds as part of the rescheduling package. Their reluctance to make new, "involuntary" loans has meant tougher and more prolonged bargaining among creditors.

In view of the severity of these problems, most observers have focused on the immediate and overriding policy issues: the stability of Western banking, the economic and political impact of I.M.F. stabilization programs,[8] and the prospects for institutional reform.[9] In the process, other important issues have been neglected. Little effort has been made to explore the strategic interaction of the various actors—their goals, their calculations, and the institutional framework within which bargaining takes place.

As a result, we have overlooked the whole issue of how, and why, creditors manage to cooperate. Yet cooperation among creditors has been the very basis of recent international debt management. Large money-center banks, relying on their own prior ties and institutional arrangements, have devised common positions to preserve the value of their foreign assets. And they have secured ratification from reluctant smaller institutions.

The task of rescheduling is a complicated one, involving hundreds of international banks and a wide array of financial assets. Aside from the technical difficulties of rescheduling so many types of financial instruments, there is no simple harmony of interest among creditors. Private banks have different exposures, different ties to each borrower, and vastly different roles in international banking. Moreover, when a joint solution is finally proposed, individual banks may be reluctant to

[8] See, for example, John Williamson, ed., *IMF Conditionality* (Washington, DC: Institute for International Economics, 1983); Willaim Cline and Sidney Weintraub, eds., *Economic Stabilization in Developing Countries* (Washington, DC: Brookings Institution, 1981); Tony Killick, ed., *The Quest for Economic Stabilization: The IMF and the Third World* (New York: St. Martin's, 1984); and Killick, ed., *The IMF and Stabilization: Developing Country Experiences* (New York: St. Martin's, 1984).

[9] Numerous reform plans have been suggested, but none has garnered much political support. Among the best-known plans are those by Norman A. Bailey, R. David Luft, and Roger W. Robinson, "Exchange Participation Notes: An Approach to the International Financial Crisis," in Thibaut de Saint Phalle, ed., *The International Financial Crisis: An Opportunity for Constructive Action* (Washington, DC: Georgetown University, Center for Strategic and International Studies, 1983), 27-36; Peter B. Kenen, "A Bailout Plan for the Banks," *New York Times* (national ed.), March 6, 1983, sec. 3, p. 3; and Felix G. Rohatyn, "A Plan for Stretching Out Global Debt," *Business Week*, February 28, 1983, pp. 15-18. These plans and many others are examined critically in Richard S. Dale and Richard P. Mattione, *Managing Global Debt* (Washington, DC: Brookings Institution, 1983), esp. 46-47, and in William R. Cline, *International Debt and the Stability of the World Economy* (Washington, DC: Institute for International Economic Policy, Analyses in International Economics, No. 4, 1983).

provide their share of the cost. They have ample opportunity to threaten defection from proposed common actions, and plausible incentives to do so.

In spite of these obstacles, creditors have shown a striking capacity to accommodate their differences, to reach joint negotiating positions, and to carry out rescheduling agreements. This capacity for joint action, so central to debt negotiations, needs to be explained and its limits explored. The limits to private, voluntary cooperation help to explain the changing role of international institutions in the debt crisis.

The widespread problems in servicing international debts also raise broader issues about the security of foreign capital. Are the rules concerning its proper treatment now changing? In the case of direct investment, for example, the rules have already changed dramatically. In the late 1960s and early 1970s, traditional legal standards were replaced by quite varied national treatment.[10] Major oil fields and mineral concessions were nationalized with little compensation, long-term contracts were nullified, and manufacturing industries were subject to more extensive regulation. This was more an assertion of economic sovereignty than a general assault on foreign capital: tough policies in some sectors were often combined with enticements to invest elsewhere. But whatever the intent of these policies, they have had a profound impact on national economic development, the organization of multinational firms, and the relationship between LDCs and the world economy.

But what of the standards for *loan* capital? Do wholesale debt renegotiations imply that the rules and procedures are changing now, as they already have for direct investment? The question is whether new standards and expectations apply. To answer that, we need to examine the fundamental features of debt restructuring and to consider the rules and principles at issue.

II. Organizing a Debt Rescheduling:
The Critical Role of Big Banks

"The basic restructuring deal, domestic or international, is struck by a few big banks," according to one participant in many such deals. "They then present it to the rest of the creditors, who have to agree after the fact."[11] This statement implies that cooperation among private banks is two-tiered. There is an inner core of true international giants—

[10] Charles Lipson, *Standing Guard: Protecting Foreign Capital in the Nineteenth and Twentieth Centuries* (Berkeley and Los Angeles: University of California Press, 1985).
[11] My analysis of debt rescheduling is based on extensive confidential interviews with bankers and public officials from the United States, Western Europe, and Latin America.

banks like Citibank, Lloyds, Chase, and Dresdner—who assemble large-scale syndicated loans and maintain affiliates in major markets around the world. It is they who lead the debt reschedulings. Smaller creditors are asked to ratify the agreement, not to haggle over its terms. This hierarchy among banks is central to debt rescheduling.

In effect, there are two games among banks in a rescheduling. In the primary game, large banks bargain with each other to set the terms. (They simultaneously bargain with the debtor, but that is another story.) The large banks thus establish the level of new funding to be provided and its apportionment among existing lenders, the rates and fees they will charge, the grace period before principal repayments must begin, the amounts of principal amortization to be postponed, and so forth.

In the secondary game, the large banks seek ratification by smaller creditors. Consent from these smaller participants is required to modify existing loan contracts that can no longer be met on schedule. Small creditors must be prevented from calling (or seriously threatening) a loan default, which could induce other creditors to invoke cross-default clauses and jeopardize the stakes of all lenders. In addition, if any new credits are needed, all creditors must be persuaded to provide their share. Thus, while small creditors do not negotiate the terms of rescheduling, their assent is vital to its success.

The major banks are well placed to win such approval. In the course of ordinary business, they work extensively with other banks, both large and small. The leading international banks share the risks of sovereign lending through syndications, and, when problems arise, sit together on creditor committees. They are heavily engaged in cross-depositing through the interbank market, and they provide a range of financial services to each other and to smaller institutions. Smaller banks—in Amsterdam, Toronto, or Dallas—may manage Euromarket syndicates occasionally, but far more often they simply buy international loan participations from the larger institutions and initiate their own loans only when existing clients need to finance exports or to expand abroad.[12] They also depend upon larger institutions for correspondent services.

These financial relationships permit both reciprocity and retaliation, and facilitate policy coordination. They are especially important because there is no formal institution for rescheduling. All agreements are *ad*

[12] These so-called smaller banks vary widely, ranging from regional American banks with extensive international interests to local institutions that only rarely have contact with the international capital market. A descriptively richer, less stylized account would capture this variety. My point here is to differentiate the large banks, which become intimately involved in debt crises, from the hundreds of banks with lesser stakes and little choice in final arrangements other than to ratify or reject them.

hoc. Such informality would seriously impede agreements if banks could not rely on their existing ties to foster cooperation.

Cooperation is further encouraged by the vast asymmetries in bank size. A small group of large international banks is able to negotiate the basic rescheduling package in which each has a powerful individual stake. Once these large banks are jointly committed to a rescheduling package, their size and their importance to other banks plays a critical role in assuring broad ratification.

Using these self-reliant arrangements, commercial lenders have successfully rescheduled international debts since the 1960s. Over the past several years, they have done so with increasing frequency and for increasingly large debts. In the process, many elements of debt restructuring have become routinized.[13]

In a typical case, a debtor, unable to pay promptly, approaches one of its largest creditors and asks for changes in the schedule of amortization payments. In addition, the debtor will probably seek an infusion of new credits to help meet any interest arrearages or other immediate obligations. The leading commercial creditor, a major bank like Citibank or Dresdner, then consults other lenders and, if they are convinced a rescheduling cannot be avoided, pulls together a committee of the largest creditors.

These procedures may sound straightforward, but they are slow and complicated, even in the early stages. Like all other features of debt rescheduling—from the *ad hoc* arrangements controlled by creditors to the commercial interest rates that are charged—they certainly do not encourage debtor states to seek relief. The first signs of trouble are usually a slow buildup of arrearages or a reluctance of some banks to roll over maturing credits. According to an I.M.F. staff study of reschedulings in the late 1970s, negotiations did not usually begin until a year or two later, when the need for a rescheduling had become obvious. The talks themselves then took another 18 months or more.[14]

This pace has accelerated in the 1980s, even though the number of reschedulings has increased significantly. The reason may be that the

[13] Debtors have sometimes urged the establishment of a permanent forum to deal with debt problems, and have raised the issue as part of the North-South dialogue. Creditors have always rejected this demand, fearing that debtors might control the institution, and that its presence would only encourage more pleas for rescheduling. M. S. Mendelsohn, *Commercial Banks and the Restructuring of Cross-Border Debt* (New York: Group of Thirty, 1983), 14.

[14] Bahram Nowzad, Richard C. Williams, and other I.M.F. staff, *External Indebtedness of Developing Countries*, Occasional Paper No. 3 (Washington, DC: International Monetary Fund, May 1981), 30-40; Richard Huff, "The Rescheduling of Country Debt: Is a More Formalized Process Necessary?" in Group of Thirty, *Risks in International Bank Lending* (New York: Group of Thirty, 1982), Appendix B.

gravity of some cases, and the combined impact of so many problems, compels immediate attention. Delays can be dangerous since many banks will not voluntarily renew their maturing short-term credits once a problem has been recognized. The process is similar to a run on a bank— but this time it is a run *by* the banks. Thus, creditors may be forced to act quickly, first to stop a hemorrhage of short-term capital, and then to piece together a debt restructuring. There are, however, real limits to how quickly banks can act, even with their full attention devoted to the problem. The Mexican rescheduling of 1982, for instance, took several months—and it was swift compared to reschedulings for Brazil and Argentina.

Once the key creditors acknowledge that a rescheduling is necessary, the first important step is to select a creditor committee.[15] The composition of this committee is important: its members must not only agree among themselves; they must also convince other creditors to support the final agreement. In view of the strong regional and national ties among banks, this "political" function of the creditor committee implies some geographic diversity among its members. Smaller creditors, who are not on the committee, are typically members of national banking networks and purchase syndicated international loans through money-center banks in their region. If they prove reluctant to endorse the agreement, they will be contacted first by these money-center banks with whom they have regular dealings. These financial relationships and communicative networks are thus important in ratifying any loan rescheduling.

After a creditor committee is in place, the first order of business is to collect financial data covering the composition and maturity of debts as well as the economic status of the borrower. The major creditors must then establish common negotiating positions and reach agreement with the troubled debtor.

The whole process requires a good deal of trust among the key creditors. Take the problem of data collection, for instance. Although some debtors have reliable figures on their own indebtedness, their economic performance, and their essential financing needs, many do not. No one agency may be in a position to control, or even to know, just how much the various state-owned enterprises, bureaucratic agen-

---

[15] That, at least, is the typical sequence. There are variations, however. In 1982, Mexico approached the U.S. Treasury, the Federal Reserve, and the I.M.F. before going to private bankers. Its reserves had declined so precipitously that a large credit was necessary immediately—and only the U.S. government could arrange a multi-billion dollar loan so quickly. More commonly, debtors work simultaneously with official and private creditors to arrange two separate rescheduling packages.

cies, and local governments have borrowed over the years. Levels of short-term borrowing are even more difficult to track and control.[16] A complete audit is possible, of course, and has been necessary in rare cases of complete financial disarray. But an outside audit is both costly and slow, and time is usually at a premium. Moreover, the prospect of foreign auditors rummaging around a state's capital and demanding documents might well stimulate nationalist fears, raise questions about the corrupt use of funds, and otherwise complicate the rescheduling exercise.[17] Ideally, the banks would prefer access to I.M.F. data. The Fund has the best independent figures, collected from member governments and checked on periodic staff missions. But such data are not generally made available to commercial banks. The Fund wants to maintain confidentiality in its dealings with members, so it only shares less sensitive information and aggregate data.

Faced with these constraints, banks must rely heavily on their collective resources. In calculating how much "new money" they need to put into a rescheduling package, the banks work back and forth between their own figures and those supplied by the debtor. They arrive at partial debt totals by adding up their assets in the debtor country, plus those they have sold to other institutions. They ask others to report on various types of loans they have made to the debtor country.

There are some incentives for individual banks to underreport these commitments. The reason is that, if new (involuntary) credits are needed, they will invariably be calculated as a *pro rata* share of previous commitments. In calculating the "new money" package, the creditor committee will tell all banks to contribute a fixed percentage (say, 7 percent) of their outstanding loans on a particular date.

A date well before the rescheduling is selected because some banks, sensing imminent trouble in the debtor country, swiftly reduce their own exposure. What is prudent for the individual lender, however, only

[16] A debtor's best information about its total obligations probably comes from its regulation of foreign exchange. Local borrowers have to register their foreign debts with the exchange-control authority in order to repay them with hard currencies.

Not all countries have such controls, however, and those that do may not adequately cover short-term trade obligations. Terry Karl's analysis of oil-rich borrowers concluded that their "controls over foreign debt were generally weak; accountability for short-term loans was virtually non-existent." She argues that in many cases foreign borrowing was simply a "mechanism to disguise the mismanagement, misallocation, or self-serving utilization of public monies." Karl, "The Paradox of the Rich Debtor: The Foreign Borrowing of Oil-Exporting Countries," unpub., American Political Science Association Convention (Chicago, 1983), 32.

[17] The debtor may, on its own, hire an investment bank to collect such data and to advise it in negotiations with commercial banks. The best-known of these advisors is actually a troika of investment and merchant banks acting jointly: Warburg's, Lazard Frères, and Lehman Brothers Kuhn Loeb.

exacerbates the collective problem posed by the debtor's illiquidity. Hence, the creditor committee picks an early date for purposes of calculating exposure. It thus attempts to limit the divergence between individual and collective rationality. In domestic bankruptcies, U.S. law does the same thing, requiring that creditors return assets collected within ninety days of bankruptcy.

Negotiations about the level of involuntary lending and its apportionment among banks are difficult and prolonged. Some banks maintain that specific types of lending, such as bearer bonds, ought to be excluded from the totals. In addition, there are disputes between banks that have bought and sold loans. Was the seller to be responsible if the loan went sour? Which bank will have to count the loans as part of its prior commitment? And what about loans to foreign companies (such as Caterpillar Tractor in Brazil) that may be guaranteed by the American parent company? Are such loans to be counted? Throughout these negotiations, individual banks try to limit their exposures and thus to minimize the new funds they must provide. What banks do *not* do, according to specialists, is simply misrepresent their assets.

What is the basis for such trust and, more generally, for cooperation among the major private creditors in a rescheduling? Our answer must begin by looking at their stakes in the various disputes, the choices they confront, and the probable consequences of their actions.

The largest creditors share two overriding characteristics:
  1. They have a lot at stake relative to other creditors, measured both in terms of their capital base and the prospective impact on operating profits.
  2. They are permanent fixtures in international banking.
Let us consider each in turn.

Not surprisingly, the largest international banks are also the largest creditors in Latin America and East Europe. What is less obvious is that their exposure has been high relative to their capital base and annual operating profits. This high *relative* exposure is particularly important because, as one senior banker told me (in the language of modern business schools), "the risks increase non-monotonically with exposure."

High exposure threatens, in successive order:
—a net loss for the quarter;
—a net loss for the year;
—a run on the bank by major depositors; and, finally,
—bank failure.
Even the less drastic outcomes imply lower share prices and may threaten

a bank's senior management. Because of their high exposure, then, large banks have a compelling interest in successful debt restructuring. Failure to complete such a rescue could lead to a write-down of assets and charge-offs against operating profits (if loan loss reserves have to be increased, or if federal regulators require that interest income be treated less favorably). Indeed, there are perverse incentives to throw good money after bad—lending even to the worst risks rather than voluntarily accepting lower short-term earnings.

Thus, in their negotiations with each other, major creditors cannot easily threaten to walk away from rescheduling talks or to write off assets with real underlying value. These hard-line tactics are plausible, however, for smaller creditors, who would suffer much less from a failure to reschedule, and whose withdrawal or obstinance could impede a settlement. They aim to secure more favorable terms, or even a buy-out of their assets by larger creditors, by threatening to sabotage an overall settlement. For the largest lenders, such a threat would be suicidal and is not credible.

Yet a major bank's stake in a particular rescheduling is hardly its only consideration. It *does* help to explain why the biggest West German banks led the East European reschedulings, where they were heavily committed, and why they sometimes met resistance from New York banks with smaller exposures and fewer trade links. For the same reason, it is the heavily exposed U.S. banks that have led the Latin American reschedulings and the less vulnerable European banks that have been more reluctant to accept the terms and procedures. Despite these differences, the giant banks have hammered out common positions and have lined up support from smaller banks in their own areas. The reason is that, aside from having a stake in Poland or in Mexico, a large bank perceives itself to be an *international bank with longstanding ties to other major institutions and permanent interests in the stable operation of international capital markets*.

The fact that key creditors are "permanent players" frames the meaning of their participation in individual debt reschedulings. They have ongoing relationships with sovereign borrowers. They arrange loans and hold deposits for state agencies and local firms, and, in some larger markets like Brazil, they may even operate domestic banking networks. They expect to resume voluntary lending to large LDC economies in the future, and to participate profitably in their domestic growth. They cannot walk away from a rescheduling and maintain these ties—and they say so frankly.

Moreover, they are permanent players in international capital markets and expect to keep working closely with other major financial institutions in a variety of ways. These banks know that they will meet repeatedly at the negotiating table and will participate in each other's future syndications. Although they must compete aggressively in booking loans, they also recognize their shared interest in arranging "workouts" for troubled debts. Equally important in terms of fostering cooperation, they are linked by a dense network of financial ties, so there is ample room for reciprocity and retribution.

These synchronic and dyachronic links among the key actors do not preclude tough bargaining over the terms of rescheduling, or individual efforts to reduce loan exposure. The complexity of the issues, the different stakes of individual banks, and the different national regulations governing each institution all leave plenty of room for disagreement and conflict. In the Mexican case, for example, there were at least 25 distinct types of loans outstanding, and different banks held quite different portfolios.[18] Should they all be treated alike?

Sorting out such issues and achieving a rough parity of sacrifice is a central problem in creditor negotiations. In general, the hardest bargaining among banks is over

- the kinds of obligations to be included in the rescheduling;
- the levels of new money to be put in; and
- the length of the amortization period.

The difficult issue of the debtor's future policies is removed from these negotiations. The creditors simply insist on I.M.F. conditional lending and economic supervision. Beyond that, the creditors' overall aim is to avoid write-downs if possible, to preserve the present value of their assets, and to eliminate any negative impact on operating profits.

Two points stand out in the bargaining among creditors. One is the need to minimize transaction costs. There is a compelling logic, well understood by the actors, to finding a formula to handle the diversity of bank assets. The basic norm is that all assets should be treated alike. This norm has "the great advantage of speeding negotiations," as one banker told me—adding that the amounts to be rescheduled "are too large to leave in limbo." Said another, "exceptions would take endless time." This strong emphasis on uniformity—with only a few standardized exceptions and qualifications—has several advantages, according to one experienced negotiator. It not only minimizes negotiating time in the first rescheduling for any country, but makes subsequent rounds much easier. By creating a clear standard, it also eases negotiations with other debtors. Thus, the major Mexican rescheduling of 1982 provided

[18] Joseph Kraft, *The Mexican Rescue* (New York: Group of Thirty, 1984), 44.

a set of guidelines and legal documents that served as a template in subsequent Latin American reschedulings. Finally, the emphasis on uniformity also appeals to "simple-minded equity among banks," as one negotiator put it, and so makes it harder for individual banks to hold out for special treatment.

It is true that some financial assets *are* treated differently—but they fall into well-defined categories. Officially guaranteed loans are handled, quite understandably, in negotiations of creditor governments (known informally as the Paris Club). Individually held bonds are exempted because they are widely disbursed, and because each holder has legal rights to petition for default if payments are not made as scheduled.[19] Short-term trade credits extended by manufacturers are not included because they cannot be monitored.[20] Likewise, only a concerted and continuous effort can sustain the levels of very short-term credit provided through interbank lending to countries such as Brazil. Monitoring these commitment levels is difficult, and many banks try to extinguish such credits as they mature. In short, there are surveillance problems and legal obstacles to any comprehensive restructuring of sovereign debt. Still, as one bank lawyer told me, when one considers the diversity of assets, "the uniformity of treatment is striking."

A second point is that even though the key creditors have overwhelming incentives to cooperate and no individual incentives to defect, they do not necessarily prefer the same point of agreement. The main reason for this difference, aside from varying loan commitments to particular debtors, is the regulatory context of the parent banks. German banks, for instance, have legally hidden reserves against loan losses; U.S. banks do not. Moreover, American banks are legally required to downgrade the status of loans that have not paid interest within the past 90 days. Serious arrearages thus affect American bank profits immediately, and may affect the price of bank shares. No other country has such statutes and regulations.

These regulatory differences help to explain why large German and Swiss banks would prefer to handle arrears by capitalizing the overdue interest. That is, they would prefer to add the overdue interest (or some portion of it) to the outstanding principal. For most continental banks,

---

[19] The bond question also suggests just how difficult it is to establish a common baseline to calculate new, involuntary commitments. In the major Mexican rescheduling, creditors finally agreed to increase their outstanding commitments by 7%. But according to Kraft, the entire banking systems of Japan, France, and Switzerland objected to the proposed baseline. "The Japanese claimed they had not made loans to Mexico but [had] acquired promissory notes from US banks. The Swiss said the Mexican numbers included many sales of bonds which were supposed to be excluded from the rescue operation." *Ibid.*, 52.

[20] Huff (fn. 14), 51-52.

such treatment does not require approval by the board of directors and would not require new funds to be raised by Euromarket subsidiaries. Moreover, it is obviously a simple way to handle the problem and would minimize negotiating time in restructuring troubled debts.

U.S. banks, on the other hand, would suffer immediate losses from such a policy since they would have to reclassify these loans as non-performing.[21] In view of these regulations, American banks demand that interest payments be kept current and that new funds be supplied to the debtor to meet these needs. Since these new funds are a loan, albeit an involuntary one, the interest is in effect capitalized. But the new funds have to be raised from hundreds of creditors—an arduous process. The advantage for American banks is that, unless the regulators disapprove, the new loans can be treated as ordinary assets and the interest payments as income, even though they are really being financed by the banks themselves. Indeed, since interest rates are set above the banks' cost of funds, and since additional fees are charged, the lenders' profits appear strong—on paper.

These differences over interest capitalization have been resolved in favor of the U.S. banks, leaving the Europeans slightly aggrieved. The reason for this outcome is straightforward. Larger European banks do not suffer badly under the current arrangements and could not credibly threaten to defect from them. They can argue, at best, that the arrangements are so complicated that they do not work well and may break down in the future if smaller banks refuse to provide new credits. Large U.S. banks would, however, suffer sharp and immediate losses from any explicit and large-scale capitalization of interest. Constrained by their regulatory setting, and by the financial markets' close scrutiny of their operating profits, these banks have resisted any alteration in the treatment of overdue interest. If pushed, they can plausibly claim that they would rather see a particular debt restructuring fail than accept this new and costly arrangement as the pattern for the future. They can also argue, again quite convincingly, that other American banks would reject any such solution and would halt negotiations if necessary. In short, the large American and European banks are playing a coordination game that leaves one group aggrieved because the other is precommitted.

[21] Some Europeans have asked, in exasperation, why the U.S. regulators do not change the 90-day rule on overdue foreign loans. In fact, the Comptroller of the Currency has been flexible on loan classification where the law allows. The Federal Reserve Board has supported this posture. They do not want to impede reschedulings. But they would face an uproar if overdue loans from Argentina or Mexico were treated differently from overdue loans to local factories or farms. There is, quite understandably, an equity issue here. Moreover, no regulator would want to introduce different accounting principles to handle foreign and domestic assets, performing or nonperforming.

The Americans are locked into a strategy that yields their most preferred outcome. The aggrieved Europeans are stuck with their second-best outcome because any shift in their strategy will produce disaster unless the United States also changes to accommodate them. But that is just the point: the Americans are committed to the status quo.

The larger point to be emphasized, however, is not the conflicting preferences about the form of new credits, but *the capacity of large private banks to coordinate effectively in cases of troubled debt despite their differences, and despite their vigorous competition as Euromarket lenders.*[22]

III. RATIFYING A RESCHEDULING:
THE ROLE OF SMALLER BANKS

If we expect large banks to cooperate with each other because of their heavy commitments to sovereign borrowers and because they are permanent fixtures in the Euromarkets, we would expect to find the holdouts and mavericks among the smaller banks with fewer international links. That is exactly where they are to be found—among the regional banks in the United States, and among the Arab, Italian, Spanish, and consortium banks.

Essentially, the aim of holdouts is to reduce their exposure without any loss of asset value.[23] Lenders who conduct little international business may see obvious benefits in cutting back their exposure in cases of troubled debt. For them, the costs of providing additional funds are not offset by any long-term ties to the beleaguered borrower. Nor are small lenders especially concerned about maintaining their reputation as reliable partners in international syndications. They may also argue that their exposure is small and that the rescheduling package can easily be completed without them.

Large banks respond that successful holdouts have serious ramifica-

---

[22] This role of large creditors in managing debt problems is not new. Armando Sapori, in his analysis of medieval Italian merchant-bankers, concludes that "their solidarity is shown by their behavior when their debtors went bankrupt. The best-established business house in the city assumed the handling of the bankruptcy for all the other companies without charge, whether they had business ties with them or not. It managed the case in court, dealt with the trustees, signed the agreement, and then divided the expenses pro rata among the creditors, giving each the net sum obtained." Armando Sapori, *The Italian Merchant in the Middle Ages*, trans. Patricia Ann Kennen (New York: W. W. Norton, 1970), 15.

[23] While all holdouts want to reduce their exposure without cost, some are especially insistent. Typically, these are banks with already-weak balance sheets and few international ties. To book additional low-quality, illiquid assets is relatively expensive and risky for them and contributes little to their main business. That is why the toughest battles over new Mexican credits have been with banks in the southwestern United States. Already saddled with bad energy debts, their loans to Mexico were usually undertaken to support local trade and were never intended to be long-term assets.

tions. They immediately reduce the debt relief available to the borrower. More important, if other creditors demand equal treatment, they may imperil the entire rescheduling. As a result, holdouts are resisted aggressively by major creditors and, if the restructuring is sufficiently important, by national monetary authorities in the United States and Europe. This emphasis on the uniform treatment of creditors—that each should contribute a *pro rata* share—is a basic norm of debt renegotiation. As Richard Huff, an analyst working for the Comptroller of the Currency, observes,

> One reason for interbank discord, beyond the normal commercial rivalries of this intensely competitive business, has been the fear that debt relief advanced by one creditor might simply be used to pay off someone else, thus leaving the debtor's financial position unchanged. ... Thus the doctrine of "fair treatment" has emerged as the guiding principle of debt-restructuring negotiations: each bank is expected to participate in debt relief (either new funding or rescheduling) in proportion to its existing exposure.[24]

But while "uniform participation" is a central tenet of rescheduling, "the enforcement of that doctrine," is, as Huff notes, "no easy matter."[25] Some banks may object to the terms of rescheduling, but more often they simply want to avoid the burdens of new, involuntary loans. At first glance, these holdouts would seem to be in a strong bargaining position. Their leverage, like that of small creditors in general, derives from their contractual rights as lenders and from the larger banks' greater need to complete the rescheduling. They are not legally required to supply any new credits, and their consent is needed for changes in the repayment schedule of existing loans. Since the exercise of these rights could sabotage a rescheduling or slow its progress, a smaller lender can strategically withhold its cooperation in an effort to extract concessions.

Another source of leverage for smaller creditors is the threat to call a formal default. Since all international loans contain cross-default clauses, some observers have suggested that a single such default could start a prairie fire.

The rationale behind this assertion is that there are no bankruptcy procedures for sovereign states, and no orderly procedures to establish the priority of creditors' claims.[26] The first creditor to attach assets can

---

[24] Huff (fn. 14), 51.
[25] *Ibid.*
[26] I am indebted to Douglas Baird, James Fooreman, and Cynthia Lichtenstein for their discussions of the legal issues. See "Symposium on Default by Foreign Government Debtors." in *The University of Illinois Law Review* (No. 1, 1982), particularly articles by Reade H.

claim them in subsequent judicial proceedings. It does not have to share the proceeds with other lenders unless it has agreed to do so in loan contracts. Thus, if a debtor falls behind in payments, individual creditors may be tempted to declare default and establish the priority of their claims. This prospect, it is said, could turn an arrearage or technical default into a wild rush of default declarations, as each creditor scrambled to protect itself against the others. An outcome that no one really wants could thus be encouraged by the absence of institutional barriers.

Such fears have been considerably exaggerated, however. First, it is difficult to get even one syndicate to call a default when major creditors object. Voting in these matters is always weighted by each lender's share of the loan, so the larger lenders are well placed to block any move they oppose. Second, in nearly all cases, major creditors would object because a default would cost them dearly. There are few substantial assets to seize, and the confrontation would jeopardize other ties to the borrower (and to other creditors if they objected). Any real hope for repayment depends upon export earnings and capital imports, which would be slashed by a formal declaration of default. Thus, even if a few smaller syndicates did declare default and did sue for assets, larger lenders would still be reluctant to invoke their cross-default clauses. They would be reluctant, that is, unless the debtor had violated basic principles of international finance by declaring unilaterally that it would not pay. To invoke cross-default clauses in less extreme circumstances would be to lose all control over the restructuring process and to move into an unexplored and risky world.

There is clear confirmation of this reluctance: very few defaults have been called despite widespread arrearages. The only significant use of cross-default clauses occurred during the freeze of Iranian assets, when syndicates led by Chase Manhattan Bank declared defaults.[27] Some other declarations followed, and some American creditors did move quickly to attach assets. Morgan Guaranty even managed to attach Iran's share of the Krupp steelworks in Germany.[28] But European commercial banks

---

Ryan, Jr., "Defaults and Remedies Under International Bank Loan Agreements with Foreign Sovereign Borrowers—A New York Lawyer's Perspective," pp. 89-132; Bruce W. Nichols, "The Impact of the Foreign Sovereign Immunities Act on the Enforcement of Lenders' Remedies," pp. 251-64; and Frank D. Mayer, Jr., and Michele Odorrizi, "Foreign Government Deposits: Attachment and Set-Off," pp. 289-304.

[27] Anthony Sampson, *The Money Lenders* (Harmondsworth, U.K.: Penguin, 1983), 309-312.

[28] On the disorderly process of attachments, where the first creditor to the courthouse ends up with the assets, see Robert D. Steele, ed., *The Iranian Crisis and International Law* (Charlottesville, VA: John Bassett Moore Society of International Law, 1981), Panel II: "Commercial Aspects of the Iran Crisis: The Asset Freeze."

(and their monetary authorities) were furious at what they considered precipitous and unnecessary action by U.S. banks. They refused to join the rush. Directors of the Dresdner Bank, for instance, publicly announced that they would *not* call Iranian loans in default. Even in this case, then, the cross-default clauses did not produce a "domino effect" reaching beyond the control of key creditors.

The larger banks are nevertheless concerned about such "domino effects" and about the bargaining leverage they give to smaller banks. As a result, legal counselors for large banks have begun drafting syndicated loan contracts that establish better obstacles to "hair-trigger" defaults. They allow longer grace periods to cure the effects of technical defaults (ten days, perhaps) and may exempt failures to meet payment deadlines when the fault is a technical one beyond the debtor's control. There has also been some change of legal language, limiting cross-defaults to cases in which other loans have actually been accelerated (thus excluding cases of technical default where an acceleration *might* occur but has not been called). Finally, the newer loan contracts typically require a higher percentage of votes to call a default. It is now common to ask for approval from banks holding two-thirds of any syndicated loan. This gives large banks a more effective veto and protects European banks against overly aggressive actions by their New York counterparts.

Creditor committees are also organized to deal with banks that would threaten a default or impede restructuring. They usually include international banks based in the United States, Britain, Germany, Japan, Switzerland, France, and Canada—a group large enough to cover major national banking networks, but small enough to operate effectively.[29] In the Mexican rescheduling, for instance, the Bank of Tokyo was assigned responsibility for other banks in Asia, while the Bank of Montreal handled banks in Canada. Lloyds was assigned not only banks in Britain and Ireland, but also those in other areas traditionally linked to British finance: Greece, Turkey, the Middle East, India, and Australia. Each U.S. member of the advisory committee took responsibility for ten American regional banks, and then asked each of these to take responsibility for ten more.[30] These elaborate arrangements were necessary since hundreds of banks worldwide held loans to Mexico. The creditors had to be convinced that their interests were represented in the negotiations

[29] Peter Leslie, "Techniques of Rescheduling: The Latest Lessons," *Banker* (April 1983), 26.

[30] Kraft (fn. 18), 26-27. The role of large *regional* banks in reschedulings has gradually increased. They typically serve as conduits of communication between the largest international banks and smaller regional banks. This role, which does not entail sanctioning the smaller banks, gives the large regional banks an opportunity to voice their own concerns.

and well served by the final agreement. If additional persuasion was needed, that, too, could best be done by a bank with local connections, both financial and political.

Large creditors have proved willing to do this kind of arm-twisting, if called upon. Shirking the individual costs has not been a problem on creditor committees for several reasons. First, the costs of dealing with holdouts are not especially high. They mainly involve lost management time. If mutually profitable banking relationships are somehow threatened, it is usually a minor matter for the larger bank. Second, the most heavily committed creditors have strong *individual* incentives to bear these costs in order to complete the rescheduling package in which they have so much at stake. Third, there are routine ways of assigning "holdout banks" to larger creditors (based on location and business ties), so any evasion would be obvious to other members of the creditor committee and costly to the bank's reputation.

Ultimately, large creditors are willing to pay the price of dealing with holdouts because these costs are integral to serving on creditor committees. And serving on such committees is valuable to larger banks. It offers them the chance to shape the terms of debt rescheduling, and thus to protect their own asset positions. It also offers them direct contact with senior officials from debtor countries, which can be useful for banks with ongoing business there. And it yields information about policy trends and economic performance in the debtor, and about other banks' attitudes. All in all, it is an opportunity for sustained contact with other large financial institutions, and a chance to be identified clearly by all banks as a responsible major actor in international credit markets.

These arrangements among major creditors are crucial to the secondary game of ratifying the new debt package. The creditor committee first concludes a draft agreement with the debtor. If the stakes are large enough, it may then present the agreement to other creditors in a series of regional meetings, which feature presentations by the debtor's senior economic officials. After the smaller creditors have communicated their concerns, the creditor committee completes the final document. It then telexes all creditors, informing them of the terms and requesting ratification plus their share of any required funds. The deadline gives them little time to assess the agreement, and none to organize a united opposition. Most small and medium-sized creditors simply accept the terms as presented. A few may not—probably hoping that a major creditor will offer them private concessions.[31]

---

[31] On rare occasions, a banker will object to a deal on principle. Such a stand is not easily overturned by the usual economic pressures on outliers. One domestic example is a small

There are seldom objections to restructuring loans that are already outstanding. The revised terms typically include healthy margins for the lenders (at least 1 percent above their cost of funds, and sometimes considerably more) and perhaps fees and commissions. Some recent deals have offered European banks additional incentives, such as the chance to convert their dollar loans into other currencies (which eases funding for non-American banks).

The difficult issue is the provision of new money. Here, too, the packages have been shaped to encourage participation. Some banks have asked for, and received, permission to allocate their new (involuntary) loans to borrowers of their choice within the debtor country. This option allows them to maintain banking ties to old clients and to select assets with less risk. Recent packages have also included a small margin of safety; if all banks contribute their share, the loans will be slightly oversubscribed. There is considerable pressure on the smallest banks to contribute; but if they cannot be persuaded and decide simply to write off their old loans, they are no longer allowed to obstruct the rescheduling. What is essential is that the agreement cover virtually all the outstanding credits (but not necessarily every small lender). Rescheduling thus requires full participation by medium-sized banks, which have millions of dollars in outstanding loans and which contribute a significant portion of any new funds.

For any bank to hold out is a perilous and lonely course. "There is a pretty firm unwritten, unspoken rule against buy-outs," one international bank lawyer told me. "The only exceptions I know of involve risk participants in letters of credit who had not already put up funds." A London syndications manager put the matter more bluntly: no banks have been bought out of a rescheduling. "If we did that," he said, "that would be the end. [The rescheduling] would unravel like a cheap sweater" as other smaller creditors stood in line for the same deal.[32]

The larger banks could, of course, offer a less visible carrot to holdouts than buying out loan participations. They might simply offer to pay higher rates on the holdout's correspondent deposits. This arrangement would be private and would directly affect the small bank's earnings.

---

bank that objected to the U.S. government's effort to bail out Chrysler. The rescue package required 100% creditor participation, and this bank held out for days against the pleadings of the highest U.S. officials.

[32] Nevertheless, there are occasional rumors of such buy-outs, and they cannot be ruled out entirely. What is clear is that any such arrangements must have been minor and highly confidential. They have not led to any significant erosion of the norm of uniform treatment for creditors.

Bankers with whom I have spoken deny the existence of such deals, but it is impossible to rule out side payments completely.

In any case, the stick is much more prominent than the carrot. There are strong sanctions that can be used against a bank that refuses to contribute to a refunding. A Euromarket syndications manager noted that such a bank would be blacklisted in international banking. Since this sanction might not hurt some smaller banks, which rarely participate in international lending anyway, additional pressures on their domestic operations may be necessary. The focus, in the first instance, is on the holdout's immediate banking relationships. Senior officials at the smaller bank, who were not necessarily involved before now, may be contacted by senior management of a money-center bank and told of the problem's importance to the larger institution. If this is insufficient, the larger bank could stress the difficulties that the smaller bank would experience in buying domestic loan participations and using other banking services. Even if alternative institutions could supply these services (and they might hesitate), few banks could easily contemplate the severance of such correspondence services. Moreover, since many banking arrangements involve close relationships with other financial institutions, a bank can be hurt if it becomes known as an unreliable partner in difficult situations. Larger banks are well placed to spread this damaging news. The reputational effects in banking are even more important than in other businesses since, as one portfolio manager told me, "banks are the very products of imperfect information; if information were perfect, you wouldn't need banks [because investors and savers would contract with each other directly]. The channel of that imperfect information is other banks, so the penalties of being frozen out are very great indeed."

The essential idea here is to isolate the few holdouts and then use their immediate banking relationships to point out the error of their ways and the costs they might entail. *The whole point is to break down the large secondary game, involving hundreds of banks and considerable opportunities for free-riding, into a series of bilateral games pitting a few small holdouts against major money-center banks*. These arrangements imply that noncooperation is transparent; that defectors may be discriminated against in the future; and that the asymmetry of bank size permits effective, low-cost sanctions.

IV. The Limits of Private Coordination and the Evolution of Institutional Arrangements

Smaller creditors, recognizing their weakness, seldom hold out. If some do, and if the rescheduling is a significant one, the national mon-

etary authority and other interested political figures may become involved. A lawyer working on the Mexican rescheduling describes the
process as follows: "One by one, we identified the hard cases. We
pinpointed their argument or excuse for not going along. Then we
brought the appropriate pressure to bear—sometimes from state or federal regulators; sometimes from figures in the local community; sometimes from other bankers."[33]

Thus, even though commercial loans are largely rescheduled by the
lenders themselves, they still may require backing from governmental
authorities to eliminate the last significant holdouts. Cooperation among
banks does not occur in complete anarchy. Central banks, particularly
the Federal Reserve Board and the Bank of England, do put pressure
on holdouts when the stakes and risks are high. Their power derives
from their regulatory control over bank operations and, in a larger sense,
from their centrality to the financial system as a whole.

But the role of governmental authorities in dealing with creditors
should not be exaggerated. It is best understood as a supplement to
private pressure in major cases. It plays little role in rescheduling smaller
debtors, and has only an indirect impact on banks outside the United
States and the United Kingdom. Not only are commercial banks effective
in their own efforts to cooperate, but the Federal Reserve is constrained
by its legal mandate, its governmental role, and its limitation to American
banks and their international operations. And within the United States,
it cannot command banks to make involuntary loans or provide guarantees against losses, even informally. Nor is it charged with supervising
bank assets or insuring bank liabilities; those tasks are assigned to the
Comptroller of the Currency and the Federal Deposit Insurance Corporation. Finally, unlike many foreign central banks, it maintains some
distance from major banks, relies heavily on laws and formal regulations,
and often assumes an adversarial role in implementing its policies and
regulations, as do the banks themselves.[34] While it has quietly favored
cooperation among banks in dealing with major debtors, its role has
largely been one of support for the efforts of major private creditors. A
much more important role for the Fed and for other central banks has
been to provide emergency financing for the largest debtors—a task that
private creditors simply cannot perform.

Recently, the I.M.F. has also played a role in creditor relationships.
It demanded, and received, pledges of new private loans to Mexico
before it would sign a stabilization agreement in 1982. I have argued

[33] Kraft (fn. 18), 53.
[34] Andrew Spindler, *The Politics of International Credit: Private Finance and Foreign Policy
in Germany and Japan* (Washington, DC: Brookings Institution, 1984).

222 LIPSON

elsewhere that the evolving role of the Fund as well as that of central banks can best be understood as incremental reforms designed to overcome gaps in cooperation among creditors.[35]

There are several such gaps. I have already noted the banks' problems in collecting timely, comprehensive data. Private banks are now attempting joint action on this front. Working through the new Institute for International Finance in Washington, they hope to improve their data on short-term debts, maturity distributions, prospective financing needs, and emerging credit problems. But, inevitably, the I.M.F. and the World Bank will continue to have superior data. The problem, as far as the lenders are concerned, is to develop ways to share this information without violating confidential channels for its collection. Better knowledge of short-term debts is especially important since the rapid buildup of such claims often indicates a deterioration in the debtor's current account and an inability to borrow over the longer term.

Second, the procedures for private bank coordination, no matter how effective, are slow—even when the need for swift action is apparent. Although many negotiating procedures are routinized, each new rescheduling must be organized from scratch. Specific details, such as the composition of creditor committees, must be arranged anew for the first round of rescheduling. (They can be repeated, much more efficiently, in subsequent rounds with the same debtor.) A variety of technical issues must be sorted out and the outstanding debt figures cumulated. Although some negotiating norms such as "equal treatment" have developed and do speed discussions, large debts invariably require months of negotiation.

Private lenders are thus virtually helpless if capital flight and the inability to roll over short-term debts combine to produce a real financial crisis. Nor is the I.M.F. authorized to step in and provide swift emergency funding. Only national central banks and treasuries are capable of organizing multi-billion dollar credits quickly. They have done so individually (as the Fed and the U. S. Treasury did for Mexico), and jointly (as the Bank for International Settlements did for Brazil). Although these "bridging" loans were intended only to meet short-term financing needs until an I.M.F. program was in place, such actions, together with mounting concerns about the quality of international bank assets, drew national monetary authorities much more deeply into Third World debt problems than ever before.

Finally, there have been growing doubts about the ability of large

[35] Charles Lipson, "International Debt and International Institutions," in Miles Kahler, ed., *The Politics of International Debt* (Cornell University Press, forthcoming 1986).

banks to secure cooperation from all creditors. The sheer size and number of reschedulings have strained their resources. They have also killed
the market for voluntary Third World lending, and diminished the taste
of many smaller banks for further international activities (eliminating,
in the process, an important reason for banks to provide forced loans).

These doubts, combined with the massive scale of Mexico's debt
problem, produced a dramatic policy shift at the I.M.F. In November
1982, the Fund's Managing Director, Jacques de Larosière, took the
unprecedented step of establishing mandatory levels of forced private
lending before the I.M.F. would sign a stabilization agreement with
Mexico. This bold action, repeated in the Brazilian case, was a turning
point in the treatment of sovereign debt. It staked out a new leadership
role for the Fund, and a new relationship between the Fund and private
banks.

But one should not infer from the I.M.F.'s larger role that private
cooperation had broken down. It had not. Rather, the I.M.F. (with U.S.
approval) saw an opportunity to improve the chances for success in a
rescheduling where the stakes were unusually high. The Mexican case
was a particularly difficult one for private creditors, not only because
of its size, but also because it involved so many small banks in the
Southwest—banks that lacked ties to international capital markets and
had already suffered heavy losses in energy lending. But the task of the
I.M.F. was not to supplant large creditors in organizing the private
banks; it was to reinforce the banks' own claims against potential holdouts. The Fund, in effect, worked through the existing structures of
private finance and ultimately relied on the banks to deal with holdouts
and problem cases. Indeed, the Fund had no direct contact with holdouts
and no real leverage over them. Rather, it reiterated the norm of equal
participation and raised the stakes if banks failed to cooperate in providing new credits.

It is clear, in any case, that the private coordination of creditors has
some gaps and weaknesses. The transaction costs are high. It is difficult
to mobilize substantial credits quickly. And there are incentives for one-
shot players to defect. These problems have fostered a larger role for
public institutions and some incremental changes in the creditors' own
procedures. These small steps do not involve fundamental concessions
on outstanding principal or debt service and do not ensure that LDCs
have access to future capital exports. As a result, these informal and
largely privatized arrangements may not be flexible enough to survive
the next global recession.

To lower transaction costs, creditors have begun to accept longer

restructuring programs. In order to provide incentives for tough stabilization programs, they have rewarded successful austerity with improved terms (though not with concessionary rates). Once again, the
case of Mexico has paved the way. A 1985 agreement, covering half of
Mexico's foreign debt (about $49 billion), spreads the payments that
originally fell due between 1985 and 1990 over 14 years. The interest
rate will be 1.125 percent above the London interbank rate. This rate
is significantly lower, and the term much longer, than previous rounds
of restructuring. It is likely to set a precedent.[36]

As noted earlier, large banks are also edging away from their prior
insistence on unanimity, which required that even the smallest banks
provide a proportionate share of new funds. The European banks and
the I.M.F. never favored this all-inclusive approach, since it is costly and
time-consuming and focuses on a trivial percentage of the overall package. To demand unanimity is to allow minor actors to impede the
agreement. To demand less, however, might lead other banks to seek
similar treatment and thus undermine the stability of rescheduling. That,
at least, has been the concern of leading U.S. banks. In practice, recent
agreements have not covered every small bank, and the effects of non-
participation seem to be contained. Allowing some banks to avoid new
funding, as in the most recent Mexican negotiations, has not affected
larger lenders—at least not yet.

The shadow of the future may be important here. "You don't need
100 percent bank cooperation in refunding if you are not doing it again,"
said one Euromarket syndication specialist. "Mexico is likely to get
voluntary funds [in the near future] so there is no reason to rope every-
body in." Note, however, that Mexico's economic improvement gives
the large banks additional incentives to contribute their share.

The real problem is that many debtors face long periods of austerity,
with little hope of reentering international credit markets in the next
several years. The next recession in the United States and Europe will
undoubtedly create even more serious problems for debtors, jeopardizing
their revised payment schedules and perhaps requiring write-offs on a
broad scale. This apprehension forms the backdrop for rescheduling
exercises in the mid-1980s.

Such bleak prospects make debt restructuring much harder. Weak
incentives for international lending make it increasingly difficult to
convince smaller banks to lend funds involuntarily. It is still an open

[36] *New York Times* (national ed.), February 4, 1985, pp. 21, 25; *Wall Street Journal*, April
1, 1985, p. 26; *Euromoney* (March 1985), 164.

question whether their refusal will eventually spread and destabilize the rescheduling process. So far it has not.

These changes in the terms and procedures of rescheduling are not striking, but they do indicate some evolution.[37] The latest major changes came at the height of the debt crisis, in 1982 and 1983, when gaps in private cooperation threatened the banking system as a whole. It was only then that central banks made emergency loans to key debtors while the I.M.F told commercial lenders what levels of new credit it required. What is happening now is that lenders are slowly moving away from urgent confrontations with debtors and from crisis management, to longer-term restructuring.

Private coordination, despite its limitations, has been remarkably successful in restructuring dozens of troubled debts, involving hundreds of banks. In this endeavor, basic principles have been preserved regarding the debtor's obligation to pay interest promptly and the responsibilities of successor governments to service previously contracted debts. The banks have repeatedly acknowledged the need to reschedule troubled debts, but never the borrowers' *right* to restructuring, much less to concessionary terms. They have sustained the principle, long supported by official creditors, that any changes in debt service must be mutually agreed upon and cannot be imposed unilaterally by the debtor. Furthermore, by refusing to reschedule without an I.M.F. stabilization agreement, the banks have effectively extended to the international arena a basic requirement of domestic loan "workouts"—that any involuntary lending must be accompanied by substantial changes in the borrower's policies, including austerity measures. Finally, despite all the economic problems associated with these loans, the private banks have negotiated remarkably hard-nosed deals, including penalty interest rates in some cases. They cannot avoid some economic losses: no bank would buy the existing loans to Brazil or Poland at face value. But the banks' rescheduling procedures have done nothing to erode the values further. Taken together, the coordinated activities of private creditors have sustained the value of their assets under trying circumstances and have provided a significant measure of security for the internationalization of capital.

[37] Other small changes could also be cited. Consultation between the creditor committee and the large regional banks has been improved and formalized. Moreover, all banks have used the economic recovery to write-down some bad debts and provide more reserves for future losses. The stronger balance sheets undoubtedly add to their leverage in negotiating with sovereign debtors.

ACHIEVING COOPERATION UNDER ANARCHY:
Strategies and Institutions

By ROBERT AXELROD and ROBERT O. KEOHANE*

ACHIEVING cooperation is difficult in world politics. There is no common government to enforce rules, and by the standards of domestic society, international institutions are weak. Cheating and deception are endemic. Yet, as the articles in this symposium have shown, cooperation is sometimes attained. World politics is not a homogeneous state of war: cooperation varies among issues and over time.

Before trying to draw conclusions about the factors that promote cooperation under anarchy, let us recall the definitions of these key terms. Cooperation is not equivalent to harmony. Harmony requires complete identity of interests, but cooperation can only take place in situations that contain a mixture of conflicting and complementary interests. In such situations, cooperation occurs when actors adjust their behavior to the actual or anticipated preferences of others. Cooperation, thus defined, is not necessarily good from a moral point of view.

Anarchy also needs to be defined clearly. As used here, the term refers to a lack of common government in world politics, not to a denial that an international society—albeit a fragmented one—exists. Clearly, many international relationships continue over time, and engender stable expectations about behavior. To say that world politics is anarchic does not imply that it entirely lacks organization. Relationships among actors may be carefully structured in some issue-areas, even though they remain loose in others. Likewise, some issues may be closely linked through the operation of institutions while the boundaries of other issues, as well as the norms and principles to be followed, are subject to dispute. Anarchy, defined as lack of common government, remains a constant; but the degree to which interactions are structured, and the means by which they are structured, vary.

It has often been noted that military-security issues display more of the characteristics associated with anarchy than do political-economic

* We would like to thank the other authors in this project for their helpful suggestions. Robert Axelrod gratefully acknowledges the financial support of the National Science Foundation and the Harry Frank Guggenheim Foundation.

ones. Charles Lipson, for instance, has recently observed that political-economic relationships are typically more institutionalized than military-security ones.[1] This does not mean, however, that analysis of these two sets of issues requires two separate analytical frameworks. Indeed, one of the major purposes of the present collection is to show that a single framework can throw light on both.

The case studies in this symposium have shown that the three dimensions discussed in the introduction—mutuality of interest, the shadow of the future, and the number of players—help us to understand the success and failure of attempts at cooperation in both military-security and political-economic relations. Section I of this essay synthesizes some of the findings of these case studies, and thereby helps to specify some of the most important ways in which these three factors affect world politics. It deals with issues in isolation from one another, as separate games or as a series of games, in order to clarify some basic analytic points. In this section, we follow the lead of game theorists, who have tried to avoid complicating their models with extraneous material in order to reach interesting conclusions. If the problem is a small event, such as a duel between two airplanes, our analysis of it may not depend on knowledge of the context (e.g., the purpose of the war). If the issue is of very high salience to participants, such as the 1914 crisis or the Cuban missile crisis, the extraneous issues (such as tariffs, or pollution of the Caribbean) may be so insignificant that they can be ignored. Either way, the strategy of focusing only on the central interaction is clearly justified.

Yet if the issue is neither isolated nor all-consuming, the context within which it takes place may have a decisive impact on its politics and its outcomes. As the case studies illustrate, world politics includes a rich variety of contexts. Issues arise against distinctive backgrounds of past experience; they are linked to other issues being dealt with simultaneously by the same actors; and they are viewed by participants through the prisms of their expectations about the future. To ignore the effects of context would be to overlook many of the most interesting questions raised by a game-theoretic perspective on the problem of cooperation.

In Section II, we therefore consider the context of issues; in so doing, we move outward from the three dimensions on which this collection focuses toward broader considerations, including linkages among issues, multilevel games, complications encountered by strategies of reciprocity

[1] Lipson, "International Cooperation in Economic and Security Affairs," *World Politics* 37 (October 1984), 1-23.

in complex situations, and the role of international institutions. Analysis of the context of games leads us to regard context as malleable: not only can actors in world politics pursue different strategies within an established context of interaction, they may also seek to alter that context through building institutions embodying particular principles, norms, rules, or procedures for the conduct of international relations. In the conclusion, we will argue that a contextual approach to strategy—by leading us to see the importance of international institutions—helps us to forge necessary links between game-theoretic arguments and theories about international regimes.

I. The Effects of Structure on Cooperation

Three situational dimensions affect the propensity of actors to cooperate: mutuality of interest, the shadow of the future, and the number of actors.

A. Payoff Structure: Mutual and Conflicting Preferences

It is well established that the payoff structure for a game affects the level of cooperation. For comparisons within a given type of game, this idea was first formalized by Axelrod, who established a measure of conflict of interest for specific games, including Prisoners' Dilemma.[2] Experimental evidence demonstrated that the greater the conflict of interest between the players, the greater the likelihood that the players would in fact choose to defect. Jervis has elaborated on these theories and shown that different types of games, such as Stag Hunt and Chicken, have different potentials for cooperation.[3] He has also applied his strategic analysis to historical and contemporary problems related to the security dilemma. His work clearly indicates that international cooperation is much easier to achieve in some game settings than in others.

Payoff structures often depend on events that take place outside of the control of the actors. The economic depressions of 1873-1896 and of the early 1930s stimulated demands for protection by firms and individuals in distress, and therefore reduced the incentives of governments to cooperate with one another. The weakness and vacillation of the British and French governments before 1939 reduced the potential value

[2] Robert Axelrod, "Conflict of Interest: An Axiomatic Approach," *Journal of Conflict Resolution* 11 (March 1967), 87-99; and *Conflict of Interest: A Theory of Divergent Goals with Applications to Politics* (Chicago: Markham, 1970).

[3] Robert Jervis, "Cooperation under the Security Dilemma," *World Politics* 30 (January 1978), 167-214.

of anti-German alliances with those countries for the Soviet Union, making a Nazi-Soviet pact seem relatively more attractive.

This is obvious enough. Slightly less obvious is another point about mutuality of interests: the payoff structure that determines mutuality of interests is not based simply upon objective factors, but is grounded upon the actors' perceptions of their own interests. Perceptions define interests. Therefore, to understand the degree of mutuality of interests (or to enhance this mutuality) we must understand the process by which interests are perceived and preferences determined.

One way to understand this process is to see it as involving a change in payoffs, so that a game such as Prisoners' Dilemma becomes either more or less conflictual. To start with, Prisoners' Dilemma is a game in which both players have an incentive to defect no matter whether the other player cooperates or defects. If the other player *cooperates*, the first player prefers to defect: $DC > CC$. On the other hand, if the other player *defects*, the first player still prefers to defect: $DD > CD$. The dilemma is that, if both defect, both do worse than if both had cooperated: $CC > DD$. Thus, Prisoners' Dilemma has a preference ordering for both players of $DC > CC > DD > CD$.[4]

Now consider a shift in the preferences of both players, so that mutual cooperation is preferred to unilateral defection. This makes the preference ordering $CC > DC > DD > CD$, which is a less conflictual game called Stag Hunt.

Jervis's study of the shift from balance-of-power systems to concerts suggests that after world wars, the payoff matrix for the victors may temporarily be one of Stag Hunt: fighting together results in a short-lived preference for staying together. After a war against a hegemonic power, the other great powers often perceive a mutual interest in continuing to work together in order to ensure that the defeated would-be hegemon does not rise again. They may even feel empathy for one another, and take an interest in each other's welfare. These perceptions seem to have substantial momentum, both among the mass public and in the bureaucracy. Yet, the cooperation that ensues is subject to fairly easy disruption. As recovery from the war proceeds, one or both parties may come to value cooperation less and relative gains more. And if one side believes that its counterpart prefers to defect, its own preference will shift to defection in order to avoid the worst payoff, CD.

Actors can also move from Prisoners' Dilemma to more conflictual

[4] The definition of Prisoners' Dilemma also includes one additional restriction: $CC > (DC + CD)/2$. This is to ensure that it is better to have mutual cooperation than to have an even chance of being the exploiter or the exploited.

games. If both players come to believe that mutual cooperation is worse than mutual defection, the game becomes Deadlock, with both sides having preferences of DC > DD > CC > CD. Since the dominant strategy of each player is to defect regardless of what the other does, the likely outcome is DD. Players in Deadlock, unlike those in Prisoners' Dilemma, will not benefit from repeated plays since mutual cooperation is not preferred to mutual defection.

Kenneth Oye provides a fine example of the movement from Prisoners' Dilemma to Deadlock in his essay on monetary diplomacy in the 1930s, in this collection. Shifts in beliefs, not only about international regimes, but particularly about desirable economic policy, led leaders such as Franklin D. Roosevelt to prefer unilateral, uncoordinated action to international cooperation on the terms that appeared feasible. Oye argues that the early 1930s do not mark a failure of coordination where common interests existed (as in Prisoners' Dilemma); rather, they indicate the decay of these common interests, as perceived by participants. In their essay in the present collection, Downs, Rocke, and Siverson argue that arms races are often games of Deadlock rather than Prisoners' Dilemma, making them much more difficult to resolve.

Beliefs are as important in the military area as in economics. Consider, for example, Van Evera's study of the beliefs leading to World War I. By 1914, what Van Evera labels "the cult of the offensive" was universally accepted in the major European countries. It was a congenial doctrine for military elites everywhere, since it magnified the role of the military and reduced that of the diplomats. It also happened to be disastrously wrong, since its adherents failed to appreciate the overwhelming advantage that recent technological change had given to the defensive (in what was soon to become trench warfare), and overlooked the experiences of the American Civil War and the Russo-Japanese War.

Gripped by this cult of the offensive, European leaders sought to gain safer borders by expanding national territories, and took more seriously the possibility of successful aggressive war; hence Germany and (to a lesser extent) other European powers adopted expansionist policies that brought them into collision with one another. European leaders also felt greater compulsion to mobilize and strike first in a crisis, since the penalty of moving late would be greater in an offense-dominant world; this compulsion then fueled the spiral of mobilization and counter-mobilization that drove the July 1914 crisis out of control. Had Europeans recognized the actual power of the defense, expansionism would have lost much of its appeal, and the compulsion to mobilize and countermobilize would have diminished. Put differently, the European payoff

structure actually would have rewarded cooperation; but Euro
perceived a payoff structure that rewarded *non*cooperation, and responded accordingly. Beliefs, not realities, governed conduct.

The case of 1914 also illustrates a point made above: subjective interpretations by one side become objective reality for the other side. When
a European state adopted expansionist policies, those nearby found themselves with an expansionist neighbor, and had to adjust accordingly. For
instance, Germany's expansionism, though largely based on illusions,
led to a genuine change in Russia's environment. Russia adopted its
inflexible war plan (which required mobilization against Germany as
well as against Austria) partly because the Russians feared that Germany
would strike into Russia's northern territories once the Russian armies
were embroiled with Austria. Thus the Russian calculus was importantly
affected by Russia's image of German intent, and Russia was driven to
bellicose measures by fear of German bellicosity. German expansionism
was premised largely on illusions, but for Russia this expansionism was
a real danger that required a response.

This discussion of payoff structures should make it clear that the
contributors to this volume do not assume that Prisoners' Dilemmas are
typical of world politics. More powerful actors often face less powerful
ones, yielding asymmetric payoff matrices. Furthermore, even symmetrical games can take a variety of forms, as illustrated by Stag Hunt,
Chicken, and Deadlock. What is important for our purposes is not to
focus exclusively on Prisoners' Dilemma *per se*, but to emphasize the
fundamental problem that it (along with Stag Hunt and Chicken) illustrates. In these games, myopic pursuit of self-interest can be disastrous.
Yet both sides can potentially benefit from cooperation—if they can only
achieve it. Thus, choices of strategies and variations in institutions are
particularly important, and the scope for the exercise of intelligence is
considerable.

Our review of payoff structures also illustrates one of the major themes
of this collection of essays: that political-economic and military-security
issues can be analyzed with the same analytical framework. Admittedly,
economic issues usually seem to exhibit less conflictual payoff structures
than do those of military security. Coordination among bankers, as
described by Lipson, has been more extensive and successful than most
arms control negotiations, as analyzed by Downs and his colleagues;
and the patterns of trade conflict and cooperation described by Conybeare
are hardly as conflictual as Van Evera's story of World War I. On the
other hand, the great power concerts discussed by Jervis, as well as
several of the arms control negotiations, were more cooperative than the

trade and monetary measures of 1930-1933 delineated in Oye's essay. And postwar economic relations between the United States and Japan have been more conflictual than military-security relations. As an empirical matter, military issues may more often have payoff structures involving a great deal of conflict of interest; but there is no theoretical reason to believe that this must always be the case.[5]

B. THE SHADOW OF THE FUTURE

In Prisoners' Dilemma, concern about the future helps to promote cooperation. The more future payoffs are valued relative to current payoffs, the less the incentive to defect today—since the other side is likely to retaliate tomorrow.[6] The cases discussed in the present essays support this argument, and identify specific factors that help to make the shadow of the future an effective promoter of cooperation. These factors include:

1. long time horizons;
2. regularity of stakes;
3. reliability of information about the others' actions;
4. quick feedback about changes in the others' actions.

The dimension of the shadow of the future seems to differentiate military from economic issues more sharply than does the dimension of payoffs. Indeed, its four components can be used to analyze some of the reasons why issues of international political economy may be settled more cooperatively than issues of international security, even when the underlying payoff matrices are similar—for example, when Prisoners' Dilemma applies. Most important is a combination of the first two factors: long time horizons and regularity of stakes. In economic relations, actors have to expect that their relationships will continue over an indefinite period of time; that is, the games they play with each other will be iterated. Typically, neither side in an economic interaction can eliminate the other, or change the nature of the game decisively in a single move. In security affairs, by contrast, the possibility of a successful preemptive war can sometimes be a tempting occasion for the rational timing of surprise.[7] Another way to put this is that, in the international political economy, retaliation for defection will almost always be possible;

[5] For an earlier discussion of contemporary events, using a common analytical framework to examine both economic and security relations, see Oye, "The Domain of Choice," in Kenneth A. Oye, Donald Rothchild, and Robert J. Lieber, eds., *Eagle Entangled: U.S. Foreign Policy in a Complex World* (New York: Longman, 1979), 3-33.

[6] Robert Axelrod, *The Evolution of Cooperation* (New York: Basic Books, 1984).

[7] Robert Axelrod, "The Rational Timing of Surprise," *World Politics* 31 (January 1979), 228-46.

therefore a rational player, considering defection, has to consider its probability and its potential consequences. In security affairs, it may be possible to limit or destroy the opponent's capacity for effective retaliation.

To illustrate this point, let us compare the case of 1914 with contemporary international debt negotiations. In 1914, some Germans, imbued with the cult of the offensive, thought that a continental war would permanently solve Germany's security problems by restructuring power and territorial relations in Europe. For these German leaders, the temptation to defect was huge, largely because the shadow of the future seemed so small. Indeed, it seemed that future retaliation could be prevented, or rendered ineffective, by decisive German action. Moreover, in the opening move of a war the stakes would be far greater than usual because of the value of preempting before the other side was fully mobilized. This perceived irregularity in the stakes further undercut the potential for sustained cooperation based upon reciprocity.

By contrast, contemporary negotiations among banks, and between banks and debtor countries, are heavily affected by the shadow of the future. That is not to say that the stakes of each game are the same; indeed, there are great discontinuities since deadlines for rescheduling take on importance for regulators, banks, and the reputations of borrowers. But the banks know that they will be dealing both with the debtor countries and with one another again and again. Continuing interbank relationships imply, as Lipson points out, that small banks will think twice before doublecrossing large banks by refusing to participate in rescheduling. This is particularly true if the small banks are closely tied, in a variety of ways, to the large banks. Continuing relations between banks and debtor countries give the banks incentives to cooperate with the debtor countries, not merely in order to facilitate debt servicing on loans already made, but to stay in their good graces—looking toward a more prosperous future. The fact that Argentina, Brazil, and Mexico are so large, and are perceived to be potentially wealthy, is a significant bargaining asset for them now, since it increases the banks' expected profits from future lending, and therefore enlarges the shadow of the future. Indeed, if these governments could credibly promise to favor, in the future, banks that help them now, and to punish or ignore those that defect in these critical times, they could further improve their bargaining positions; but, as sovereign governments whose leaders will be different in the future, they cannot effectively do so.

Reliability of information about the others' actions and promptness of feedback are also important in affecting the shadow of the future, although they do not seem to differentiate military-security from polit-ical-economic issues so clearly. Because of the absence of military secrecy, actors may sometimes have more reliable information on political-economic than on military-security issues. Banks thrive on differential access to information, and therefore hold it closely. Furthermore, since the systemic effects of political-economic actions are often difficult to judge, and "cheating at the margin" is frequently easy, feedback between policy and results may be slow. For instance, the distribution of benefits from the Tokyo Round of trade negotiations is still a matter of conjecture and political contention rather than economic knowledge. By contrast, the superpowers publish lists of the precise number of missiles in each other's inventories, and we can assume that information about the effect of a military action by either side—short of a devastating surprise attack that would destroy command and control facilities—would be com-municated almost immediately to the leaders of both states.

The length of the shadow of the future, like the character of payoff structures, is not necessarily dictated by the objective attributes of a situation. On the contrary, as we have just seen, expectations are im-portant. International institutions may therefore be significant, since institutions embody, and affect, actors' expectations.[8] Thus institutions can alter the extent to which governments expect their present actions to affect the behavior of others on future issues. The principles and rules of international regimes make governments concerned about precedents, increasing the likelihood that they will attempt to punish defectors. In this way, international regimes help to link the future with the present. That is as true of arms control agreements, in which willingness to make future agreements depends on others' compliance with previous arrangements, as it is in the General Agreement on Tariffs and Trade, which embodies norms and rules against which the behavior of members can be judged. By sanctioning retaliation for those who violate rules, regimes create expectations that a given violation will be treated not as an isolated case but as one in a series of interrelated actions.

C.   NUMBER OF ACTORS: SANCTIONING PROBLEMS

The ability of governments to cooperate in a mixed-motive game is affected not only by the payoff structure and the shadow of the future, but also by the number of players in the game and by how their rela-tionships are structured. Axelrod has shown that reciprocity can be an

[8] Stephen D.Krasner, ed., *International Regimes* (Ithaca, NY: Cornell University Press, 1983); Robert O. Keohane, *After Hegemony: Cooperation and Discord in the World Political Economy* (Princeton: Princeton University Press, 1984).

effective strategy to induce cooperation among self-interested players in the iterated, bilateral Prisoners' Dilemma, where the values of each actor's options are clearly specified.[9] However, effective reciprocity depends on three conditions: (1) players can identify defectors; (2) they are able to focus retaliation on defectors; and (3) they have sufficient long-run incentives to punish defectors. When there are many actors, these conditions are often more difficult to satisfy. In such situations, it may be impossible to identify, much less to punish, defection; even if it is possible, none of the cooperators may have an incentive to play the role of policeman. Each cooperator may seek to be a free-rider on the willingness of others to enforce the rules.

We may call the difficulty of preventing defection through decentralized retaliation the "sanctioning problem." Its first form, the inability to identify defectors, is illustrated by the terrorist bombings against American installations in Lebanon in 1983. The United States did not know, at the time the bombings took place, who was responsible. The only state that could plausibly have been held responsible was Syria; but since the Syrians denied responsibility, retaliation against Damascus could have spread and deepened the conflict without punishing the terrorist groups themselves. The issue of identifying defectors is one aspect of a fundamental problem besetting efforts to cooperate in world politics: acquiring, in a timely fashion, adequate amounts of high-quality information. In order to maintain cooperation in games that reward unreciprocated defection, such as Prisoners' Dilemma, governments must have confidence in their ability to monitor their counterparts' actions sufficiently well to enable them to respond effectively to betrayal. As Lipson has pointed out, the greater perils of betrayal (to the side that is betrayed) in military-security than in political-economic relations put more severe demands on gathering information in the former than in the latter area.[10]

The second form of the sanctioning problem occurs when players are unable to focus retaliation on defectors. This difficulty is illustrated by Conybeare's analysis of the Anglo-Hanse trade wars. The Hanseatic League was unable to punish English privateers for their depredations, and instead retaliated against English merchants in Hanseatic towns. This produced escalation rather than cooperation.

The third form of the sanctioning problem arises when some members of a group lack incentives to punish defectors. This obstacle to cooperation often arises where there are many actors, some of which fail

[9] Axelrod (fn. 6).
[10] Lipson (fn. 1).

to cooperate in the common effort to achieve some collective good. Oye observes that although British devaluation in 1931 hurt other countries, no single government had the incentive to devote its own resources to bring about a revision of British policy. This form of the sanctioning problem—lack of incentives to punish defectors—also arose in the debt negotiations of the 1980s. To prevent default, it was necessary to arrange rescheduling agreements involving additional bank lending. Smaller banks were tempted to refuse to provide new funds. Only the fact that the large banks had strong incentives to put pressure on smaller ones to ante up prevented rescheduling agreements from unravelling "like a cheap sweater."

When sanctioning problems are severe, cooperation is in danger of collapsing. One way to bolster it is to restructure the situation so that sanctioning becomes more feasible. Sometimes this is done unilaterally. Oye points out that external benefits or costs may be "privatizable"; that is, changes can be made in the situation so that the benefits and costs of one's actions are directed specifically at those with whom one has negotiated. He argues that in the early 1930s Britain eventually succeeded in privatizing its international currency relationships by adopting exchange controls and attaching conditions, negotiated bilaterally, to new loans. This transformation of the game permitted a modest revival of international lending, based not on open access to British capital markets but on bilateral reciprocity.

As our examples indicate, sanctioning problems can occur both in the international political economy and on military-security issues. They tend to be more severe on military-security than on political-economy issues, due to the high costs of punishing defections, the difficulties of monitoring behavior, and the stringent demands for information that are imposed when successful defection can dramatically shorten the shadow of the future. But since sanctioning problems occur on both types of issues, issue-area alone cannot account for their incidence or severity. To explain the incidence and severity of sanctioning problems, we need to focus on the conditions that determine whether defection can be prevented through decentralized retaliation: the ease of identifying sources of action, the ability of governments to focus retaliation or reward on particular targets, and the incentives that exist for members of a group to punish defectors.

While the likelihood that these problems will arise may be enhanced by an increase in the number of actors involved, difficulties may also appear on issues that seem at first glance to be strictly bilateral. Consider, for instance, the example of 1914. In the Balkan crisis, Austria sought to impose sanctions against Serbia for its support of revolutionaries who tried to destroy the ethnically heterogeneous Austro-Hungarian empire. But sanctions against Serbia implied punishment for Russia, Serbia's ally, since Russian leaders were averse to accepting another Balkan setback. Russian mobilization, however, could not be directed solely against Austria, since Russia only had plans for general mobilization.[11] Thus, neither Austria nor Russia was able to focus retaliation on the defector; the actions of both helped to spread rather than to contain the crisis. With more clever and moderate leadership, Austria might have found a way to punish Serbia without threatening Russia. And a detailed plan for mobilization only against Austria could have provided Russia with a more precisely directed measure to retaliate against Austria's ultimatum to Serbia.

Privatization is not the only way to maintain cooperation. Moreover, as some of our examples indicate, it can be difficult to achieve. Another way to resolve sanctioning problems is to construct international regimes to provide standards against which actions can be measured, and to assign responsibility for applying sanctions. Regimes provide information about actors' compliance; they facilitate the development and maintenance of reputations; they can be incorporated into actors' rules of thumb for responding to others' actions; and they may even apportion responsibility for decentralized enforcement of rules.[12]

Charles Lipson's discussion of the international lending regime that has been constructed by bankers reveals how regimes can promote cooperation even when there are many actors, no dominant power, and no world central bank. Creditor committees were established under the leadership of large money-center banks. Each money-center bank then took responsibility for a number of relatively large regional banks, which in turn were assigned similar responsibilities for smaller banks.[13] As a result, a hierarchy of banks was created, isolating smaller banks from one another and establishing responsibility for enforcing sanctions. Small banks displaying tendencies toward defection were threatened with being outside the flow of information in the future and, implicitly, with not being offered participation in lucrative future loans. This informal hierarchy, of course, was reinforced by the presence of the U.S. Federal Reserve System looming in the background: stories, whether apocryphal or not, of small bankers being told to "cough up" by high officials of

[11] Robert E. Osgood and Robert W. Tucker, *Force, Order and Justice* (Baltimore: Johns Hopkins University Press, 1967), esp. chap. 2, "The Expansion of Force."

[12] Keohane (fn. 8), 49-132.

[13] Lipson, "Bankers' Dilemmas," in this collection, 200-225.

the Fed circulated in banking circles during the early 1980s. It would have taken a bold president of a small bank to ignore both the banking hierarchy and the danger of arousing the Fed's wrath by not participating in a rescheduling.

This reference to the role of institutions in transforming N-person games into collections of two-person games suggests once again the importance of the context within which games are played. In isolation, the basic concepts discussed in the introduction—payoff structures, iteration, and the number of players—provide only a framework for analysis. They take on greater significance, as well as complexity, when they are viewed within the broader context of other issues, other games, and the institutions that affect the course of world politics. We now turn to the question of how the context of interaction affects political behavior and outcomes.

II. THE CONTEXT OF INTERACTION

Whether cooperation can take place without central guidance depends not merely on the three game-theoretic dimensions we have emphasized so far, but also on the context within which interaction takes place. Context may, of course, mean many different things. Any interaction takes place within the context of norms that are shared, often implicitly, by the participants. John Ruggie has written of the "deep structure" of sovereignty in world politics,[14] and also of the way in which shifting values and norms of state intervention in society—the emergence and legitimation of the welfare state—affected the world political economy between 1914 and 1945. International political-economic bargaining was fundamentally changed by the shift, during this period, from laissez-faire liberalism as a norm to what Ruggie calls "embedded liberalism."[15]

Interactions also take place within the context of institutions. Robert Keohane has argued elsewhere that even if one adopts the assumption that states are rational and self-interested actors, institutions can be shown to be important in world politics.[16] Institutions alter the payoff structures facing actors, they may lengthen the shadow of the future,

[14] John G. Ruggie, "Continuity and Transformation in the World Polity: Toward a Neorealist Synthesis," *World Politics* 35 (January 1983), 261-85.

[15] John G. Ruggie, "International Regimes, Transactions and Change: Embedded Liberalism in the Postwar Economic Order," *International Organization* 36 (Spring 1982), 379-416, reprinted in Krasner (fn. 8), 195-231; Fred Hirsch, "The Ideological Underlay of Inflation," in John Goldthorpe and Fred Hirsch, eds., *The Political Economy of Inflation* (London: Martin Robertson, 1978), 263-84.

[16] Keohane (fn. 8).

and they may enable N-person games to be broken down into games with smaller numbers of actors.

Using the game-theoretic perspective of this symposium, another way of looking at context may be especially revealing. This aspect has to do with what we call multilevel games. In such situations, different games affect one another, so that their outcomes become mutually contingent. Three such situations are particularly important for world politics: issue-linkage, domestic-international connections, and incompatibilities between games among different sets of actors. After considering these situations, we will turn to the implications of these multilevel games for the efficacy of a strategy of reciprocity in fostering cooperation.

A.   MULTILEVEL GAMES

Issue-linkage. Most issues are linked to other issues. This means that games being played on different issues—different "chessboards," in Stanley Hoffmann's phrase[17]—affect one another. Connections between games become important when issues are linked.

Issue-linkage in this sense involves attempts to gain additional bargaining leverage by making one's own behavior on a given issue contingent on others' actions toward other issues.[18] Issue-linkage may be employed by powerful states seeking to use resources from one issue-area to affect the behavior of others elsewhere; or it may be employed by outsiders, attempting to break into what could otherwise be a closed game. Linkage can be beneficial to both sides in a negotiation, and can facilitate agreements that might not otherwise be possible.[19] Actors' resources may differ, so that it makes sense to trade one for the other: the United States, for instance, may provide economic aid to Egypt in exchange for Egyptian support for American policy in the Middle East. Furthermore, different players may have preferences of different intensities: thus, in a log-rolling game, each party trades its "vote," or policy position, on an issue it values less highly for the other's vote on one it values more highly.

The outstanding example of a successful bargaining linkage in our

[17] Stanley Hoffmann, "International Organization and the International System," *International Organization* 24 (Summer 1970), 389-413.

[18] Ernst B. Haas refers to this as "tactical" issue-linkage, contrasting it with "substantive" issue-linkage resulting from causal knowledge. See Haas, "Why Collaborate? Issue-linkage and International Regimes," *World Politics* 32 (April 1980), 357-405, at 372. For a sophisticated analysis of tactical issue-linkage, see Michael McGinnis, "Issue Linkage and the Evolution of International Cooperation," *Journal of Conflict Resolution*, forthcoming.

[19] Robert E. Tollison and Thomas D. Willett, "An Economic Theory of Mutually Advantageous Issue Linkage in International Negotiations," *International Organization* 33 (Fall 1979), 425-49.

case studies is that of the Washington Naval Treaty of 1922. As Downs, Rocke, and Siverson show, these arms control negotiations were successful in part because they linked bargaining over arms with bargaining over other issues. As part of an agreement to limit battleship construction, Japan gave Britain and the United States guarantees regarding trade in China and limitations of fortification on certain Pacific islands; Japan received legal recognition of its right to certain territory taken from Germany after World War I. Bringing these issues into the negotiations to limit the building of battleships helped to make cooperation possible, not only on these specific issues but on the whole package.

Of course, not all issue-linkages promote agreement, any more than each exercise of power can be expected to lead to cooperation. Oye has distinguished between "backscratching," which he regards as welfare-enhancing, and "blackmailing," which may reduce welfare levels.[20] The "backscratcher" merely offers, in return for compensation, to refrain from acting in what would otherwise be its own best interest. For instance, a debtor country, unable to make its payments on time without facing severe hardship or political revolution, may offer to continue servicing its debts only if compensated with new loans and an easier payment schedule. If this offer is rejected, the debtor does what it would have done without the offer: it defaults.

Backscratching entails a promise. Blackmailing, by contrast, implies a threat. As Schelling has pointed out, "the difference is that a promise is costly when it succeeds, and a threat is costly when it fails."[21] Black-mailers threaten to act against their own interests unless compensated. Thus, a debtor country that would be hurt by defaulting may nevertheless threaten to do so unless compensation is offered. This threat, if carried out, would leave both the debtor (the blackmailer, in this case) and its creditors worse off than if it had merely acted in its own interest without bargaining at all. If the blackmailing strategy works, on the other hand, the effect will be to transfer resources from the creditors to the debtor, an action that will not necessarily improve overall welfare.

Although it may be difficult to differentiate between backscratching and blackmailing in practice, the distinction helps us to recognize that issue-linkages have dangers as well as opportunities. One side may demand so much of the other in other areas that cooperation will not take place even in the area of shared interests. This accusation is fre-

---

[20] Oye (fn. 5).
[21] Thomas C. Schelling, *The Strategy of Conflict* (New York: Oxford University Press, 1960), 177.

quently made against Henry Kissinger's version of linkage. Kissinger insisted that the Soviets exercise great restraint in the Third World in return for American cooperation on arms control.[22] In Oye's terms, Kissinger was trying to "blackmail" the Soviets by threatening to act against the United States' own interests (delay arms control) unless the Soviets compensated the United States with unilateral restraint.[23]

The most intriguing point about linkage that is highlighted by the case studies is the existence of what could be called "contextual" issue-linkage. In such a situation, a given bargain is placed within the context of a more important long-term relationship in such a way that the long-term relationship affects the outcome of the particular bargaining process. Two cases of contextual issue-linkage show that this form can often work to reduce conflict even without affecting the preferences of the participants on the specific issues being discussed. Oye notes that in 1936, the United States, Britain, and France were able to reach an agreement on international monetary reform because of the common security concern over a rising Nazi Germany. And as Downs and his colleagues point out, by far the most important cause of cooperation in arms races that ended peacefully has been the activity of a third power. For example, the Anglo-French naval arms race of 1852-1853 was resolved when the two states formed an alliance in order to fight the Russians in the Crimean War.

International relations and domestic politics. Similar analytic questions arise in considering connections between international relations and domestic politics. Arms control negotiations involve not merely bargaining between governments, but within societies as well; the Carter administration was able to resolve the SALT II game with the Soviet Union, but not with the U.S. Senate. Trade issues typically also involve both international and domestic games. In the Tokyo Round, the same Carter administration—with a different responsible party, Robert Strauss—was able to mesh international and domestic games, playing them simultaneously rather than sequentially (international first), as had been done on some issues in the Kennedy Round a decade earlier. The result in this case was that the Tokyo Round trade agreements with

[22] George W. Breslauer, "Why Détente Failed: An Interpretation," in Alexander L. George and others, *Managing U.S.-Soviet Rivalry: Problems of Crisis Prevention* (Boulder, CO: Westview Press, 1983), 319-40; John L. Gaddis, "The Rise, Fall and Future of Détente," *Foreign Affairs* 62 (Winter 1983/84), 354-77; Stanley Hoffmann, "Détente," in Joseph S. Nye, ed., *The Making of America's Soviet Policy* (New Haven: Yale University Press for the Council on Foreign Relations, 1984), 231-64.
[23] Oye (fn. 5), 17.

other countries were all ratified overwhelmingly by Congress, in contrast to the rejection of some of the international agreements made in the Kennedy Round.[24]

Such domestic-international connections are commonplace. Frequently, the incentives provided by domestic bargaining games inhibit effective foreign policy and may exacerbate international conflict. A well-known case is that of American decision making during the early months of the Korean War. General MacArthur was such a formidable figure in American politics that even his military superiors were reluctant to challenge his judgment in marching toward the Yalu River in the fall of 1950; yet this maneuver was so questionable that, if it had not been for the domestic political games taking place, serious reservations would have been expressed in the Pentagon and the White House.[25]

Another type of domestic-international linkage is discussed by Conybeare in this collection. During the 15th century, the Hanseatic League responded to naval setbacks at the hands of Britain by financing and equipping Edward IV, who, upon defeating the Lancastrians in the War of the Roses, signed a treaty that was one-sidedly favorable to the Hanse's trading interests. By intervening in British domestic politics, the Hanse was thus able to triumph despite military weakness. This technique—intervening in a domestic political game as compensation for weakness at the international level—has recently been employed in more subtle ways by small powers with strong interests in American foreign policy.[26]

Compatibilities and incompatibilities among games. Many different games take place in world politics, involving different but overlapping sets of actors. Sometimes the existence of more than one game makes it easier to attain cooperation, but related games may also create difficulties for one another. That is, games in world politics can be compatible or incompatible with each other.

One example of a set of compatible games is provided by cooperation in international economic negotiations among the major industrialized countries. After World War II, such cooperation was facilitated by the fact that these countries were military allies. In contrast to Britain's situation in the 19th century, America's ability to persuade other major trading states to accept the rules that it preferred was greatly enhanced by the fact that in the military-political game the United States was a

[24] Gilbert Winham, "Robert Strauss, the MTN, and the Control of Faction," *Journal of World Trade Law* 14 (September-October 1980).

[25] Alexander George and Richard Smoke, *Deterrence in American Foreign Policy* (New York: Columbia University Press, 1974).

[26] Robert O. Keohane, "The Big Influence of Small Allies," *Foreign Policy*, No. 2 (Spring 1971), 161-82.

senior partner, rather than an adversary, of the other major actors in the world economy. To take another example: Lipson's analysis of debt negotiations suggests that the negotiating game among large banks was rendered compatible with games between large and small banks by structuring the situation so that small banks could not coordinate with each other. That is, two sets of negotiations were made compatible by precluding a third one.

The case of 1914 illustrates the problem of incompatibility among games. In non-crisis periods, loyalty within an alliance was compatible with friendly relations across alliances. But when the 1914 crisis occurred, loyalty within an alliance—such as Germany's support for Austria, Russia's for Serbia, and France's for Russia—implied defection across alliances. The increased cooperativeness of intra-alliance games destroyed broader patterns of cooperation.

In the contemporary international political economy, problems of incompatibility may also arise. For instance, negotiations on questions such as tariffs or energy policies are most likely to yield positive results for the advanced industrialized countries when only a few major players are involved in the initial negotiation. Friction with others, however, especially the less developed countries, may produce conflict on a larger scale. Or, to take a different example from the politics of international debt, close and explicit collaboration among debtor countries could, some fear, disrupt relations between debtor governments and banks in the richer countries.

The contrast between the fate of Soviet-American arms control in the 1970s and the Tokyo Round of trade negotiations illustrates the importance of multilevel games. In the face of linkages to other contentious issues, complex domestic political games, and a lack of reinforcement between political-economic and military-security games, even shared interests, a long shadow of the future, and bilateralism may be insufficient to promote cooperation. If the interaction happens to be an iterated game of Chicken, the problem is even worse because each player has a strong incentive to avoid cooperation in the short run in order to develop a reputation for firmness in the long run. Conversely, even when there are quite severe conflicts of interest, these may be overshadowed by more important mutual interests, perhaps institutionalized in organizations such as NATO. Once again, it is not sufficient to analyze a particular situation in isolation from its political context. We must also analyze the patterns of expectations, and the institutions created by human beings, within which particular negotiations are located and in the light of which they are interpreted by participants.

B.   RECIPROCITY AS A STRATEGY IN MULTILEVEL GAMES

Robert Axelrod has employed computer tournaments and theoretical analysis of the iterated, two-player Prisoners' Dilemma to show that a strategy based on reciprocity—such as Tit-for-Tat—can be remarkably effective in promoting cooperation.[27] Even among pure egoists, cooperation can "emerge" if a small initial cluster of potential cooperators exists.

This argument suggests that governments may have incentives to practice reciprocity in a variety of situations that are characterized by mixtures of conflicting and complementary interests—that is, in certain non-zero-sum games. Evidence for this proposition is established best for the particular case of Prisoners' Dilemma. Axelrod's theory suggests that in this game a strategy based on reciprocity can yield relatively high payoffs against a variety of other strategies. Furthermore, such a strategy helps the whole community by punishing players who use uncooperative strategies. When payoff structures are those of Prisoners' Dilemma, therefore, we can expect practitioners of reciprocity to attempt to institutionalize it as a general practice, so that they will benefit from others' use of the strategy as well as their own.

As we have noted above, not every situation in which conflict or cooperation may occur can be categorized as Prisoners' Dilemma. Games such as Chicken and Stag Hunt are also significant. Evidence on these cases is not as extensive as on Prisoners' Dilemma. Yet, as Oye's introduction points out, there are good reasons to believe that reciprocity is an attractive strategy in a variety of non-zero-sum situations. The key conditions for the successful operation of reciprocity are that mutual cooperation can yield better results than mutual defection, but that temptations for defection also exist. In such situations, reciprocity may permit extensive cooperation without making cooperative participants inordinately vulnerable to exploitation by others. Furthermore, it may deter uncooperative actions.[28]

[27] Axelrod (fn. 6).

[28] Consider the example of Stag Hunt, defined by the preference ordering of both players as $CC > DC > DD > CD$. If Player A is credibly committed to a strategy of reciprocity, beginning with cooperation, B's incentives to cooperate are enhanced. A's commitment to cooperate ensures that B will not be double-crossed (which would leave B with the worst payoff). Furthermore, A's commitment to retaliate against defection ensures that any defection by B would lead, after the first move, not to B's second-best outcome (DC), but to its third-best outcome (DD). The game of Chicken provides another appropriate case in point. In Chicken, mutual cooperation is only the second-best outcome for both players, but mutual defection is worst for both. Thus, $DC > CC > CD > DD$. A credible strategy of reciprocity by Player A in Chicken ensures B of its second-best outcome if it cooperates, and guarantees that continual defection will in the long run provide it with its worst payoff. Assuming that B's shadow of the future is sufficiently long, it should respond to A's strategy of reciprocity by cooperating.

It is not surprising, therefore, that reciprocity is a popular strategy for practical negotiators as well as for analysts in the laboratory. Oye's analysis of monetary politics in the 1930s reveals that Britain developed such a strategy in its relations with the Scandinavian countries. Contemporary discussions of international trade provide another case in point. U.S. officials have frequently defended reciprocity in trade relations on the grounds that pursuit of this strategy would deter discrimination against American products by other countries, and that relaxation of reciprocity would invite retaliation by others. Even observers skeptical about reciprocity often agree. In a policy-oriented article critical of current proposals that the United States should practice "aggressive reciprocity" in trade negotiations, William Cline argues that such action is rendered less effective by a high probability of foreign counter-retaliation.[29] In Axelrod's terms, Tit-for-Tat (which begins by cooperating and then retaliates once for each defection by the other player) discourages exploitative strategies—"aggressive reciprocity."

Thus, the applicability of Tit-for-Tat does not seem to be limited to Prisoners' Dilemma. Yet it is not a perfect strategy. In the first place, it can perpetuate conflict through an "echo effect": "if the other player defects once, Tit-for-Tat will respond with a defection, and then if the other player does the same in response, the result would be an unending echo of alternating defections."[30] In real-world politics as well as in the laboratory, reciprocity can lead to feuds as well as to cooperation, particularly when players have different perceptions of past outcomes.[31] Soviet-American détente collapsed partly because each side concluded that the other was not practicing reciprocity, but was, on the contrary, taking unilateral advantage of its own restraint.[32] Second, even when many shared interests exist and judgments of equivalence are not distorted, reciprocity may lead to deadlock. John W. Evans has pointed out that in tariff negotiations conducted according to the principle of reciprocity, potential concessions may become "bargaining chips" to be hoarded: "Tariffs that have no intrinsic economic value for a country that maintains them have acquired value because of the insistence of other countries on reciprocity in the bargaining process." As a result, "tariff levels may be maintained in spite of the fact that a lower level

[29] Cline, " 'Reciprocity': A New Approach to World Trade Policy?" Institute for International Economics, Policy Analyses in International Economics 2 (Washington: September 1982), 25.

[30] Axelrod (fn. 6), 176.

[31] For an analysis of the spiral mode of conflict, see Robert Jervis, *Perception and Misperception in International Politics* (Princeton, NJ: Princeton University Press, 1976), esp. 58-113.

[32] See references cited in fn. 22.

would raise the country's real income."[33] Third, when several actors negotiate separately and sequentially over issues that are substantively interdependent, subsequent bargains may call previous agreements into question by altering the value of concessions that have been made. This "issue interdependence problem" bedeviled trade negotiations under the conditional most-favored-nation clause prior to the institution of multilateral trade negotiations after World War II. Conditional most-favored-nation treatment permitted discrimination among suppliers. Later agreements between an importer and other suppliers therefore eroded the value of earlier concessions. This led to complex, acrimonious, and frustrating patterns of bargaining.[34]

Despite these difficulties, reciprocity remains a valuable strategy for decentralized enforcement of cooperative agreements. Players who are aware of the problems of echo effects, bargaining deadlocks, and issue interdependence can compensate for these pitfalls. Axelrod observes that a better strategy than Tit-for-Tat "might be to return only nine-tenths of a tit for a tat."[35] The Tokyo Round dealt with the deadlock problem by beginning negotiations not on the basis of current tariff rates, but rather on the basis of a formula for hypothetical large across-the-board tariff cuts, with provisions for withdrawing offers on sensitive products, or if adequate compensation was not received. The problem of issue interdependence was dealt with in the trade area through multilateralization of tariff negotiations and adoption of unconditional most-favored-nation treatment.

These difficulties in applying reciprocity, and the responses of players to them, illustrate the significance of the institutions within which reciprocity is practiced. As noted above, multilateral trade negotiations are a case in point. In the military-security area, reciprocity has also been institutionalized. For example, stationing of American troops in Europe is linked to purchases of American military equipment by European governments. NATO as an institution has helped member governments achieve a variety of such reciprocal arrangements.

The debt negotiations discussed by Lipson also illustrate how reciprocity can be institutionalized in an N-person game. First, the major actors are identified, and bilateral negotiations take place between them or their agents. The I.M.F. and committees of banks negotiate with debtor countries. At a second stage, smaller banks are given the oppor-

[33] Evans, *The Kennedy Round in American Trade Policy: The Twilight of the GATT?* (Cambridge: Harvard University Press, 1971), 31-32.
[34] See Robert O. Keohane, "Reciprocity in International Relations," *International Organization* 40 (Winter 1986).
[35] Axelrod (fn. 6), 138.

tunity to adhere to these bargains, but not to influence their terms. At this stage, emphasis is placed on reciprocity at a different level: although the smaller actors have the potential to act as free-riders, efforts are made to ensure that they have incentives not to do so for fear that they may suffer in a larger game. Small banks face the threat of being excluded from crucial relationships with big banks, and from future lending consortia, if they fail to provide funds for rescheduling loans. As in the other cases described above, strategies of reciprocity for debt rescheduling are adapted creatively to avoid the problems of issue-interdependence that arise when there are many actors.

III. Conclusion

A. THE IMPORTANCE OF PERCEPTION

The contributors to *Cooperation under Anarchy* did not specifically set out to explore the role of perception in decision making, but the importance of perception has kept asserting itself. The significance of perception, including beliefs and cognition, will come as no surprise to students of international politics.[36] Yet it is worth pointing out once again that decision making in ambiguous settings is heavily influenced by the ways in which the actors think about their problem.

While this point has been made in laboratory studies many times,[37] there is an important twist in international politics that does not get sufficient attention from the psychologists who study decision making in the laboratory. Leaders of one state live far away from the leaders of other states. They are far away not only in space, but also in their cognitive framework: their tacit assumptions differ about what is important, what needs to be done, and who bears the responsibility for change. Put simply, those acting on behalf of states often do not appreciate how their own actions will affect others and how they will be interpreted by others. As Van Evera concludes from his study of World War I, preventing that war would have required dispelling extensive misperceptions that were prevalent in Europe before 1914.

Other striking examples of the importance of perception also come from the security area. For example, Downs, Rocke, and Siverson have found that even when nations in arms races built defensive rather than

---

[36] Jervis (fn. 31).

[37] For example, Amos Tversky and Daniel Kahneman, "Judgment under Uncertainty: Heuristics and Biases," *Science* 185 (September 1974), 1124-31; Richard Nisbet and Lee Ross, *Human Inference: Strategies and Shortcomings of Social Judgment* (Englewood Cliffs, NJ: Prentice-Hall, 1980).

offensive weapons, it was usually done not to defuse the arms race, but simply because they believed that such weapons offered the greatest amount of security per dollar. Even more to the point is that many arms races were started or accelerated without serious appreciation of the consequences. For example, when the Soviet leaders deliberately exaggerated their bomber strength in 1955 and their ICBM capabilities several years later, they did so for short-term political advantages; there is no evidence that they fully appreciated the long-term consequences that would follow when the United States geared up to take the threat seriously. In general, Downs, Rocke, and Siverson find that arms races are not often perceived as the result of actions chosen by others. In the events leading to the outbreak of war, national leaders may completely misunderstand the consequences of their acts. Van Evera notes, for example, that in 1914 the Russian government did not realize that Russia's mobilization would lead directly to Germany's mobilization, and to war. Another example of the impact of biased interpretations of events is provided by Jervis in his discussion of the decay of great-power concerts, which were undermined by divergent views of which side had made greater concessions to maintain cooperation.

While security issues provide the most dramatic examples, governments may be no better at understanding how their actions in the realm of political economy will be seen by others. Conybeare's study shows that trade wars have sometimes begun when states held mistaken beliefs that other countries would be reluctant to raise tariffs on imported food in retaliation for new tariffs placed on their exported manufactured goods. Trade wars have begun when states had exaggerated expectations about the tolerance of others for attempts at minor exploitation in widely accepted terms of trade.

B.   GROPING TOWARD NEW INSTITUTIONS AND NORMS

Our project began with a set of hypotheses about how specific features of an international setting would affect the chances for the development of cooperation. Factors included were mutuality of interests, the shadow of the future, and the number of actors. These hypotheses have been supported by a broad set of cases that began in the 14th century, and covered trade disputes, monetary policy, and debt rescheduling as well as arms races, the outbreak of war, and diplomatic concerts. The three factors did, in fact, help to account for both cooperation and conflict.

We also discovered something else: over and over again we observed that the actors were not satisfied with simply selecting strategies based upon the situation in which they found themselves. In many cases we saw deliberate efforts to change the very structure of the situation by changing the context in which each of them would be acting. Decision makers themselves perceived (more or less consciously) that some aspects of the situations they faced tended to make cooperation difficult. So they worked to alter these background conditions. Among the problems they encountered were the following:

1. how to provide incentives for cooperation so that cooperation would be rewarded over the long run, and defection punished;
2. how to monitor behavior so that cooperators and defectors could be identified;
3. how to focus rewards on cooperators and retaliation on defectors;
4. how to link issues with one another in productive rather than self-defeating ways and, more generally, how to play multilevel games without tripping over their own strategies.

A fundamental strategic concept in attaining these objectives is that of reciprocity. Cooperation in world politics seems to be attained best not by providing benefits unilaterally to others, but by conditional co-operation. Yet reciprocity encounters many problems in practice. As Axelrod has demonstrated, and as Van Evera's discussion of 1914 illustrates, payoff structures in the strategic setting may be so malign that Tit-for-Tat cannot work. Reciprocity requires the ability to recognize and retaliate against a defection. And retaliation can spread acrimoniously.

Actors in world politics seek to deal with problems of reciprocity in part through the exercise of power. Powerful actors structure relationships so that countries committed to a given order can deal effectively with those that have lower levels of commitment. This is done by establishing hierarchies, as one would expect from Herbert Simon's assertion that complex systems will be hierarchic in character.[38] In the present symposium, the construction of hierarchy for the sake of co-operation is best illustrated by Lipson's discussion of inter-bank networks to facilitate rescheduling of Third World debts; but it is also evident in Jervis's discussion of great-power concerts.

Another way to facilitate cooperation is to establish international regimes. Regimes can be defined as "sets of implicit or explicit principles, norms, rules, and decision-making procedures around which actors' expectations converge in a given area of international relations."[39] International regimes have been extensive in the post-1945 international

[38] Simon, *The Sciences of the Artificial* (Cambridge: MIT Press, 2d ed. 1982), chap. 4, "The Architecture of Complexity," p. 99.
[39] Krasner (fn. 8), 3.

political economy, as illustrated by the international trade regime (centered on the GATT) and the international monetary regime (including the I.M.F. as well as other organizations and networks).[40] Since the use of power can facilitate the construction of regimes, this approach should be seen as complementary to, rather than in contradiction with, an emphasis on hierarchical authority. Regimes do not enforce rules in a hierarchical sense, but they do change patterns of transaction costs and provide information to participants, so that uncertainty is reduced. Jervis argues that the Concert of Europe helped to facilitate cooperation by making it easier for governments to understand one another. Lipson shows how, in the regime for debt rescheduling, the control of information is used to faciliate cooperation on terms favored by the big banks. He also indicates that one weapon in the hands of those banks is their ability to structure transaction costs: the costs of negotiations involving major money-center banks are reduced while the costs of coordinating resistance by small banks are not. Conybeare's analysis implies that if England and the Hanseatic League had been able to form an international trade regime, they might have been able to make mutually advantageous bargains and to discipline some of their more unruly constituents.

International regimes do not substitute for reciprocity; rather, they reinforce and institutionalize it. Regimes incorporating the norm of reciprocity delegitimize defection and thereby make it more costly. Insofar as they specify precisely what reciprocity means in the relevant issue-area, they make it easier to establish a reputation for practicing reciprocity consistently. Such reputations may become important assets, precisely because others will be more willing to make agreements with governments that can be expected to respond to cooperation with cooperation. Of course, compliance is difficult to assure; and international regimes almost never have the power to enforce rules. Nevertheless, since governments with good reputations can more easily make agreements than governments with bad ones, international regimes can help to facilitate cooperation by making it both easier and more desirable to acquire a good reputation.[41]

International regimes may also help to develop new norms, as Ruggie has argued.[42] Yet few such examples are evident in the cases discussed in this volume. The great-power concerts discussed by Jervis embodied new norms, but these did not last long; and the new norms of the 1930s

[40] Keohane (fn. 8), chaps. 8-9.
[41] *Ibid.*, esp. chaps. 5-7.
[42] Ruggie (fn. 15).

monetary system described by Oye were largely uncooperative and connected with the breakdown rather than the institutionalization of a regime. Major banks today are trying mightily to strengthen norms of repayment (for debtors) and of relending (for banks), but it is not at all clear that this will be successful. Better examples of creating norms may be provided by the evolution of thinking on chemical and biological warfare, and by the development, under GATT, of norms of non-discrimination—which are now, as we have seen, under pressure. Evidently, it is difficult to develop new norms, and they often decay in reaction to conspicuous violations.

Establishing hierarchies, setting up international regimes, and attempting to gain acceptance for new norms are all attempts to change the context within which actors operate by changing the very structure of their interaction. It is important to notice that these efforts have usually not been examples of forward-looking rationality. Rather, they have been experimental, trial-and-error efforts to improve the current situation based upon recent experience. Like other forms of trial-and-error experimentation, they have not always worked. Indeed, it is instructive to enumerate the variety of ways in which such experiments can fail.

1. The most important source of failure is that efforts to restructure the relationships may never get off the ground. As Downs, Rocke, and Siverson note, there was an active peace movement in the years before 1914, and World War I was preceded by a series of conferences designed to secure arms control and strengthen international law; but these efforts did not significantly affect the nature of world politics. Similarly, the shakiness of monetary arrangements in the 1920s was perceived by many of the participants, but conferences to deal with these weaknesses, such as that at Genoa in 1922, failed to cope with them effectively. The great-power concerts discussed by Jervis seemed to get somewhat farther, but were never sufficiently institutionalized to have much prospect of longevity.

2. Some agreements are instituted, but turn out to be self-contradictory. We have noted that sequential bilateral negotiations under conditional most-favored-nation treatment may lead to a problem of infinite regress: each bargain tends to require the renegotiation of many others. Bilateral arms control agreements, whose restraints could encourage third parties to increase their armaments in order to catch up with the major powers, face a similar difficulty.

3. Even successful arrangements are subject to decay. Decay can result

from actors' attempts to find loopholes in established rules. The very success of GATT in reducing tariff rates contributed to an expansion of nontariff barriers; and efforts to evade those barriers led to their progressive extension and tightening.[43] Likewise, successful cooperation in the area of security may lead governments to believe that their partners' cooperation is not based on reciprocity but is unconditional. Insofar as this belief is incorrect, discord may ensue.

4. In some cases, changes that have nothing to do with the arrangements make them obsolete. Thus the international debt regime in place before the crisis of August 1982 was manifestly ill-equipped to handle a situation in which most Third World debts had to be rescheduled. In this instance, the old regime was adapted to meet new needs. The Depression of the 1930s made the monetary orthodoxy of the gold exchange standard obsolete. Indeed, Oye argues that the cooperative international monetary arrangements of the 1920s hindered attempts at monetary cooperation during the 1930s. The collapse of the old regime was a necessary condition for creation of a new one.

Eventually, any institution is likely to become obsolete. The question is under what conditions international institutions—broadly defined as "recognized patterns of practice around which expectations converge"[44]—facilitate significant amounts of cooperation for a period of time. Clearly, such institutions can change the incentives for countries affected by them, and can in turn affect the strategic choices governments make in their own self-interest.

This interaction between incentives and institutions suggests the importance of linking the upward-looking theory of strategy with the downward-looking theory of regimes. The strategic approach is upward-looking in that it examines what individual actors will choose to do, and derives consequences for the entire system based on these choices. Most of the analysis in this volume has followed this upward-looking approach. On the other hand, much regime analysis has been downward-looking in that it examines the implications, for actors, of the way the entire system is organized. Some recent work has attempted to combine

[43] Vinod Aggarwal, "The Unraveling of the Multi-Fiber Arrangement, 1981: An Examination of Regime Change," *International Organization* 37 (Autumn 1983), 617-46; David B. Yoffie, *Power and Protectionism: Strategies of the Newly Industrializing Countries* (New York: Columbia University Press, 1983).

[44] Oran R. Young, "Regime Dynamics: The Rise and Fall of International Regimes," *International Organization* 36 (Spring 1982), 277-98; reprinted in Krasner (fn. 8), 93-114.

these two approaches,[45] but it has not yet been done in either a formally rigorous or an empirically comprehensive way.

The experimental groping by policy makers does not necessarily lead to stronger and ever more complex ways of achieving cooperation. The process proceeds by fits and starts. The success of each step is uncertain, and there is always danger that prior achievements will come unstuck. New experiments are often tried only under obvious pressure of events (as in debt rescheduling). And they are often dependent upon the active leadership of a few individuals or states who feel a serious need for change and who have the greatest resources.

The essays in this collection show that we are beginning to understand the structural conditions that affect strategic choices leading to cooperation or discord. These factors are mutuality of interest, the shadow of the future, and the number of actors. Over a wide range of historical cases, these three dimensions of situations do help account for the emergence, or nonemergence, of cooperation under anarchy.

But in the course of this collective research we have also found that states are often dissatisfied with the structure of their own environment. We have seen that governments have often tried to transform the structures within which they operate so as to make it possible for the countries involved to work together productively. Some of these experiments have been successful, others have been stillborn, and still others have collapsed before fully realizing the dreams of their founders. We understand the functions performed by international regimes, and how they affect strategies pursued by governments, better than we did a number of years ago. What we need now are theories that account for (1) when experiments to restructure the international environment are tried, and (2) whether a particular experiment is likely to succeed. Even within a world of independent states that are jealously guarding their sovereignty and protecting their power, room exists for new and better arrangements to achieve mutually satisfactory outcomes, in terms both of economic welfare and military security.

This does not mean that all endeavors to promote international cooperation will yield good results. Cooperation can be designed to help a few at the expense of the rest; and it can accentuate as well as alleviate injustice in an imperfect world. Yet the consequences of failure to co-

[45] In *After Hegemony* (fn. 8), Robert Keohane has sought to show how game theory (which is "upward-looking") can be combined fruitfully with the "downward-looking" theories of public goods and market failure to develop a functional theory of international regimes. But he has not formalized his theory, and has applied it only to the post-World War II international political economy.

operate—from warfare to the intensification of depressions—make us believe that more cooperation is often better than less. If governments are prepared to grope their way toward a better-coordinated future, scholars should be prepared to study the process. And, in a world where states have often been dissatisfied with international anarchy, scholars should be prepared to advance the learning process—so that despite the reality of anarchy, beneficial forms of international cooperation can be promoted.

Books Written Under the Auspices of
CENTER OF INTERNATIONAL STUDIES
PRINCETON UNIVERSITY
1952-85

Gabriel A. Almond, *The Appeals of Communism* (Princeton University Press 1954)

William W. Kaufmann, ed., *Military Policy and National Security* (Princeton University Press 1956)

Klaus Knorr, *The War Potential of Nations* (Princeton University Press 1956)

Lucian W. Pye, *Guerrilla Communism in Malaya* (Princeton University Press 1956)

Charles De Visscher, *Theory and Reality in Public International Law*, trans. by P. E. Corbett (Princeton University Press 1957; rev. ed. 1968)

Bernard C. Cohen, *The Political Process and Foreign Policy: The Making of the Japanese Peace Settlement* (Princeton University Press 1957)

Myron Weiner, *Party Politics in India: The Development of a Multi-Party System* (Princeton University Press 1957)

Percy E. Corbett, *Law in Diplomacy* (Princeton University Press 1959)

Rolf Sannwald and Jacques Stohler, *Economic Integration: Theoretical Assumptions and Consequences of European Unification*, trans. by Herman Karreman (Princeton University Press 1959)

Klaus Knorr, ed., *NATO and American Security* (Princeton University Press 1959)

Gabriel A. Almond and James S. Coleman, eds., *The Politics of the Developing Areas* (Princeton University Press 1960)

Herman Kahn, *On Thermonuclear War* (Princeton University Press 1960)

Sidney Verba, *Small Groups and Political Behavior: A Study of Leadership* (Princeton University Press 1961)

Robert J. C. Butow, *Tojo and the Coming of the War* (Princeton University Press 1961)

Glenn H. Snyder, *Deterrence and Defense: Toward a Theory of National Security* (Princeton University Press 1961)

Klaus Knorr and Sidney Verba, eds., *The International System: Theoretical Essays* (Princeton University Press 1961)

Peter Paret and John W. Shy, *Guerrillas in the 1960's* (Praeger 1962)

George Modelski, *A Theory of Foreign Policy* (Praeger 1962)

Klaus Knorr and Thornton Read, eds., *Limited Strategic War* (Praeger 1963)

Frederick S. Dunn, *Peace-Making and the Settlement with Japan* (Princeton University Press 1963)

Arthur L. Burns and Nina Heathcote, *Peace-Keeping by United Nations Forces* (Praeger 1963)

Richard A. Falk, *Law, Morality, and War in the Contemporary World* (Praeger 1963)

James N. Rosenau, *National Leadership and Foreign Policy: A Case Study in the Mobilization of Public Support* (Princeton University Press 1963)

Gabriel A. Almond and Sidney Verba, *The Civic Culture: Political Attitudes and Democracy in Five Nations* (Princeton University Press 1963)

Bernard C. Cohen, *The Press and Foreign Policy* (Princeton University Press 1963)

Richard L. Sklar, *Nigerian Political Parties: Power in an Emergent African Nation* (Princeton University Press 1963)

Peter Paret, *French Revolutionary Warfare from Indochina to Algeria: The Analysis of a Political and Military Doctrine* (Praeger 1964)

Harry Eckstein, ed., *Internal War: Problems and Approaches* (Free Press 1964)

Cyril E. Black and Thomas P. Thornton, eds., *Communism and Revolution: The Strategic Uses of Political Violence* (Princeton University Press 1964)

Miriam Camps, *Britain and the European Community 1955-1963* (Princeton University Press 1964)

Thomas P. Thornton, ed., *The Third World in Soviet Perspective: Studies by Soviet Writers on the Developing Areas* (Princeton University Press 1964)

James N. Rosenau, ed., *International Aspects of Civil Strife* (Princeton University Press 1964)

Sidney I. Ploss, *Conflict and Decision-Making in Soviet Russia: A Case Study of Agricultural Policy, 1953-1963* (Princeton University Press 1965)

Richard A. Falk and Richard J. Barnet, eds., *Security in Disarmament* (Princeton University Press 1965)

Karl von Vorys, *Political Development in Pakistan* (Princeton University Press 1965)

Harold and Margaret Sprout, *The Ecological Perspective on Human Affairs, With Special Reference to International Politics* (Princeton University Press 1965)

Klaus Knorr, *On the Uses of Military Power in the Nuclear Age* (Princeton University Press 1966)

Harry Eckstein, *Division and Cohesion in Democracy: A Study of Norway* (Princeton University Press 1966)

Cyril E. Black, *The Dynamics of Modernization: A Study in Comparative History* (Harper and Row 1966)

Peter Kunstadter, ed., *Southeast Asian Tribes, Minorities, and Nations* (Princeton University Press 1967)

E. Victor Wolfenstein, *The Revolutionary Personality: Lenin, Trotsky, Gandhi* (Princeton University Press 1967)

Leon Gordenker, *The UN Secretary-General and the Maintenance of Peace* (Columbia University Press 1967)

Oran R. Young, *The Intermediaries: Third Parties in International Crises* (Princeton University Press 1967)

James N. Rosenau, ed., *Domestic Sources of Foreign Policy* (Free Press 1967)

Richard F. Hamilton, *Affluence and the French Worker in the Fourth Republic* (Princeton University Press 1967)

Linda B. Miller, *World Order and Local Disorder: The United Nations and Internal Conflicts* (Princeton University Press 1967)

Henry Bienen, *Tanzania: Party Transformation and Economic Development* (Princeton University Press 1967)

Wolfram F. Hanrieder, *West German Foreign Policy, 1949-1963: International Pressures and Domestic Response* (Stanford University Press 1967)

Richard H. Ullman, *Britain and the Russian Civil War: November 1918-February 1920* (Princeton University Press 1968)

Robert Gilpin, *France in the Age of the Scientific State* (Princeton University Press 1968)

William B. Bader, *The United States and the Spread of Nuclear Weapons* (Pegasus 1968)

Richard A. Falk, *Legal Order in a Violent World* (Princeton University Press 1968)

Cyril E. Black, Richard A. Falk, Klaus Knorr and Oran R. Young, *Neutralization and World Politics* (Princeton University Press 1968)

Oran R. Young, *The Politics of Force: Bargaining During International Crises* (Princeton University Press 1969)

Klaus Knorr and James N. Rosenau, eds., *Contending Approaches to International Politics* (Princeton University Press 1969)

James N. Rosenau, ed., *Linkage Politics: Essays on the Convergence of National and International Systems* (Free Press 1969)

John T. McAlister, Jr., *Viet Nam: The Origins of Revolution* (Knopf 1969)

Jean Edward Smith, *Germany Beyond the Wall: People, Politics and Prosperity* (Little, Brown 1969)

James Barros, *Betrayal from Within: Joseph Avenol, Secretary-General of the League of Nations, 1933-1940* (Yale University Press 1969)

Charles Hermann, *Crises in Foreign Policy: A Simulation Analysis* (Bobbs-Merrill 1969)

Robert C. Tucker, *The Marxian Revolutionary Idea: Essays on Marxist Thought and Its Impact on Radical Movements* (W. W. Norton 1969)

Harvey Waterman, *Political Change in Contemporary France: The Politics of an Industrial Democracy* (Charles E. Merrill 1969)

Cyril E. Black and Richard A. Falk, eds., *The Future of the International Legal Order*. Vol. I: *Trends and Patterns* (Princeton University Press 1969)

Ted Robert Gurr, *Why Men Rebel* (Princeton University Press 1969)

C. Sylvester Whitaker, *The Politics of Tradition: Continuity and Change in Northern Nigeria 1946-1966* (Princeton University Press 1970)

Richard A. Falk, *The Status of Law in International Society* (Princeton University Press 1970)

John T. McAlister, Jr. and Paul Mus, *The Vietnamese and Their Revolution* (Harper & Row 1970)

Klaus Knorr, *Military Power and Potential* (D. C. Heath 1970)

Cyril E. Black and Richard A. Falk, eds., *The Future of the International Legal Order*. Vol. II: *Wealth and Resources* (Princeton University Press 1970)

Leon Gordenker, ed., *The United Nations in International Politics* (Princeton University Press 1971)

Cyril E. Black and Richard A. Falk, eds., *The Future of the International Legal Order*. Vol. III: *Conflict Management* (Princeton University Press 1971)

Francine R. Frankel, *India's Green Revolution: Economic Gains and Political Costs* (Princeton University Press 1971)

Harold and Margaret Sprout, *Toward a Politics of the Planet Earth* (Van Nostrand Reinhold Co. 1971)

Cyril E. Black and Richard A. Falk, eds., *The Future of the International Legal Order*. Vol. IV: *The Structure of the International Environment* (Princeton University Press 1972)

Gerald Garvey, *Energy, Ecology, Economy* (W. W. Norton 1972)

Richard H. Ullman, *The Anglo-Soviet Accord* (Princeton University Press 1973)

Klaus Knorr, *Power and Wealth: The Political Economy of International Power* (Basic Books 1973)

Anton Bebler, *Military Rule in Africa: Dahomey, Ghana, Sierra Leone, and Mali* (Praeger Publishers 1973)

Robert C. Tucker, *Stalin as Revolutionary 1879-1929: A Study in History and Personality* (W. W. Norton 1973)

Edward L. Morse, *Foreign Policy and Interdependence in Gaullist France* (Princeton University Press 1973)

Henry Bienen, *Kenya: The Politics of Participation and Control* (Princeton University Press 1974)

Gregory J. Massell, *The Surrogate Proletariat: Moslem Women and Revolutionary Strategies in Soviet Central Asia, 1919-1929* (Princeton University Press 1974)

James N. Rosenau, *Citizenship Between Elections: An Inquiry Into The Mobilizable American* (Free Press 1974)

Ervin Laszlo, *A Strategy for the Future: The Systems Approach to World Order* (George Braziller 1974)

R. J. Vincent, *Nonintervention and International Order* (Princeton University Press 1974)

Jan H. Kalicki, *The Pattern of Sino-American Crises: Political-Military Interactions in the 1950s* (Cambridge University Press 1975)

Klaus Knorr, *The Power of Nations: The Political Economy of International Relations* (Basic Books, Inc. 1975)

James P. Sewell, *UNESCO and World Politics: Engaging in International Relations* (Princeton University Press 1975)

Richard A. Falk, *A Global Approach to National Policy* (Harvard University Press 1975)

Harry Eckstein and Ted Robert Gurr, *Patterns of Authority: A Structural Basis for Political Inquiry* (John Wiley & Sons 1975)

Cyril E. Black, Marius B. Jansen, Herbert S. Levine, Marion J. Levy, Jr., Henry Rosovsky, Gilbert Rozman, Henry D. Smith, II, and S. Frederick Starr, *The Modernization of Japan and Russia* (Free Press 1975)

Leon Gordenker, *International Aid and National Decisions: Development Programs in Malawi, Tanzania, and Zambia* (Princeton University Press 1976)

Carl von Clausewitz, *On War*, edited and translated by Michael Howard and Peter Paret (Princeton University Press 1976)

Gerald Garvey and Lou Ann Garvey, *International Resource Flows* (D. C. Heath 1977)

Walter F. Murphy and Joseph Tanenhaus, *Comparative Constitutional Law: Cases and Commentaries* (St. Martin's Press 1977)

Gerald Garvey, *Nuclear Power and Social Planning: The City of the Second Sun* (D. C. Heath 1977)

Richard E. Bissell, *Apartheid and International Organizations* (Westview Press 1977)

David P. Forsythe, *Humanitarian Politics: The International Committee of the Red Cross* (Johns Hopkins University Press 1977)

Paul E. Sigmund, *The Overthrow of Allende and the Politics of Chile, 1964-1976* (University of Pittsburgh Press 1977)

Henry S. Bienen, *Armies and Parties in Africa* (Holmes and Meier 1978)

Harold and Margaret Sprout, *The Context of Environmental Politics: Unfinished Business for America's Third Century* (University Press of Kentucky 1978)

Samuel S. Kim, *China, The United Nations, and World Order* (Princeton University Press 1979)

S. Basheer Ahmed, *Nuclear Fuel and Energy* (D.C. Heath 1979)

Robert C. Johansen, *The National Interest and the Human Interest: An Analysis of U.S. Foreign Policy* (Princeton University Press 1980)

Richard A. Falk and Samuel S. Kim, eds., *The War System: An Interdisciplinary Approach* (Westview Press 1980).

James H. Billington, *Fire in the Minds of Men: Origins of the Revolutionary Faith* (Basic Books 1980)

Bennett Ramberg, *Destruction of Nuclear Energy Facilities in War: The Problem and the Implications* (D. C. Heath 1980)

Gregory T. Kruglak, *The Politics of United States Decision-Making in United Nations Specialized Agencies: The Case of the International Labor Organization* (University Press of America 1980)

W. P. Davison and Leon Gordenker, eds., *Resolving Nationality Conflicts: The Role of Public Opinion Research* (Praeger Publishers 1980)

James C. Hsiung and Samuel S. Kim, eds., *China in the Global Community* (Praeger Publishers 1980)

Douglas Kinnard, *The Secretary of Defense* (University Press of Kentucky 1980)

Richard Falk, *Human Rights and State Sovereignty* (Holmes & Meier 1981)

James H. Mittelman, *Underdevelopment and the Transition to Socialism: Mozambique and Tanzania* (Academic Press 1981)

Gilbert Rozman, ed., *The Modernization of China* (The Free Press 1981)

Robert C. Tucker, *Politics as Leadership.* The Paul Anthony Brick Lectures. Eleventh Series (University of Missouri Press 1981)

Robert Gilpin, *War and Change in World Politics* (Cambridge University Press 1981)

Nicholas G. Onuf, ed., *Law-Making in the Global Community* (Carolina Academic Press 1982)

Ali E. Hillal Dessouki, ed., *Islamic Resurgence in the Arab World* (Praeger Publishers 1981)

Richard Falk, *The End of World Order* (Holmes & Meier 1983)

Klaus Knorr, ed., *Power, Strategy, and Security* (Princeton University Press 1983)

Finn Laursen, *Superpower at Sea* (Praeger 1983)

Samuel S. Kim, *The Quest for a Just World Order* (Westview Press 1984)

Gerald Garvey, *Strategy and the Defense Dilemma* (D.C. Heath 1984)

Peter R. Baehr and Leon Gordenker, *The United Nations: Reality and Ideal* (Praeger Publishers 1984)

Joseph M. Grieco, *Between Dependency and Autonomy: India's Experience with the International Computer Industry* (University of California Press 1984)

Jan Hallenberg, *Foreign Policy Change: United States Foreign Policy Toward the Soviet Union and the People's Republic of China, 1961-1980* (University of Stockholm 1984)

Michael Krepon, *Strategic Stalemate: Nuclear Weapons and Arms Control in American Politics* (New York: Macmillan 1984)

Gilbert Rozman, *A Mirror for Socialism: Soviet Criticisms of China* (Princeton University Press 1985)

LIBRARY OF CONGRESS CATALOGING-IN-PUBLICATION DATA

Main entry under title:

Cooperation under anarchy.

1. World politics—20th century—Addresses, essays, lectures.
2. International relations—Addresses, essays, lectures.
3. International economic relations—Addresses, essays, lectures.
4. International cooperation—Addresses, essays, lectures.
I. Oye, Kenneth A., 1949-

D445.C736   1985   327.1′1   85-42936
ISBN 0-691-07695-2
ISBN 0-691-02240-2 (pbk.)